BASICS OF ECONOMIC BOTANY

Ramesh Umrani

ANMOL PUBLICATIONS PVT. LTD.
NEW DELHI - 110 002 (INDIA)

ANMOL PUBLICATIONS PVT. LTD.
H.O.: 4374/4B, Ansari Road, Daryaganj,
New Delhi-110 002 (India)
Ph.: 23278000, 23261597
B.O.: No. 1015, Ist Main Road, BSK IIIrd Stage
IIIrd Phase, IIIrd Block,
Bangalore - 560 085 (India)
Visit us at: www.anmolpublications.com

Basics of Economic Botany

First Edition, 2009
ISBN 978-81-261-3768-8

PRINTED IN INDIA

Printed at Balaji Offset Press, Delhi.

Contents

Preface

Animals have to depend directly or indirectly upon plants. Even increasing population sizes have been made us think about ways to feed large numbers of people, most of whom live under substandard conditions. At the same time, the Natural or Organic food movement has necessitated that individuals become educated consumers of Plant products. As a consequence, interest in studying plants of actual or potential use in Feeding, Clothing, Housing, and Warming human kind has arisen. This book provides a detailed coverage of the major uses of plants. To keep the text readable and relevant, efforts have been made to provide a balanced treatment of the plants discussed by including aspects of History, Morphology, Chemistry and Modern usage.

Author

Chapter 1

Taxonomy

Taxonomy, science of classifying organisms. Probably the first scientific study of plants was the attempt to classify them. At first, because of the limited knowledge of plant structures, artificial classifications, beginning with the most ancient one into herbs, shrubs, and trees, were necessary. These simple categories merely cataloged, in a tentative way, the rapidly accumulating material, in preparation for a classification based on natural relationsbhips. Modern taxonomic classification, based on the natural concepts and system of the Swedish botanist Carolus Linnaeus, has progressed steadily since the 18th century, modified by advances in knowledge of morphology, evolution, and genetics.

CLASSIFICATION

Classification, in biology, identification, naming, and grouping of organisms into a formal system based on similarities such as internal and external anatomy, physiological functions, genetic makeup, or evolutionary history. With an estimated 10 million to 13 million species on Earth, the diversity of life is immense. Determining an underlying order in the complex web of life is a difficult undertaking that encompasses advanced scientific methods as well as fundamental philosophical issues about how to view the living world. Among the scientists who work on classification problems are systematists, biologists who study the diversity of organisms and their evolutionary relationship. In a related field known as taxonomy, scientists identify new organisms and determine how to place them into an existing classification scheme.Classification determines methods for organizing the diversity of life on Earth. It is a dynamic process that reflects the very nature of organisms, which are subject to modification and change over many, many generations in the process of evolution. Since life first appeared on Earth 3.5 billion years ago, many new types of organisms have evolved. Many of these organisms have become extinct, while some have developed into the present fauna and flora of the world. Extinction and diversification continue nonstop, and scientists are frequently encountering fluctuations that may affect the way an organism is classified.

In addition to ordering organisms, scientists give a new species a scientific name, typically a two-word name in Latin, to distinguish it from similar organisms. This naming process creates a standard way for scientists around the world to communicate about the same organism. This standard minimizes confusion, particularly when common names are applied to organisms. For instance, the bird Europeans commonly call a robin is a different species of bird from the robin Americans recognize. The confusion ends when the birds are referred to by their scientific names: the European robin is *Erithacus rubecula,* while the American robin is *Turdus migratorius.*When classifying organisms, scientists study a wide range of features, including those visible to the naked eye, those detectable only under a microscope, and those that can be determined only by chemical tests. Scientists compare the external shapes and sizes of organisms as well as the anatomy and function of internal organs and organ systems, such as the digestive or reproductive systems. Biochemists study and compare the molecular interactions within an organism that enable it to grow, make and store energy, and reproduce.

The early stages of an organism's development, or embryology, as well as an organism's behaviour, or ethology, are also useful in grouping organisms. Even the role an organism plays in its habitat can help place it in a particular group. Scientists use the fossil record to learn how certain animals have changed and evolved through Earth's history, which may provide clues for classification.

More recently, scientists have employed the techniques of molecular biology to compare the units of heredity, or genes, among organisms. Scientists study the fundamental units of deoxyribonucleic acid (DNA), the molecule that makes up genes, and organisms that share a similar DNA structure may be more closely related. Called molecular systematics, this approach is a powerful analytical tool. Used in combination with the other features studied in classification, molecular systematics can provide valuable insight into classification problems. For many organisms, molecular systematics studies have supported traditional classification; however, in some cases, the evidence from genetics studies has indicated that organisms should be reclassified. Skunks, traditionally have been classified with badgers, ferrets, and minks in the family Mustelidae. But recent studies of molecular traits indicate that skunks differ significantly from these animals and may warrant classification in their own family.

Species are Grouped

Scientists classify organisms using a series of hierarchical categories called taxa (taxon, singular). This hierarchical system moves upward from a base containing a large number of organisms with very specific characteristics. This base taxon is part of a larger taxon, which in turn becomes part of an even larger taxon. Each successive taxon is distinguished by a broader set of characteristics.

The base level in the taxonomic hierarchy is the species. Broadly speaking, a species is a group of closely related organisms that are able to interbreed and produce fertile offspring. On the next tier of the hierarchy, similar species are grouped into a broader taxon called a genus (genera, plural). The remaining tiers within the hierarchy are formed by grouping genera into families, then families into orders, and orders into classes. In the classification of animals, bacteria, protists (unicellular organisms, such as amoebas, with characteristics of both plants and animals), and fungi, classes are grouped into phyla, while plant classes are grouped into divisions. Both phyla and divisions are grouped into kingdoms. Some scientists go on to group kingdoms into domains.

Classification Methods

Grouping organisms according to shared characteristics is not a simple task, and scientists often disagree about the best way to classify organisms. Some think that organisms should be grouped according to differences or similarities in the way they look or act. Other scientists argue that classification should be based on characteristics derived from a shared evolution. Conflicting philosophies about classification have resulted in a variety of classification methods, each with their own set of assumptions, techniques, and results. The classification of insects, birds, and bats illustrates a traditional classification process. Insects, birds, and bats are all animals—that is, they are multicellular organisms that obtain energy from food. Scientists group these organisms into the Kingdom Animalia.

Birds and bats both have spinal cords, causing scientists to classify both birds and bats in the phylum Chordata. Within the phylum Chordata, key features cause scientists to separate birds and bats. Birds are placed in the class Aves, which includes egg-laying animals, while bats are placed in the class Mammalia, which includes animals that give birth to live young and nurse their young from mammary glands. Insects, which lack spinal cords, are classified in the phylum Arthropoda, the taxon that includes animals with jointed legs and a skeleton on the outside of the body.

Insects are further divided based on such broad physical features as the presence or absence of wings.Scientists using the classical approach must judge the relative importance of characteristics. They may decide that wing structure is more important than the presence of fingernails in certain cases of classification. Some critics argue that this interpretation and evaluation is too subjective. To introduce more objectivity into classification, some scientists devised the phenetics approach to classification.

In the phenetics approach, scientists rely on quantitative methods and consider only the observable characteristics of modern organisms. Pheneticists identify a set of characteristics to measure and assign a certain numerical value to each characteristic. The tally is used to determine the extent of similarity between organisms. Pheneticists may find that, overall, birds and reptiles have a 77 percent similarity of body structure, or morphology, compared to a 55 percent morphological similarity between birds and mammals. From this measurement, pheneticists would suggest a classification that grouped birds and reptiles more closely than birds and mammals. A third classification method is the cladistic approach, which strives to classify organisms by natural evolutionary relationships, known as phylogeny. Cladists use the fossil record, molecular genetics, and other techniques to create an evolutionary tree called a cladogram. This branched diagram shows the relationship of a group of species based on the fewest number of shared changes that have occurred from generation to generation.

History of Classification Systems

Classification is one of the oldest sciences, but despite its age it is still a vigourous field full of new discoveries and methods. Much like other fields of science, great thinkers have shaped the course of classification. One of the earliest classification schemes was established by Greek philosopher Aristotle, who lived in the 300s BC. Aristotle believed that the complexity of life could be divided into a natural order based on dichotomies, or polar opposites. Aristotle divided animals into those with blood and those without blood, a classification that roughly corresponds to the division between vertebrates and invertebrates used in contemporary classification schemes. Aristotle wrote extensively on both plants and animals, but his writings on plants were lost.

Fortunately, his pupil Theophrastus applied Aristotle's taxonomic approach to the study of plants in his work *Inquiry into Plants*. Theophrastus subdivided plants, based on shape, into such broad categories as trees, shrubs, and herbs. A more pragmatic approach to classification was developed by Greek physician Dioscorides, who separated, for instance, medicinal herbs from those used in making perfumes.

To unify the naming of organisms and to communicate

more precisely about the increasing number of species being discovered, scholars in the Middle Ages (around the 5th century to the 15th century AD) translated the common names of organisms into Latin—at the time the language of educated persons. These names were often long and cumbersome, and included numerous descriptive terms. This complex naming process was simplified into a two word, or binomial, naming system in the mid-16th century to mid-17th century by a group of naturalists known as herbalists.Sixteenth-century Italian botanist Andrea Cesalpino was the first scientist to classify plants primarily according to structural characteristics, such as their fruits and seeds.

Cesalpino developed a method of character weighting in which he defined certain key characteristics that were important for recognizing plant groups. This method was adapted by Swiss botanist Caspar Bauhin, who catalogued an extensive list of plants. More importantly, Bauhin was the first to organize plants into a crude system that resembles modern genera and species.

Animal classification also advanced in the 16th century. French naturalist Pierre Belon extensively studied and catalogued birds. He was the first to use adaptation to habitat to divide birds into such groups as aquatic birds, wading birds, birds of prey, perching birds, and land birds, categories still used informally today. In the 17th century, English naturalist John Ray was the first to apply the character weighting method to structural features in animals. He used key characteristics, such as the shape and size of the bird beak, to classify birds.Swedish naturalist Carolus Linnaeus developed formal rules that provided consistency for a two-name system in common use called the binomial system of nomenclature.

In this system, similar organisms are grouped into a genus, and each organism is given a two-word Latin name. The first word is the genus name, and the second word is usually an adjective describing the organism, its geographic location, or the person who discovered it. Using this system, the domestic dog is *Canis familiaris*. *Canis* is the genus name for the group of animals that includes dogs, wolves, coyotes, and jackals. The word *familiaris* acts as a descriptor to further differentiate the domestic dog from its wild cousins.

Prior to Linnaeus, biologists nad established random categories of classification, such as the category of genus for a group of species. Before the 19th century, Linnaeus and other taxonomists classified organisms in an arbitrary but logical way that made it easier to communicate scientific information. But with the publication of *On the Origin of Species* in 1859 by British naturalist Charles Darwin, the purpose of classification took on new meaning.

Darwin argued that classification systems should reflect the history of life—that is, species should be related based on their shared ancestry. He defined species as groups that have diverged from a shared ancestry in recent history, while organisms in higher taxa, such as genera, class, or order, diverged from a shared ancestor.

Making evolutionary history compatible with the classification systems already established was no easy task, however. Critics argued that classification should be consistent with phylogeny, but not based solely upon evolutionary history. They advocated using other factors, such as behaviour or anatomy, along with phylogeny to better classify organisms. This controversy over the fundamental approach to classification continues today.

The development and use of microscopes in the late 16th century revealed a diverse array of single-celled organisms. These organisms presented new classification problems for the science community, which still relied on a two-kingdom classification system. At first, single-celled organisms that carried out photosynthesis were classified in Kingdom Plantae, and organisms that ingested food were placed in Kingdom Animalia. By the 19th century, scientists had identified a wide variety of microscopic organisms with diverse cell anatomies, specialized internal structures called organelles, and reproductive patterns that did not easily fit into the plant or animal classification system.

This great diversity prompted German biologist Ernst Haeckel to propose placing these unicellular forms in a third kingdom, the Protista. Haeckel placed bacteria within the Kingdom Protista in a separate group that he called Monera, recognizing that these organisms differed from all other cells because they lacked nuclei. As biologists learned more about bacteria, they became aware of the further differences between these organisms and all other life forms. In addition to lacking nuclei, bacteria differ from other types of cells in that they do not have membrane-bound organelles, such as mitochondria, the cell structures involved in energy metabolism. In the 1930s, these differences led French marine biologist Edouard Chatton to make a crucial distinction between prokaryotes, organisms such as bacteria that lack nuclei, and eukaryotes, more complex organisms that have nuclei. In 1938 American biologist Herbert Copeland argued that the distinctions between prokaryotes and eukaryotes were so fundamental that prokaryotes merited a fourth kingdom of their own called Kingdom Monera (now called Kingdom Prokaryotae).

American biologist Robert H. Whittaker proposed adding a fifth kingdom, Fungi, based on fungi's unique method of obtaining food. Fungi had previously been classified with plants, but Whittaker argued that fungi do not make their own food, as plants do, and they do not ingest it, as animals do. Rather, fungi secrete digestive enzymes around their food, breaking it down before absorbing it into their cells.

Advances in molecular systematics provided new insights about relationships among organisms and revealed imperfections in the current classification systems. New molecular biology techniques, such as polymerase chain reaction, which permits the easy analysis and comparison of DNA structures, enabled American microbiologist Carl Woese to determine that a group of organisms formerly classified as bacteria actually belong to a separate taxon. Archaea, also known as archaebacteria, were found to have unique molecular structures and physiological characteristics.

Archaea are represented by a relatively small group of single-celled organisms that mostly live in extremely hot, salty, or acidic anaerobic environments. Woese initially proposed a six-kingdom classification system, in which he separated prokaryotic organisms into two kingdoms, the Archaebacteria and Eubacteria, or true bacteria, and placing eukaryotic organisms into the Kingdoms Plantae, Animalia, Fungi, and Protista. He later advocated the use of a new category called the domain. In his new system, all life forms are grouped into three domains: bacteria, archaea, and eukarya.

Other scientists propose an eight-kingdom system. In addition to the Plantae, Animalia, and Protista kingdoms, this system also includes two prokaryote kingdoms of Archaea and Eubacteria, and divides Kingdom Protista into three separate kingdoms. No matter what method is used to classify an organism, its place in the hierarchy of life is not fixed. Scientists continue to uncover new evidence from the fossil record, molecular biology, or other fields that may change an organism's place in the classification hierarchy.

EXTINCTION (BIOLOGY)

Extinction (biology), the end of existence of a group of organisms, caused by their inability to adapt to changing environmental conditions. Extinction affects individual species—that is, groups of interbreeding organisms—as well as collections of related species, such as members of the same family, order, or class. The dodo a species of flightless pigeon formerly living on the island of Mauritius, became extinct in 1665. About 10,000 to 12,000 years ago, the most of the woolly mammoths and the last of the mastodons, both members of the elephant family, died. And about 245 million years ago at the end of the Paleozoic Era, an entire class of primitive marine animals called trilobites disappeared forever.

Fossils, the remains of prehistoric plants and animals buried and preserved in sedimentary rock or trapped in amber or other deposits of ancient organic matter, provide a record of the history of life on Earth. Scientists who study this fossil record, called paleontologists, have learned that extinction is a natural and ongoing phenomenon. In fact, of the hundreds of millions of species that have lived on Earth over the past 3.8 billion years, more than 99 percent are already extinct. Some of this happens as the natural result of competition between species and is known as natural selection. According to natural selection, living things must compete for food and space. They must evade the ravages of predators and disease while dealing with unpredictable shifts in their environment. Those species incapable of adapting are faced with imminent extinction. This constant rate of extinction, sometimes called background extinction, is like a slowly ticking clock. First one species, then another becomes extinct, and new species appear almost at random as geological time goes by. Normal rates of background extinction are usually about five families of organisms lost per million years.

More recently, paleontologists have discovered that not all extinction is slow and gradual. At various times in the fossil record, many different, unrelated species became extinct at nearly the same time. The cause of these large-scale extinctions is always dramatic environmental change that produces conditions too severe for organisms to endure. Environmental changes of this caliber result from extreme climatic change, such as the global cooling observed during the ice ages, or from catastrophic events, such as meteorite impacts or widespread volcanic activity. Whatever their causes, these events dramatically alter the composition of life on Earth, as entire groups of organisms disappear and entirely new groups rise to take their place.

Mass Extinctions

In its most general sense, the term mass extinction refers to any episode of multiple loss of species. But the term is generally reserved for truly global extinction events—events in which extensive species loss occurs in all ecosystems on land and in the sea, affecting every part of the Earth's surface. Scientists recognize five such mass extinctions in the past 500 million years. The first occurred around 438 million years ago in the Ordovician Period.

At this time, more than 85 percent of the species on Earth became extinct. The second took place 367 million years ago, near the end of the Devonian Period, when 82 percent of all species were lost. The third and greatest mass extinction to date occurred 245 million years ago at the end of the Permian Period. In this mass extinction, as many as 96 percent of all species on Earth were lost. The devastation was so great that paleontologists use this event to mark the end of the ancient, or Paleozoic Era, and the beginning of the middle, or Mesozoic Era, when many new groups of animals evolved.

About 208 million years ago near the end of the Triassic Period, the fourth mass extinction claimed 76 percent of the species alive at the time, including many species of amphibians and reptiles. The fifth and most recent mass extinction occurred about 65 million years ago at the end of the Cretaceous Period and resulted in the loss of 76 percent of all species, most notably the dinosaurs.

Many geologists and paleontologists speculate that this fifth mass extinction occurred when one or more meteorites struck the Earth. They believe the impact created a dust cloud that blocked much of the sunlight—seriously altering global temperatures and disrupting photosynthesis, the process by which plants derive energy. As plants died, organisms that relied on them for food also disappeared. Supporting evidence for this theory comes from a buried impact crater in the Yucatán Peninsula of Mexico.

Measured at 200 km (124 mi) in diameter, this huge crater is thought to be the result of a large meteorite striking the Earth. A layer of the element iridium in the geologic sediment from this time provides additional evidence. Unusual in such quantities on Earth, iridium is common in extraterrestrial bodies, and theory supporters suggest iridium traveled to Earth on a meteorite.

Other scientists suspect that widespread volcanic activity in what is now India and the Indian Ocean may have been the source of the atmospheric gases and dust that blocked sunlight. Ancient volcanoes could have been the source of the unusually high levels of iridium, and advocates of this theory point out that iridium is still being released today by at least one volcano in the Indian Ocean. No matter what the cause, the extinction at the end of the Cretaceous Period was so great that scientists use this point in time to divide the Mesozoic Era (also called the Age of Reptiles) from the Cenozoic Era (otherwise known as the Age of Mammals).

Role of Mass Extinction in Evolution

Historically biologists—most famous among them British naturalist Charles Darwin—assumed that extinction is the natural outcome of competition between newly evolved, adaptively superior species and their older, more primitive ancestors. These scientists believed that newer, more highly evolved species simply drove less well-adapted species to extinction. That is, historically, extinction was thought to result from evolution. It was also thought that this process happens in a slow and regular manner and occurs at different times in different groups of organisms.

In the case of background extinction, this holds true. An average of three species becomes extinct every million years, usually as a result of the forces of natural selection. When this happens, new species—differing only slightly from the organisms that disappeared—rise to take their places, creating evolutionary lineages of related species. The modern horse comes from a long evolutionary lineage of related, but now extinct, species. The earliest known horse had four toes on its front feet, three toes on its rear feet, and weighed just 36 kg (80 lb). About 45 million years ago, this horse became extinct. It was succeeded by other types of horses with slightly different characteristics, such as teeth better shaped for eating different plants, which made them better suited to their environments. This pattern of extinction and the ensuing rise of related species continued over the course of 55 million years, ultimately resulting in the modern horse and its relatives the zebras and asses.

In mass extinctions, entire groups of species—such as families, orders, and classes—die out, creating opportunities for the survivors to exploit new habitats. In their new niches, the survivors evolve new characteristics and habits and, consequently, develop into entirely new species. What this course of events means is that mass extinctions are not the *result* of the evolution of new species, but actually a *cause* of evolution. Fossils from periods of mass extinction indicate that most new species evolve *after* waves of extinction. Mass extinctions cause periodic spurts of evolutionary change that shake up the dynamics of life on Earth.

This is perhaps best demonstrated in the development of our own ancestors, the early mammals. Before the fall of the dinosaurs, which had dominated Earth for more than 150 million years, mammals were small, nocturnal, and secretive. They devoted much of their time and energy to evading meat-eating dinosaurs. With the extinction of dinosaurs, the remaining mammals moved into habitats and ecological niches previously dominated by the dinosaurs. Over the next 200 million years, those early mammals evolved into a wide variety of species, assuming many ecological roles and rising to dominate the Earth as the dinosaurs had before them.

The Current Extinction Crisis

Most scientists agree that life on Earth is now faced with the most severe extinction episode since the event that drove the dinosaurs extinct. No one knows exactly how many species are being lost because no one knows exactly how many species exist on Earth. Estimates vary, but the most widely accepted figure lies between 10 and 13 million species. Of these, biologists estimate that as many as 27,000 species are becoming extinct each year. This translates into an astounding 3 species every hour.

Instead of global climate change, humans are the cause of this latest mass extinction. With the invention of agriculture some 10,000 years ago, humans began destroying the world's terrestrial ecosystems to produce farmland. Today pollution destroys ecosystems even in remote deserts and in the world's deepest oceans. In addition, we have cleared forests for lumber, pulp, and firewood. We have harvested the fish and shellfish of the world's largest lakes and oceans in volumes that make it impossible for populations to recover fast enough to meet our harvesting needs. And everywhere we go, whether on purpose or by accident, we have brought along species that disrupt local ecosystems and, in many cases, drive native species extinct. For instance, Nile perch were intentionally introduced to Lake Victoria for commercial fishing in 1959. This fish proved to be an efficient predator, driving 200 rare species of cichlid fishes to extinction.

This sixth extinction, as it has come to be known, poses a great threat to our continued existence on the planet. As the sum of all species living in the world's ecosystems, known as biodiversity, dwindles, so too go many of the resources on which we depend. Humans use at least 40,000 different plant, animal, fungi, bacteria, and virus species for food, clothing, shelter, and medicines. In addition, the fresh air we breathe, the water we drink, cook, and wash with, and the many chemical cycles—including the nitrogen cycle and the carbon cycle, so vital to sustain life—depend on the continued health of ecosystems and the species within them.

The list of victims of the sixth extinction grows by the year. Forever lost are the penguinlike great auk, the passenger pigeon, the zebralike quagga, the thylacine, the Balinese tiger, the ostrichlike moa, and the tarpan, a small species of wild horse, to name but a few. More than 15,000 plants and animals are threatened by extinction. Each of these organisms has unique attributes—some of which may hold the secrets to increasing world food supplies, eradicating water pollution, or curing disease.

A subspecies of the endangered chimpanzee has recently been identified as the probable origin of the human immunodeficiency virus, the virus that causes acquired immunodeficiency syndrome (AIDS). But these animals are widely hunted in their west African habitat, and just as researchers learn of their significance to the AIDS epidemic, the animals face extinction. If they become extinct, they will take with them many of the secrets surrounding this devastating disease.

Species Conservation

Legislation to protect endangered species from impending extinction includes the Endangered Species Act. The Convention on International Trade in Endangered Species of

Wild Fauna and Flora (CITES), established in 1975, enforces the prohibition of trading of threatened plants and animals between countries. The Convention on Biological Diversity, an international treaty developed in 1992 at the United Nations Conference on the Environment and Development, obligates more than 160 countries to take action to protect plant and animal species.

Scientists meanwhile are intensifying their efforts to describe the species of the world. So far biologists have identified and named around 1.75 million species—a mere fraction of the species believed to exist today. Of those identified, special attention is given to species at or near the brink of extinction. The World Conservation Union (IUCN) maintains an active list of endangered plants and animals called the Red List. In addition, captive breeding programmes at zoos and private labouratories are dedicated to the preservation of endangered species. Participants in these programmes breed members of different populations of endangered species in an effort to increase their genetic diversity, thus enabling the species to better cope with further threats to their numbers.

All these programmes together have had some notable successes. The peregrine falcon, nearly extinct in the United States due to the widespread use of the pesticide DDT, rebounded strongly after DDT was banned. The brown pelican and the bald eagle offer similar success stories.

The California condor, a victim of habitat destruction, was bred in captivity, and small numbers of them are now being released back into the wild. Growing numbers of legislators and conservation biologists, scientists who specialize in preserving and nurturing biodiversity, are realizing that the primary cause of the current wave of extinction is habitat destruction. Efforts have accelerated to identify ecosystems at greatest risk, including those with high numbers of critically endangered species. Programmes to set aside large tracts of habitats, often interconnected by narrow zones or corridors, offer the best hope yet of sustaining ecosystems, and thereby the majority of the world's species.

ROBIN

Robin, name first given to a small European bird of the thrush family, familiar in England from living in close proximity to humans. The name was later applied by settlers in other parts of the world to birds of somewhat similar appearance—in North America to another species of the thrush and to members of several endemic genera of songbirds of Australia and New Guinea.

The European robin is technically a chat thrush, not a true thrush. The plump body is about 14 cm (about 5.5 in) long; its general colour is olive-brown, with a characteristic reddish-orange breast. The species ranges from Siberia to North Africa and, depending on its location, may migrate short distances during the year.

The American robin, a true thrush, is one of the largest and most numerous of American thrushes, with a body about 25 cm (about 10 in) long. The male is olive-gray; the top and sides of the head are black, the chin and throat are white with black streaks, and the breast and underparts are reddish orange. The female is of duller hues. The bird, like its European namesake, migrates and lives close to human dwellings. Its nest is built of coarse grass and reeds, plastered inside with mud and lined with grasses. The eggs, laid in a clutch of four to five, are a uniform greenish blue.

THRUSH (BIRD)

Thrush (bird), common name applied to any of a large family of widely distributed passerine (perching) birds. Thrushes are found in almost all parts of the world and include some of the most melodious singers among birds. They are small to medium-sized and feed chiefly on insects or worms, though many thrushes also eat fruits and berries when other food is not plentiful. Thrushes tend to feed on the ground. They typically have relatively long, slender bills and legs. Thrush nests are usually cup-shaped, and the females lay from three to six eggs. The eggs are pale and in many cases bluish.

Experts have classified thrushes into two major groups, the true thrushes (to which the American robin belongs) and the chat thrushes (to which the European robin belongs). The true thrushes are found on every continent and on many islands. The chat thrushes are largely confined to Europe and Asia. Today, many experts place the chat thrushes into a separate family: the Old World flycatcher family, *Muscicapidae*.

The largest group of true thrushes belongs to the genus *Turdus*, which comprises about 65 species. These thrushes are found in both temperate and tropical areas around the world. However, only one species of *Turdus*, the American robin, inhabits North America. A strictly American genus, *Catharus*, includes tropical and temperate species that rank among the finest songsters of the bird world. The best-known member of this group is the hermit thrush.

It nests in forests and woodlands over most of the United States and Canada. Like many of its relatives, the hermit thrush is brown above and creamy white below, and heavily spotted with dark gray on its breast. It is distinguished by its contrasting reddish tail. The more heavy-bodied wood thrush is also a fine singer. It is found in deciduous forests of the eastern United States and southeastern Canada. Other North American thrushes include the veery, Swainson's thrush, and gray-cheeked thrush.

In Europe and Asia the European blackbird is the most common thrush and a member of the genus *Turdus*. The male blackbird is all black with a yellow bill and the female is dull brown. The blackbird forages in parks and gardens much as the robin does in the United States, and its song and calls are quite similar to the robin's. The common blackbird measures about 23 cm (9 in) long and is similar in size to the song thrush, a bird that is found throughout Europe and into Asia. Like the blackbird and other thrushes, the song thrush has an attractive, flutelike song.

The name *thrush* is often applied to birds of different families reminiscent of thrushes in colouration, voice, or ecological niche. Among such birds are the ant thrushes, the shrike thrushes, and the North American waterthrushes.

WOOD THRUSH

Wood Thrush, common name for a songbird found

throughout the woodlands of the eastern United States. It is known for its melodic flutelike songs. The wood thrush is the official bird of Washington, D.C.

The wood thrush measures about 20 cm (about 8 in) from beak to tail. The plumage is the same for both sexes and does not change with the seasons. It has a brown body, a rusty-brown colour on its shoulders and head, and white rings around the eyes. Its throat, chest, and belly are white with large, dark brown spots. The wood thrush feeds primarily on insects, including beetles, butterflies, and caterpillars, and will also eat fruit.

After a courtship behaviour in which the pair fly together in tight circles, the female builds a cuplike nest close to the ground. She incubates, or warms, the three or four greenish-blue eggs by sitting on them for about two weeks until they hatch. Both the male and female bring food to the young who leave the nest within two weeks of hatching.

Wood thrush populations have been in decline for the past 50 years due in part to the destruction of the lowland tropical forest habitat in which it winters. Several private efforts are underway to maintain wood thrush populations.

GENUS

Genus, in biology, category of classification of living things; specifically, a group of species closely related in structure and evolutionary origin. The position of a genus, in classification of the kingdoms of living forms, is below family or subfamily, and above species. A genus name always differs from the name used for any other genus of living forms.

An organism is named by assigning it a binomial, consisting of a genus name followed by a species name. In the scientific name of the tiger lily, *Lilium tigrinum, Lilium* is the genus name and *tigrinum* is the species name. In zoological nomenclature, the genus and species names may be identical; the gorilla, is *Gorilla gorilla.* In botanical nomenclature, the genus name may never be assigned as a species name. The scientific name applied to a family is always a modification of the name of one of the genera; the genus involved is termed the type genus

SPECIES AND SPECIATION

Species and Speciation, basic concepts in the classification of organisms. In simple terms, a single species is a distinct kind of organism, with a characteristic shape, size, behaviour, and habitat that remains constant from year to year. A biological species is defined as a group of natural populations that mate and produce offspring with one another, but do not breed with other populations. This definition includes genealogical relationships as well as physical properties, and emphasizes that species evolve independently of one another.

The Nature of Species

Other conceptions of species exist, the oldest of which is the typological-species concept that originated with Plato and Aristotle. According to this concept, a species represents some ideal form, of which individual variation is merely the imperfect expression. The morphological-species definition, on the other hand, is purely observational: a group of individuals that resemble one another and are separated from other such groups by gaps in morphological variation, that is, variation in structure and form.

These concepts are adequate for classification of inanimate objects such as minerals, where a particular degree of similarity reflects the effects of the same degree of similarity in the physical processes that formed the objects. Organisms, however, are also influenced by genealogy (hereditary characteristics from preceding generations), therefore, these definitions are inappropriate. Certain properties of organisms may reflect past history but may be irrelevant to or only partly affected by current environmental conditions. The human vermiform appendix, a classic example, is a vestige of a more herbivorous ancestor.

In addition to being inappropriate, the typological and morphological concepts prove inadequate when the attempt is made to apply them over geological time or over a broad geographical area; a characteristic used to distinguish between two species in one place is often not valid in another. This is because, in space and geologic time, species change in morphology, behaviour, and habitats. The biological-species concept takes this into account, but the typological and morphological definitions refer to only one static type.

Speciation

Speciation is the process whereby new species are formed. The following events are thought to occur in most cases. In the first step, extrinsic isolation, an existing species becomes subdivided by some extrinsic event, such as a climatic change, the formation of a physical barrier (such as a mountain range), or its invasion of a new habitat or island. Subdivision may also occur merely because many hundreds of generations may be required for individuals to disperse from one end of the species' geographic range to another.

In the second step, differentiation, the isolated populations diverge genetically, which they can do more rapidly than populations exchanging individuals with other populations. Populations may diverge either at random or as a result of natural selection. In the third step, intrinsic isolation, some form of isolation evolves among the populations; this is dependent on the organisms rather than the environment. Such isolation may result from preferences during courtship or from genetic incompatibility, in which offspring of matings between the differentiated populations are no longer viable or fertile; the mule is an example.

In the final step, independence, the newly separated populations continue to evolve independently and may subsequently invade each other's geographic ranges without hybridization. Each of these steps has been demonstrated in the field and labouratory with various organisms.

Two major modes of speciation are theoretically possible: geographic and nongeographic. In geographic speciation, initial isolation results from geographic separation of the populations. In nongeographic speciation, initial isolation results from changes in behaviour or genetics of part of a local population. Many insects will eat only one species of plant and will use this plant's shape, colour, or odor as cues for location of mates and egg laying. If a group of these insects accidentally invades a new plant species and mates there, then it is as isolated as if it were far away. A great deal of controversy exists about the relative frequency of various modes of speciation, but the geographic mode is generally considered more common.

The biological-species definition is not infallible. A few borderline cases will always exist for which species identification is arbitrary. This arises because species are not static entities; they can change in time and sometimes give rise to new species. The intermediate stages in speciation cause the most difficulty in classification and identification, just as, during cell division, whether one cell or two exist is a matter of opinion. The nonexistence of borderline cases would mean only that evolution had run its course and was no longer taking place.

PHYLUM

Phylum, in biology, major category, or taxon, of organisms with a common design or organization. This design is shared by all members of the phylum, even though structural details may differ greatly because of evolution. The assumption is made by biologists that all members of a phylum have a common ancestry.

A phylum is part of the hierarchy of classification of organisms. It is an arbitrary grouping; that is, it is developed from a combination of scientific observation, theorizing, and guesswork in an attempt to find order in the complexity of living and extinct life forms. The same is true of all classification levels above and below it except for species, which consist of organisms known to be capable, at least potentially, of interbreeding.

DEOXYRIBONUCLEIC ACID

Deoxyribonucleic Acid (DNA), genetic material of all cellular organisms and most viruses. DNA carries the information needed to direct *protein synthesis* and *replication*. Protein synthesis is the production of the proteins needed by the cell or virus for its activities and development. Replication is the process by which DNA copies itself for each descendant cell or virus, passing on the information needed for protein synthesis. In most cellular organisms, DNA is organized on chromosomes located in the nucleus of the cell.

Structure

A molecule of DNA consists of two *chains*, strands composed of a large number of chemical compounds, called nucleotides, linked together to form a chain. These chains are arranged like a ladder that has been twisted into the shape of a winding staircase, called a double helix. Each nucleotide consists of three units: a sugar molecule called deoxyribose, a phosphate group, and one of four different nitrogen-containing compounds called bases. The four bases are adenine (A), guanine (G), thymine (T), and cytosine (C). The deoxyribose molecule occupies the centre position in the nucleotide, flanked by a phosphate group on one side and a base on the other. The phosphate group of each nucleotide is also linked to the deoxyribose of the adjacent nucleotide in the chain. These linked deoxyribose-phosphate subunits form the parallel side rails of the ladder. The bases face inward toward each other, forming the rungs of the ladder.

The nucleotides in one DNA strand have a specific association with the corresponding nucleotides in the other DNA strand. Because of the chemical affinity of the bases, nucleotides containing adenine are always paired with nucleotides containing thymine, and nucleotides containing cytosine are always paired with nucleotides containing guanine. The complementary bases are joined to each other by weak chemical bonds called hydrogen bonds.

Protein Synthesis

DNA carries the instructions for the production of proteins. A protein is composed of smaller molecules called amino acids, and the structure and function of the protein is determined by the sequence of its amino acids. The sequence of amino acids, in turn, is determined by the sequence of nucleotide bases in the DNA. A sequence of three nucleotide bases, called a triplet, is the genetic code word, or codon, that specifies a particular amino acid. For instance, the triplet GAC (guanine, adenine, and cytosine) is the codon for the amino acid leucine, and the triplet CAG (cytosine, adenine, and guanine) is the codon for the amino acid valine. A protein consisting of 100 amino acids is thus encoded by a DNA segment consisting of 300 nucleotides. Of the two polynucleotide chains that form a DNA molecule, only one strand contains the information needed for the production of a given amino acid sequence. The other strand aids in replication.

Protein synthesis begins with the separation of a DNA molecule into two strands. In a process called transcription, a section of one strand acts as a template, or pattern, to produce a new strand called messenger RNA (mRNA). The mRNA leaves the cell nucleus and attaches to the ribosomes, specialized cellular structures that are the sites of protein synthesis. Amino acids are carried to the ribosomes by another type of RNA, called transfer RNA (tRNA). In a process called translation, the amino acids are linked together in a particular sequence, dictated by the mRNA, to form a protein.

A gene is a sequence of DNA nucleotides that specify the order of amino acids in a protein via an intermediary mRNA molecule. Substituting one DNA nucleotide with another containing a different base causes all descendant cells or viruses to have the altered nucleotide base sequence. As a result of the substitution, the sequence of amino acids in the resulting protein may also be changed. Such a change in a DNA molecule is called a mutation. Most mutations are the result of errors in the replication process. Exposure of a cell or virus to radiation or to certain chemicals increases the likelihood of mutations.

Replication

In most cellular organisms, replication of a DNA molecule takes place in the cell nucleus and occurs just before the cell divides. Replication begins with the separation of the two polynucleotide chains, each of which then acts as a template for the assembly of a new complementary chain. As the old chains separate, each nucleotide in the two chains attracts a complementary nucleotide that has been formed earlier by the cell. The nucleotides are joined to one another by hydrogen bonds to form the rungs of a new DNA molecule. As the complementary nucleotides are fitted into place, an enzyme called DNA polymerase links them together by bonding the phosphate group of one nucleotide to the sugar molecule of the adjacent nucleotide, forming the side rail of the new DNA molecule. This process continues until a new polynucleotide chain has been formed alongside the old one, forming a new double-helix molecule.

Tools and Procedures

Several tools and procedures facilitate are used by scientists for the study and manipulation of DNA. Specialized enzymes, called restriction enzymes, found in bacteria act like molecular scissors to cut the phosphate backbones of DNA molecules at specific base sequences. Strands of DNA that have been cut with restriction enzymes are left with single-stranded tails that are called sticky ends, because they can easily realign with tails from certain other DNA fragments. Scientists take advantage of restriction enzymes and the sticky ends generated by these enzymes to carry out recombinant DNA technology, or genetic engineering. This technology involves removing a specific gene from one organism and inserting the gene into another organism.

Another tool for working with DNA is a procedure called polymerase chain reaction (PCR). This procedure uses the enzyme DNA polymerase to make copies of DNA strands in a process that mimics the way in which DNA replicates naturally within cells. Scientists use PCR to obtain vast numbers of copies of a given segment of DNA.

DNA fingerprinting, also called DNA typing, makes it possible to compare samples of DNA from various sources in a manner that is analogous to the comparison of fingerprints. In this procedure, scientists use restriction enzymes to cleave a sample of DNA into an assortment of fragments. Solutions containing these fragments are placed at the surface of a gel to which an electric current is applied. The electric current causes the DNA fragments to move through the gel. Because smaller fragments move more quickly than larger ones, this process, called electrophoresis, separates the fragments according to their size. The fragments are then marked with probes and exposed on X-ray film, where they form the DNA fingerprint—a pattern of characteristic black bars that is unique for each type of DNA.

A procedure called DNA sequencing makes it possible to determine the precise order, or sequence, of nucleotide bases within a fragment of DNA. Most versions of DNA sequencing use a technique called primer extension, developed by British molecular biologist Frederick Sanger. In primer extension, specific pieces of DNA are replicated and modified, so that each DNA segment ends in a fluorescent form of one of the four nucleotide bases.

Modern DNA sequencers, pioneered by American molecular biologist Leroy Hood, incorporate both lasers and computers. Scientists have completely sequenced the genetic material of several microorganisms, including the bacterium Escherichia coli. Scientists achieved the milestone of sequencing the complete genome of a multicellular organism—a roundworm identified as Caenorhabditis elegans.

The Human Genome Project, an international research collabouration, was established to determine the sequence of all of the 3 billion nucleotide base pairs that make up the human genetic material. In 2003 scientists completed the sequencing of the human genome. The project identified nearly all of the estimated 20,000 to 25,000 genes in the nucleus of a human cell. The project also mapped the location of these genes on the 23 pairs of human chromosomes.

An instrument called an atomic force microscope enables scientists to manipulate the three-dimensional structure of DNA molecules. This microscope involves laser beams that act like tweezers—attaching to the ends of a DNA molecule and pulling on them. By manipulating these laser beams, scientists can stretch, or uncoil, fragments of DNA. This work is helping reveal how DNA changes its three-dimensional shape as it interacts with enzymes.

Applications

Research into DNA has had a significant impact on medicine. Through recombinant DNA technology, scientists can modify microorganisms so that they become so-called factories that produce large quantities of medically useful drugs. This technology is used to produce insulin, which is a drug used by diabetics, and interferon, which is used by some cancer patients. Studies of human DNA are revealing genes that are associated with specific diseases, such as cystic fibrosis and breast cancer.

This information is helping physicians to diagnose various diseases, and it may lead to new treatments.Physicians are using a technology called chimeraplasty, which involves a synthetic molecule containing both DNA and RNA strands, in an effort to develop a treatment for a form of hemophilia.

Forensic science uses techniques developed in DNA research to identify individuals who have committed crimes. DNA from semen, skin, or blood taken from the crime scene can be compared with the DNA of a suspect, and the results can be used in court as evidence.

DNA has helped taxonomists determine evolutionary relationships among animals, plants, and other life forms. Closely related species have more similar DNA than do species that are distantly related. One surprising finding to emerge from DNA studies is that vultures of the Americas are more closely related to storks than to the vultures of Europe, Asia, or Africa.

Techniques of DNA manipulation are used in farming, in the form of genetic engineering and biotechnology. Strains of crop plants to which genes have been transferred may produce higher yields and may be more resistant to insects. Cattle have been similarly treated to increase milk and beef production, as have hogs, to yield more meat with less fat.

Social Issues

Despite the many benefits offered by DNA technology,

some critics argue that its development should be monitored closely. One fear raised by such critics is that DNA fingerprinting could provide a means for employers to discriminate against members of various ethnic groups. Critics also fear that studies of people's DNA could permit insurance companies to deny health insurance to those people at risk for developing certain diseases. The potential use of DNA technology to alter the genes of embryos is a particularly controversial issue.

The use of DNA technology in agriculture has also sparked controversy. Some people question the safety, desirability, and ecological impact of genetically altered crop plants. In addition, animal rights groups have protested against the genetic engineering of farm animals.

Despite these and other areas of disagreement, many people agree that DNA technology offers a mixture of benefits and potential hazards. Many experts also agree that an informed public can help assure that DNA technology is used wisely.

CHROMOSOME

Chromosome, microscopic structure within cells that carries the molecule deoxyribonucleic acid (DNA)—the hereditary material that influences the development and characteristics of each organism. In bacteria and bacteria-like organisms called archaebacteria, chromosomes consist of simple circles of DNA floating freely in the organism. In all other life forms, collectively called eukaryotes, chromosomes reside within a well-defined nucleus. In eukaryotes, chromosomes are highly complex structures in which the shape of the DNA molecules is linear, rather than circular.

Chromosome Structure

Chromosomes consist chiefly of proteins and DNA. Tiny chemical subunits called nucleotide bases form the structure of DNA. A sequence of bases along a DNA strand that codes for the production of a protein is known as a gene. Genes occupy precise locations on the chromosome.

Each cell contains enough DNA to form a thread

extending about 2 m (about 7 ft). Proteins called histones play a key role in packaging DNA within chromosomes. Sections of the DNA molecule wind around clusters of histones to form units called nucleosomes, which resemble spools encircled with thread. Another type of protein, called nonhistone chromosomal protein, further compresses nucleosomes into a compact, narrow coil. Chromosomes become most condensed when a cell is preparing to divide.

The chromosome structure ensures that even when the DNA is highly confined, it is free to carry out transcription, or the production of messenger ribonucleic acid (mRNA). Messenger ribonucleic acid is the molecule that carries the DNA instructions that determine the types of proteins a cell will reproduce to the sites where proteins are constructed. In addition, chromosomes permit DNA to replicate, or reproduce itself, so that as a cell divides to produce two cells, each of these new cells will contain all of the necessary genetic information.

Scientists are learning how DNA loosens its connection with histones in order to replicate itself and participate in the synthesis of mRNA. Evidence suggests that enzymes interact with the tails of histones, which protrude from the nucleosomes. These interactions may temporarily disrupt the nucleosome structure so that the DNA is free to interact with the enzymes that help to generate either mRNA or new copies of DNA.

Centromeres and Telomeres

The chromosomes of nearly all eukaryotic life forms contain two important structures: centromeres and telomeres. During cell division, the centromere—visible through a microscope as a knotlike struct ure—connects to an apparatus called the spindle. The spindle contains fibres that move the centromeres around, causing the rest of each chromosome to follow. This process ensures that each chromosome moves to its proper place during mitosis, when a cell divides to give rise to two cells, and during meiosis, the process of cell division that gives rise to eggs or sperm.

Telomeres are specialized sequences of DNA that are

found at the tips of chromosomes. Telomeres serve as a kind of cap that prevents the ends of chromosomes from attaching to the ends of other chromosomes. Scientists suspect that telomeres may influence the activity of nearby genes and may play a role in determining the life span of a cell.

Chromosome Number

In the cells of most organisms that reproduce sexually, chromosomes occur in pairs: One chromosome is inherited from the female parent, and one is inherited from the male parent. The two chromosomes of each pair contain genes that correspond to the same inherited characteristics. Each pair of chromosomes is different from every other pair of chromosomes in the same cell.

The number of chromosome pairs in an organism varies depending on the species. The number of chromosomes characteristic of a particular organism is known as the diploid number. Dogs have 39 pairs of chromosomes and a diploid number of 78, while tomato plants have 12 pairs of chromosomes and a diploid number of 24.

Sex cells (eggs or sperm) contain only half the number of chromosomes found in the other cells of an organism. This reduced number of chromosomes in the sex cells is known as the haploid number. During fertilization, an egg and sperm unite to form a cell known as a zygote, the first cell of the offspring. The zygote contains the diploid number of chromosomes characteristic of the species.

Most organisms have complete sets of matching chromosomal pairs, known as autosomes. In mammals, birds, and some other organisms, one pair of chromosomes is not identical. Known as the sex chromosomes, this pair plays a dominant role in determining the sex of an organism. Females have two copies of the X chromosome, while males have one Y chromosome and one X chromosome. Both males and females inherit one sex chromosome from the mother (always an X chromosome) and one sex chromosome from the father (an X in female offspring and a Y in male offspring). The presence of the Y chromosome determines that a zygote will develop into a male.

The Y chromosome is about one-third the size of the X chromosome and contains only a fraction of the number of genes. At one point in evolutionary history, the X and Y chromosomes were equal in size and gene number, but the two chromosomes gradually diverged over the course of 300 million years. These unmatched sex chromosomes produce a pattern of gene inheritance known as sex-linked inheritance, which differs from genes found on autosomes. In males, which carry an X and a Y chromosome, some genes found on the X chromosome may be missing on the Y chromosome. As a result, the organism will usually develop the trait associated with the gene on the X chromosome. In fruit flies, for instance, the gene for eye colour is located on the X chromosome. A male fruit fly will inherit the eye colour found on the X chromosome, since no gene for eye colour is found on the Y chromosome.

Human Chromosomes

Humans have 23 pairs of chromosomes, with a diploid number of 46. Scientists number these chromosome pairs according to their size—the largest is chromosome 1 and the smallest is chromosome 23. In human chromosomes, errors may occur that give rise to embryos with more or less genetic material, sometimes resulting in developmental disabilities or health problems.

In a process called nondisjunction, paired members of chromosomes fail to separate from one another during meiosis. Nondisjunction can lead to a condition known as Down syndrome, in which a person inherits three copies of chromosome 21. Another condition that may result from nondisjunction is Turner syndrome, a disorder in which a female inherits only a single X chromosome.

Genetic errors occur if part of a chromosome is either missing or duplicated. Chromosomes sometimes undergo changes called translocations, in which part of one chromosome breaks off and attaches to another chromosome. A translocation involving chromosomes 9 and 22 is linked to a type of leukemia called chronic myelogenic leukemia. On the sex chromosomes, problems arise in men when an abnormal gene is present on the X chromosome. With no healthy gene found on the Y chromosome to override the abnormal gene, disease may result. Men who inherit a mutated gene that causes hemophilia from their mother on the X chromosome will develop this bleeding disorder since they are missing a normal version of the gene on their Y chromosome.

Scientists called cytogeneticists look at a person's chromosomes in the labouratory to determine whether the individual has the usual number of chromosomes and whether these chromosomes have missing or extra segments. To examine chromosomes, cytogeneticists grow samples of a person's blood cells in the labouratory and expose the cells to a chemical called colchicine, which disrupts the spindle apparatus that is normally present in dividing cells. This disruption immobilizes the chromosomes during cell division, when they are most condensed and visible. Chromosomes are then stained with various dyes, which produce a pattern of vertical bands.

Cytogeneticists take photographs of the banded chromosomes through a microscope to create images called karyotypes, in which the members of each chromosome pair are arranged next to each other for easy comparison. The analysis of karyotypes reveals whether a person has extra or missing chromosomes, as well as whether large segments of chromosomes are absent, rearranged, or duplicated.

Experiments involving artificial chromosomes—chromosomes that are synthesized in the labouratory—are providing new insights into the structure and function of chromosomes. The first artificial chromosomes, produced in the 1980s, were chromosomes of yeast cells. The first artificial human chromosomes were created in 1997.

Researchers have successfully identified all the genes located on chromosomes 5, 16, 19, 21, and 22. This research has revealed a number of disease-causing genes associated with these chromosomes.

For instance, genes found on chromosome 5 have been linked to colourectal cancer, *basal cell carcinoma* (a form of skin cancer), and a type of dwarfism. Chromosome 16 contains genes implicated in adult polycystic renal disease, which affects 5 million people worldwide.

Identifying disease-causing genes and their chromosome locations will help researchers devise new diagnostic tools to determine a person's risk for disease as well as new therapies to replace or repair faulty genes.

GENETIC DISORDERS

Genetic Disorders, medical conditions caused by an error in a person's genetic material. Some genetic disorders result in medical problems that are apparent at birth, while other genetic disorders do not become evident until childhood or adult life. Genetic disorders range in severity from those that cause death to those that produce only mild problems, such as colour blindness. Scientists have identified more than 9,000 genetic disorders. Some of these disorders are extremely rare, while others are comparatively common.

Genetic disorders pose a medical challenge. Scientists have not yet developed cures or effective ways to treat many genetic conditions. Many genetic disorders are complex, involving several different parts of the body, making treatment difficult. Patients with cystic fibrosis require treatment for problems affecting the lungs, pancreas, intestines, and liver.

In some instances, doctors must diagnose and treat affected newborns immediately to prevent them from developing complications that would cause impaired development or even death. In addition, genetic disorders have unique personal, family, and social consequences. Parents who have a child with a genetic disorder may blame themselves for having passed on the genetic condition.

Healthy siblings or other members of an affected person's family may feel guilty for having escaped the disorder. Some people with a genetic condition may feel different or stigmatized because they perceive their genes as flawed. People may alter their plans to have children because they do not want their children to develop the genetic condition.

Specially trained health professionals help people deal with the complex medical and social consequences of genetic disorders. Clinical geneticists are physicians who diagnose and treat individuals with genetic disorders. These professionals explain the medical facts related to the disorder, such as the factors that cause the disease and the diagnostic and treatment options available. Genetic counselors are health professionals with graduate training in human genetics. Genetic counselors work alone and with clinical geneticists to help couples understand their risks of having a child with a genetic disorder. Genetic counselors also help patients choose a course of action to deal with their disorder that is in harmony with their feelings about the medical risks, their family goals, and their ethical and religious values.

Genes, Chromosomes, and Disease

All genetic disorders involve one or more genes found in the nuclei, or in some cases, the cytoplasm, of human cells. Genes are composed of deoxyribonucleic acid (DNA), a threadlike molecule whose structure provides instructions used by cells to direct the synthesis of proteins. Proteins regulate most of the biochemical reactions that occur within cells, and they are the building blocks of many substances in the body. Genes are precisely arranged on chromosomes, rodlike structures that each contain several thousand genes. Human cells contain 46 chromosomes arranged in 23 pairs. One of these chromosome pairs is called the sex chromosomes because they determine a person's gender.

Among females, the sex chromosomes consists of two chromosomes, both called X. The sex chromosomes in males are made up of one X chromosome and a smaller Y chromosome. The remaining 22 pairs of human chromosomes are called autosomes. These chromosomes are numbered 1 through 22, with 1 corresponding to the largest chromosome pair and 22 corresponding to the smallest.

Most, but not all, of a person's DNA is located within these 23 pairs of chromosomes, all of which are found within the nuclei of cells. In contrast, some DNA is found outside the nuclei of cells. This DNA is present in small, self-replicating structures called mitochondria and is called mitochondrial DNA.

Types of Genetic Disorders

Scientists have identified certain categories of genetic disorders, some of which have characteristic inheritance patterns. One category consists of single-gene disorders—disorders that involve an error in the DNA that makes up an individual gene. A second category of genetic disorders involves abnormalities of chromosomes in which too much or too little chromosomal material is present. Some genetic disorders are said to be multifactorial, because they are caused by the combined effects of multiple genes and environmental factors, such as diet and exposure to certain chemicals. Still other genetic disorders are caused by mutations in mitochondrial DNA.

Single-Gene Disorders

Single-gene disorders result from errors within an individual gene. Each gene contains information used by cells to manufacture a specific protein or a component of a protein. A tiny alteration, or mutation, in the DNA that makes up a gene may cause a person's cells to either fail to produce sufficient quantities of a crucial protein or to synthesize a protein with an altered form. Such a protein cannot perform its normal role.

The impact of a single-gene disorder sometimes depends on whether a person has inherited a faulty version of a gene from only one parent or from both parents. The genes that are carried on each of the 22 pairs of autosomes always occur in pairs—one of which is inherited from the mother, and the other from the father. In some instances, a faulty gene has a dominant effect, in which the person who inherits one faulty gene and one normally working gene will eventually develop a disorder. In other instances, the faulty gene is recessive—it will not cause a disorder unless a person inherits two copies of the faulty gene, one from the mother and one from the father.

About half of all single-gene disorders are said to be autosomal dominant, meaning that the faulty gene is carried on an autosomal chromosome and exerts its effects even when only one copy is present. A person with an autosomal dominant disorder has a 50 percent chance of producing a child with the disorder each time he or she has a child. An example of an autosomal dominant disorder is Huntington's disease. In this condition, which affects about 1 in 10,000 people, a person usually does not experience symptoms until they are at least 30 to 40 years old. At that time, or even later in life, a person with Huntington's disease develops uncontrolled movements called chorea and may also have problems with coordination, thinking, and judgment. These symptoms are due to the degeneration of nerve cells in a part of the brain called the basal ganglia in the cerebrum. This degeneration typically progresses until it results in the person's death.

In contrast to Huntington's disease, many other single-gene disorders are autosomal recessive. These disorders only occur when a person inherits two faulty copies of the same gene. In such cases, the parents are not affected themselves but they each carry one copy of the problematic gene, in which case they are known as carriers. If both parents are carriers of the same flawed gene, they have a 25 percent risk that they will produce a child with a genetic disorder each time they have a child.

An example of an autosomal recessive single-gene disorder is cystic fibrosis. This disease involves a gene that produces a protein that helps transport chloride molecules across cell membranes. This protein is typically present in specialized cells called epithelial cells, which line the inner surface of the lungs. If a person inherits two mutated forms of this gene, symptoms develop, including the potential build up of thick, suffocating mucus in the lungs. In some people with cystic fibrosis, pancreatic enzymes are secreted that interfere with the digestion of food. Abnormal mucus also interferes with the digestion of food. About 1 in 29 people of northern European ancestry carry a cystic fibrosis gene alteration, and about 1 in every 3,300 Caucasians in North America has the disease.

Another disorder that follows this inheritance pattern is Tay-Sachs disease. People who inherit two copies of the faulty Tay-Sachs gene lack a crucial enzyme called hexosaminidase A, which is needed to break down certain fatty substances in brain and nerve cells. As a result, these substances build up in such large quantities that the central nervous system gradually stops functioning and the person dies. Symptoms of Tay-Sachs typically become evident within the first six months of life, and most affected individuals die before reaching four years of age. Among people of eastern European Jewish ancestry, about 1 in 30 people carry a Tay-Sachs gene, and the incidence of Tay-Sachs disease for this population is 1 out of 3,600 people.

Some single-gene disorders are not entirely dominant or entirely recessive. In these disorders, each member of a pair of genes has a distinct effect. This is sometimes referred to as co-dominant, semi-dominant, or intermediate expression. An example of such a disorder is sickle-cell anemia, caused by a mutated gene that produces an abnormal form of hemoglobin, a protein in red blood cells that transports oxygen from the lungs to the tissues.

In people who have two copies of the faulty gene, this abnormal hemoglobin molecule causes red blood cells to assume a distorted shape after releasing oxygen. The distorted cells resemble a sickle—a crescent-shaped tool used in harvesting crops. The sickled shape prevents the cells from passing easily through tiny blood vessels, resulting in painful blockages.

Among people who inherit two faulty sickle-cell genes, the abnormal form of hemoglobin is predominant; these people are said to have sickle-cell disease. People who have a single faulty sickle-cell gene are said to have sickle-cell trait. These individuals have mainly the normal form of hemoglobin, but they have small amounts of the abnormal form and their cells may sickle on rare occasions. Sickle-cell anemia is most common among people who have ancestors from Africa, the Mediterranean, India, and the Middle East. In North America, about 10 percent of African Americans carry a faulty sickle-cell gene. In the United States, about 72,000 people have sickle-cell anemia.

A category of single-gene disorders known as X-linked disorders involves genes located on the X chromosome, one of the two sex chromosomes. Males are at greater risk for X-linked genetic disorders than females, because if a male inherits an X chromosome with a mutated recessive gene, he lacks a second X chromosome that might provide the normal, dominant form of the gene. The Y chromosome contains only a small number of genes that are mostly involved in determining male characteristics. Alterations to genes on the Y chromosome are a factor in some instances of male infertility.

An example of an X-linked disorder is hemophilia. People with hemophilia usually lack 1 of the 14 or more proteins called clotting factors that repair a cut or torn blood vessel. Consequently, their bodies are sometimes unable to stop bleeding after an injury. The clotting factor that is absent in hemophilia A, the most common form of hemophilia, is called factor VIII and is encoded by a gene on the X chromosome. Most people with hemophilia are males who have inherited an X chromosome with the faulty gene from their mother. It is rare for females to have hemophilia, because this would require inheriting the faulty gene from the X chromosome of both parents. About 1 in 10,000 men have hemophilia A.

Chromosomal Disorders

Chromosomal disorders are caused by the presence of an extra or missing whole or partial chromosome. In some cases, whole chromosomes or pieces of chromosomes are attached to one another in abnormal ways, which cause a person or their offspring to have an incorrect amount of chromosomal material. Chromosomal disorders are sometimes caused by an error in a type of cell division called meiosis, which occurs during the formation of eggs and sperm. Chromosomal disorders disrupt the biological functions of many genes. They produce multiple problems in the affected individual, often including mild or severe mental retardation. More than 600 chromosomal syndromes have been identified.

Down syndrome is the most common chromosomal disorder, affecting about 1 in 800 newborns. People with Down syndrome characteristically have three copies of the autosomal chromosome known as number 21 instead of the normal pair of number 21 chromosomes. For this reason, Down syndrome is commonly called trisomy 21. People with Down syndrome usually have mild to severe learning disabilities and physical symptoms that include a small skull, an extra fold of skin at the inner corner of each eye, and a flattened bridge of the nose. They also may have heart defects and other serious health problems.

Some chromosomal disorders involve the sex chromosomes. In many instances, an extra or missing sex chromosome is less life threatening than an extra or missing autosome. A person with Klinefelter syndrome, which affects about 1 in 500 males, has two X chromosomes and one Y chromosome. Males with Klinefelter syndrome are typically tall, and they may have small testes and slight breast development. They also may have minor problems with learning and are usually infertile.

Another chromosomal disorder that affects the sex chromosomes is Turner syndrome, which affects 1 in 2,500 females. In this disorder, a female has one functioning X chromosome instead of two. Females with this condition are typically short, with a thick, webbed neck. They may have mild problems with learning, and they usually are infertile because they lack normal ovaries.

Multifactorial Disorders

Multifactorial disorders are caused by several genes as well as the influence of a person's environment, such as diet or lifestyle. An example of a multifactorial disorder is a category of birth defects called neural tube defects. In a neural tube defect, a fetus's neural tube—the structure that develops into the spinal cord and brain—is damaged. The two most common types of neural tube defects are anencephaly and spina bifida. Anencephaly is a fatal condition in which a baby is born with only a partial brain or no brain at all. About 1,000 to 2,000 babies with anencephaly are born each year in the United States. Spina bifida results when a neural tube defect causes an opening in the spine.

In the United States, about one infant in every 2,000 live births is born with spina bifida. These infants need surgery to close the opening in the spine, and they may develop problems with walking or with bowel or bladder control. Geneticists believe that certain genes may play a role in damage to the neural tube, but the mother's diet during pregnancy also plays a role. A woman's risk of giving birth to an infant with a neural tube defect significantly decreases if she consumes adequate amounts of folic acid, a vitamin in the B complex, during the first three months of pregnancy and one month before conception.

Some common diseases that run in families but do not display an obvious pattern of inheritance are also thought to be multifactorial. Two examples are coronary heart disease and diabetes mellitus. In both cases, genes may cause a person to be predisposed to develop the disease, but lifestyle choices can help to prevent the disease from developing or from worsening after it occurs.

Mitochondrial Disorders

All cells contain tiny self-replicating structures called mitochondria located outside of the nucleus. Each mitochondrion contains about ten single copies of small, circular chromosomes. These chromosomes contain a type of DNA that is different from the DNA found in chromosomes inside the cell nucleus. Both sperm and eggs contain mitochondria, but at fertilization, a sperm contributes only the genetic material in its nucleus to the new life form. All of a person's mitochondria are genetic descendents of those mitochondria that were present in the egg before fertilization. Therefore, mitochondrial disorders are transmitted solely through the mother. Both males and females can be affected, but an affected male will not pass on the disorder to his children.

Conditions involving mitochondrial inheritance are rare,

and they have been recognized only since the 1980s. One example is Leber's hereditary optic neuropathy, a vision disorder characterized by shrinking of the optic nerve, which transmits visual images from the eye to the brain.

Genetic Screening

Clinical geneticists and other health professionals use several screening tests and procedures to determine whether a person has a genetic disorder or is at risk of having a child with a disorder. These tests may be performed at various times in a person's life. Some genetic screening tests are routinely performed on newborns. Among adults, genetic screening is always voluntary.

Preimplantation Diagnosis

A test that can be performed at the earliest possible stage of life is called preimplantation diagnosis. This test is used in conjunction with in vitro fertilization, a procedure for uniting an egg and sperm in a labouratory rather than in a woman's body.

Before an embryo created using in vitro fertilization is surgically implanted into the mother's uterus, physicians remove a cell from the developing embryo and analyse its DNA to learn if abnormalities associated with a specific genetic disorder are present. Although in vitro fertilization is a standard medical practice, removing cells from a developing embryo and preimplantation diagnosis are considered experimental procedures.

Prenatal Screening

Prenatal screening—genetic screening performed during a pregnancy—is used to identify fetuses at risk for certain genetic disorders. Usually, a multiple marker screen analyses a pregnant woman's blood for the presence of three substances—alpha fetoprotein, estriol, and human chorionic gonadotropin—that may signal certain problems in the fetus. This test is a screening test to identify fetuses with an extra chromosome or fetuses with a neural tube defect.

Chorionic villus sampling is a prenatal screening test performed at about the tenth week of pregnancy. A thin hollow tube called a catheter is inserted through the vagina and cervix into the uterus and is used to withdraw small amounts of the chorionic villus, which is part of the developing placenta. In some instances a sample of the chorionic villus is obtained through a needle inserted through the abdomen. Doctors isolate fetal cells from the chorionic villus and analyse them in the labouratory to determine if certain genetic abnormalities are present.

Amniocentesis is a prenatal screening test that is offered primarily to women who are 35 years or older at the time of pregnancy. This test is performed between the 14th and 20th weeks of pregnancy. Doctors insert a thin needle through the abdomen and into a woman's uterus, away from the fetus, to remove a few tablespoons of amniotic fluid.

This fluid contains fetal urine and fetal cells, which can be used to prepare a karyotype a photographic image that depicts all of the embryo's chromosomes in a cell. A karyotype reveals whether a fetus has extra chromosomes, missing chromosomes, or chromosomes that have attached to one another in unusual ways. The cells in the amniotic fluid can also be used to check for the presence of certain DNA mutations and to determine whether enzymes present in the fluid are characteristic of certain genetic disorders.

Newborn Screening

Genetic screening of newborns is necessary to identify those genetic disorders that would harm an infant if not treated immediately. Newborns with sickle-cell anemia are at risk of dying from severe infections; these infants are given antibiotics immediately after being diagnosed with this disease. Newborns with phenylketonuria lack the enzyme needed to convert phenylalanine, an amino acid present in food, into a different amino acid called tyrosine. As a result, phenylalanine can build up to toxic levels in the bloodstream, resulting in severe mental retardation.

For infants diagnosed with this disease, doctors prescribe

a special diet that lacks phenylalanine to prevent this damaging buildup. Similarly, infants with galactosemia require a diet that is low in the sugar galactose to prevent the buildup of this substance to levels that produce seizures, mental retardation, and early death. In the United States and Canada, hospitals commonly screen newborns for phenylketonuria and galactosemia. Screening for sickle-cell anemia is performed for all infants in the United States and for infants of parents from at-risk groups in Canada.

Carrier Screening

Genetic screening detects carriers of genetic disorders—people who have a single copy of a mutated recessive gene but are otherwise healthy. These tests are usually intended to diagnose autosomal recessive disorders that are common in individuals of certain ethnic backgrounds. People of Eastern European Jewish ancestry may be screened to see if they are carriers for Tay-Sachs disease, cystic fibrosis, and an inherited neurological disorder called Canavan disease. In the United States and Canada, African Americans are at high risk for developing sickle-cell anemia. A blood disorder called beta thalassemia is more common in individuals of Greek or Italian ancestry, and alpha thalassemia, a related condition, is more common in persons of Southeast Asian and Chinese ancestry.

Carrier testing identifies couples at risk of having an affected child so that they can make informed decisions about having children. Many couples choose to have children even if both partners are known to carry the same recessive gene. In such instances, some people undergo prenatal genetic testing to learn if a fetus has a disorder and decide at that time if they want to terminate the pregnancy. Others use prenatal genetic testing to learn in advance the health status of their child so that they can prepare for a specialized delivery or surgery, or other treatment the infant may need.

Family History Screening

A medical family history helps identify healthy individuals at risk of developing a genetic disorder themselves, or of having a child with a genetic condition. In obtaining a family history, a health professional asks questions about the health of family members over a span of three or more generations. The information is recorded as a graphic image that incorporates symbols, such as squares, circles, triangles, and diamonds, to present a shorthand record of the medical family history. This image, called a pedigree, can reveal the multigenerational pattern of a genetic disorder. A dominant disorder affects at least one family member in each generation, whereas a recessive disorder may cluster in a single generation.

Treatments for Genetic Disorders

Currently, there are no permanent cures for genetic disorders, but many treatments are available. A procedure called gene therapy is on the horizon; it may eventually provide permanent cures for at least some genetic disorders.

For a few genetic disorders caused by an enzyme malfunction, it is possible to replace the malfunctioning enzyme with a functioning enzyme.Gaucher disease is an autosomal recessive disorder marked by a shortage of an enzyme called glucocerebrosidase. People with one type of Gaucher disease develop progressive bone disease and an enlarged spleen. They can be treated with enzyme replacement therapy, in which they receive regular intravenous infusions of synthetic enzymes that carry out the functions of glucocerebrosidase.

Most genetic disorders are treated using more than one type of treatment, in keeping with their complex and varied symptoms. Children with cystic fibrosis usually take pancreatic enzymes to help digest food and inhale medicines that are formulated to break up mucus in air passages. Parents of these children regularly clap their hand on the child's chest and back to loosen mucus in the lungs. In some instances, surgeons may perform a lung transplantation to save a patient's life.

People with sickle-cell anemia commonly require drugs to combat pain and anemia and to prevent infections. They may receive blood transfusions to increase the number of normal red blood cells in their bloodstream. Adults with severe sickle-cell anemia sometimes benefit from an anticancer drug called hydroxyurea, which reduces the frequency of cell sickling, and from erythropoietin, a hormone that stimulates red blood cell production. Some people with severe sickle-cell anemia benefit from bone marrow transplants.

An experimental procedure called gene therapy may have the potential to cure several fatal genetic disorders. Instead of treating symptoms of a disorder, gene therapy alters the genetic makeup of certain cells. Gene therapy was first used in 1990 to treat children with an autosomal recessive condition called adenosine deaminase (ADA) deficiency. In the absence of the enzyme adenosine deaminase, T lymphocytes, a type of immune system cell, cannot develop normally. Children with ADA lack the immunity to fight off infections and typically die within the first years of life. In experiments using gene therapy, a genetically modified virus was used to carry a normal ADA gene to the patient's immune cells. The inserted ADA gene then programmememed the cells to produce the missing ADA enzyme, which led to normal immune function in those cells. Gene therapy has also produced promising results in treating a rare immunologic disorder called chronic granulomatous disease, and it is being investigated in the treatment of cystic fibrosis and hemophilia.

Chapter 2

Forest Products: Wood and Cork

TREE

Tree, woody plant with a distinct main stem, or trunk. At maturity, trees are usually the tallest of plants, and their height and single main stem differentiate them from shrubs, which are shorter and have many stems. Trees are *perennials*, plants that live for at least three years. Some species of tree only grow to 4 m (13 ft) in height, but the tallest species may reach heights of more than 112 m (more than 367 ft). The General Sherman Tree, a giant sequoia in California's Sequoia National Park, has a height of 84 m (275 ft) and a diameter of 11 m (37 ft). The largest trees, however, are not necessarily the oldest. The bristlecone pine grows to a height of only about 9 m (about 30 ft), but one specimen has been dated as at least 4,600 years old.

Trees grow throughout the world, from the extreme cold regions near the Arctic and the Antarctic to the hot tropical regions around the equator. They grow in both good and poor soil, in deserts and swamps, along shores, and at mountain elevations of several thousand feet. Although trees may grow singly, under natural conditions they more often grow in stands, which consist either of one species or of a mixture of species. A forest is a plant community made up of the trees, shrubs, and herbs that cover an area. Throughout much of North America, forests include only a few species of trees. In tropical forests, however, large numbers of different species can be found in very small areas. A survey of a 1-hectare (2.5-

acre) plot in the Brazilian rain forest determined that it contained 476 tree species.

Importance of Trees

Perhaps the most important ecological function of trees is protecting the land against erosion, the wearing away of topsoil due to wind and water. The trunks and branches of trees provide protection from the wind, and tree roots help solidify soil in times of heavy rain. In addition, trees and forests store water reserves that act as buffers for the ecosystem during periods of drought. In many areas the removal of forests has resulted in costly floods and subsequent droughts. Trees and forests also provide habitat, protection, and food for many plant and animal species. In addition, they play an important role in global climate and atmosphere regulation—the leaves of trees absorb carbon dioxide in the air and produce oxygen that is necessary for life.

Trees have many economic uses. Lumber from trees is the most widely used material in the building of homes and other structures. Many trees yield edible fruits and nuts such as oranges, grapefruits, apples, avocados, peaches, pecans, hickory nuts, and almonds. Trees and their fruits are also the source of many commercial waxes and oils, including olive oil and coconut oil.

Tree trunks are tapped for sap, which is used in making such products as maple syrup, rubber, and turpentine. The barks of certain trees are sources of cork and spices. Many trees yield important medicines, such as quinine. The bark of the yew tree is the source of the drug taxol, which in 1992 was approved for treating ovarian cancer. Chemical materials produced by trees are used in tanning leather and in the manufacture of inks, medicines, dyes, and wood alcohol. In addition, trees are used in landscaping homes, parks, and highways. In regions with extreme climates, they serve as windbreaks or as shade against the sun.

Types of Trees

There are two general types of trees, angiosperms and

gymnosperms. Angiosperms are flowering plants in which the *ovule,* or seed, is encased in a protective ovary. With about 235,000 species, the angiosperm division is the largest and most diverse plant group. It is divided into dicots, plants with two *cotyledons* (seed leaf structures), that include the familiar broadleaf trees such as maple and oak; and the monocots, plants with one cotyledon that include the palms and lily trees.

Unlike angiosperms, gymnosperms do not bear flowers. Their seeds lie exposed in structures such as cones or fleshy cups called arils. The group includes about 500 tree species—including three major types, needle-leaf trees (or conifers), ginkgos, and cycads.

Angiosperms

As angiosperms, all dicots produce flowers, and their seeds are always enclosed in a protective covering. In temperate regions, most of these broadleaf trees are *deciduous,* meaning that they shed their foliage each year. Some nontropical broadleaf trees, however, such as certain magnolias and hollies, are *evergreen*—that is, they retain foliage throughout the year. In warmer parts of the United States and in the tropics, most broadleaf trees are evergreen. Broadleaf trees include virtually all of the familiar trees and shrubs that are known to flower, such as the elm, chestnut, alder, birch, and willow, as well as tropical species such as teak and mahogany.

The most recognizable trees in the monocot angiosperm class are the palm trees. There are about 2500 species of palms, including the coconut palm and date palm. Most palms lack branches and instead have enormous *compound* leaves (leaves composed of leaflets arranged along a central stem). Lily trees are another member of the monocot class. These trees are closely related to the familiar garden lily and include yucca trees such as the odd-looking Joshua tree, which is found in the deserts of the southwestern United States.

Gymnosperms

The needle-leaf trees, or conifers, include such trees as the pine, spruce, fir, yew, redwood, and cypress. The seeds of these gymnosperms are usually produced in cones at the base of protective scales. As their name implies, needle-leaf trees have slender needle-shaped leaves. Because of their small surface area and structure, needle leaves are not seriously injured by very low temperatures or by severe droughts. For this reason, the forests of cold far northern latitudes and high-altitude arid regions consist mostly of needle-leaf trees. Most needle-leaf trees are evergreens and retain most of their foliage throughout the year. Deciduous members of the group include the bald cypress and the larch.

The ginkgo, or maidenhair tree, is the sole living survivor of the ancient division of ginkgo gymnosperms. The ginkgo was abundant in the Mesozoic era (about 240 million to 65 million years ago). Virtually unchanged since that time, this tree is recognized by its fan-shaped leaves and the forking vein patterns on its leaves.

A deciduous tree, the ginkgo grows slowly but may attain heights of more than 30 m (more than 98 ft). Ginkgos are native to Asia, where they have been preserved as sacred trees in Chinese temples since antiquity, but they are also cultivated in Europe and the United States.

Cycads are palmlike gymnosperms found mainly in tropical and subtropical regions of Africa, Asia, and Central America. There are about 100 species, with only one native to the United States. The trunk has no branches, and the long leaves are clustered near the top.

Cycads are evergreen and may grow to heights of more than 18 m (more than 59 ft). They first appeared 285 million years ago and were the dominant plant type during the age of the dinosaurs, which roughly paralleled the Mesozoic era. Because the cycad is a popular ornamental tree, most cycad species are in danger of extinction because so many of them have been collected from the wild.

Major Parts of a Tree

The major parts of a tree are its roots, trunk, leaves, flowers, and seeds. These components play vital roles in a tree's growth, development, and reproduction.

Roots

Trees are held in place by anchoring organs called roots. In addition to anchoring the tree, roots also absorb water and minerals through tiny structures called root hairs. From the roots the water and mineral nutrients are carried upward through the wood cells to the leaves. Although the internal structure of most kinds of roots is similar, there are often external differences. Pines, have a strongly developed *taproot,* or main root, in addition to branching side roots. In maples, on the other hand, there is little or no central taproot, and the other roots are produced in great numbers near the surface of the soil.

Roots grow constantly, and at the growing tip of each root is a region called the *meristem,* which is composed of special rapidly dividing cells. Just behind the meristem the cells become elongated, and farther from the tip the cells become differentiated into various kinds of plant tissue. In rapidly growing roots the root tip is covered by a root cap, a protective coat of loose cells that are constantly being rubbed off and replaced as the root grows.

Trunk

Bark is the outer protective covering of tree trunks. Because bark varies so widely in colour, texture, and thickness, its characteristics provide one of the most important means of identifying species of trees. Most of the total thickness of bark consists of outer bark, which is made up of dead cells. Outer bark may be very thick, as in the cork oak, or quite thin, as in young birches and maples. Openings in the outer bark allow the movement of carbon dioxide and oxygen to and from the inner tissues.

The inner bark layer, called the phloem, consists of a thin layer of living cells. These cells act together to transport food in the form of sugars, which are made in the tree's leaves, through the trunk and stems to other parts of the tree. Phloem cells have thin walls, and their living contents are so interconnected that the sugar solutions can pass easily and rapidly from one end of the plant to the other. As old layers of outer bark are sloughed off, new ones are constantly being added from the inside, where new phloem is always being created.

Most of a tree trunk is occupied by the wood, or xylem layer, which consists almost entirely of dead cells. The living xylem cells, however, act as the tree's plumbing system by transporting water and dissolved food through the trunk and stems. A layer of cells called the *cambium* separates the living xylem cells from the phloem. As the tree grows and develops, the cambium forms new phloem and xylem cells. The layers of xylem cells form rings; these rings can be counted to determine the age of the tree in areas with distinct growing seasons.

In young trees the centre of the woody column, inside the xylem, consists of soft thin-walled cells called the pith. The pith serves as a storage tissue for sugars and later as a reservoir for wastes. In older trees the pith is crushed by the xylem's woody tissue, and wastes are simply deposited in the wood cells near the centre of the trunk. As a result, in some trees the cells within the pith become dark in colour and form what is often called the heartwood. The lighter cells around them make up the sapwood.

In monocot trees, such as palms, the xylem and phloem tissues are grouped into bundles, which are scattered through the mass of pith that makes up most of the tree's internal structure. In the stems of such trees, the yearly growth rings are not apparent, as they are in oaks, maples, and other trees of temperate regions.

Leaves

In trees, as in other green plants, the principal function of the leaves is the manufacture of sugars by the process of photosynthesis. In this process, sugars are formed when carbon dioxide (from the air) and water (from the leaf cells) are combined in the presence of light and the green pigment chlorophyll. Oxygen is produced as a byproduct. Some of the newly formed sugar is used by the leaf cells for energy, but most is carried to other parts of the tree to provide energy for growth and development in those areas.

The leaves are also the chief organs involved in the loss of water from the plant, called transpiration. Many of the tree's tissues cannot function without a constant supply of water, and water is necessary to prevent overheating or wilting of the leaves. Transpiration is responsible for the movement of water from the roots of the tree up to the top. As water is lost through the leaves, water that enters the roots is pulled upward through the xylem tissue to replace the lost moisture, ensuring a constant circulation of water through the tissues of the tree.

Flowers

All angiosperms bear flowers, the trees' reproductive structures. In some trees, such as dogwoods, cherries, and some magnolias, the flowers are large and colourful. Oaks, willows, and other temperate forest trees, on the other hand, often bear small, pale, and inconspicuous flowers.

In maples and many other trees the male and female reproductive parts are carried in separate flowers on the same tree. This arrangement is known as monoecism, and such trees are called monoecious. In oaks the male pollen-producing flowers are borne in long hanging tassels, and the short-stalked or stalkless female flowers are located on the twigs. In some trees, such as the hollies and willows, the male and female flowers are borne on separate trees. This is known as dioecism, and these trees are called dioecious.

In needle-leaf trees the male and female reproductive structures may be produced in cones rather than flowers, and in such cases there are always separate male and female cones. The cones are often produced on the same tree, but frequently there are more female cones in the upper branches. In all reproductive arrangements, the flowers or female cones are fertilized when wind, birds, bats, mammals, or insects carry pollen from the male structures to the female ones.

Seeds

Seeds, the ripened ovules of the plant that are capable of

germination, are the product of fertilized flowers and are distributed in various ways. In pines each seed is surrounded by a winglike structure. As the winged seed falls from the cone, it floats down to the ground, riding air currents. Oak seeds are enclosed in acorns, which are either planted by squirrels or merely fall to the ground near the parent tree. Willow trees produce thin-walled, flask-shaped fruits that burst open, releasing the seeds. Each seed has a tuft of downy fibres, which enables it to be picked up by air currents and travel for considerable distances. Seeds of other tree species are dispersed by water, mammals, birds, and ants.

Tree Growth and Development

Trees grow in both height and diameter. A tree increases in height through the elongation of its trunk or branches and the seasonal production of new branches. The growth of the tree in diameter results from the activity of the cambium, the special cells lying at the inner surface of the bark.

Height

All branches arise from buds, which are located at the tips of twigs and at the bases of leaves. Within each bud is a *meristematic region,* or growing zone, similar to that in the root tip. The growing tip is surrounded by many tiny leaves, and the entire bud is covered with a series of protective scales. The cells in the growing tip, like those of the root tip, divide rapidly, elongate, and become differentiated into the various kinds of stem tissue.

Diameter

The part of the bark that causes the tree to grow in diameter is the cambium. During the growing season the cells of the cambium, like those of the stem tip and root tip, divide rapidly. They produce xylem, or wood cells, toward the centre of the trunk, and they produce phloem, or food-conducting cells, toward the bark. At places the cambium also produces rows of thin-walled cells that run horizontally through the xylem and the phloem. Known as *rays,* these horizontal cells conduct and store water and nutrients. Among tropical woody plants, growth continues throughout the year. In trees of temperate regions, however, the annual growth is usually crowded into a short period of a few weeks in early spring.

When the stem of a tree is cut fully across, one can observe each year's growth as a ring. By counting these rings, it is possible to determine the age of the tree as well as the growing conditions during its lifetime.

In favourable conditions, when the tree experiences rapid growth, it forms wide rings, but in difficult times, when growth is slower, it forms narrower rings. Each annual ring consists of two parts. One part, which makes up most of the ring, is light-coloured wood composed of relatively large cells. These cells were formed during the spring, when growing conditions were best. The second part of the ring is darker and is composed of small thick-walled cells, which were formed during the less favourable months.

Growth Rates

The rate at which trees grow varies considerably. Young bamboo stems may increase at the rate of many centimeters a day until they eventually reach a height of 36 m (118 ft) with a diameter of more than 30 cm (more than 1 ft). Many needle-leaf trees, such as the longleaf pine, grow at a much faster rate than broadleaf trees like walnuts and oaks, especially in their early years. Some broadleaf trees, however, such as black locusts and cottonwoods, may grow rapidly in suitable soils.

Planting and Caring for Trees

Whether trees are being planted for reforestation, ornament, shade, or fruit, the first step is selecting the species to be grown. The choice depends on such factors as the characteristics of the soil, the location of the site, and drainage. Sycamore and cottonwood trees will not grow on dry exposed slopes or ridges, or in fields with thin topsoil over a heavy compact subsoil. Walnut trees will not grow in swampy places, and jack pines grow especially well on loose sandy soils with good drainage. A good rule of thumb is to plant *native* trees—

trees that have demonstrated their ability to thrive in the local environment without harming other local species.

The hole for a seedling should be deep enough to hold the fully expanded root system of the seedling. Larger plants should be placed in a hole 60 cm (2 ft) deep with a diameter 60 cm greater than that of the ball of the roots. In poor soil the hole should be 1.8 m (6 ft) wide and 60 cm deep for a 2.5-m (8-ft) tree, and proportionately wider for taller trees.

After the tree is placed in the hole, the soil should be firmly pressed around the roots, and the ground should be thoroughly soaked with water. Mixing bone meal or well-rotted manure into the soil will help the tree become established quickly. Most deciduous trees should be planted in the fall when they are not growing, but evergreens are usually planted in the spring, at the beginning or middle of their period of vigourous growth.

Watering

After planting, the soil around a tree should be kept moist, but not soaked. If artificial watering is not practical, a layer of mulch 7 to 15 cm (3 to 6 in) deep should be placed around the tree to conserve moisture and to discourage the growth of weeds. Because a transplanted tree does not adequately absorb water through its damaged roots, it is important to prevent water loss from the plant by pruning top limbs to limit transpiration.

Fertilizing

In good soils it is less important to fertilize than in poor soils. However, all trees grow better and faster and are less likely to become diseased if fertilizer is supplied in the proper amounts. This may be done most easily by placing a large handful of fertilizer in holes made by a crowbar at the edge of the spread of the tree's limbs. The holes should be about 60 cm (2 ft) deep and about 5 cm (2 in) in diameter, and they should be spaced about 90 cm (3 ft) apart. After the fertilizer has been introduced, the holes should be filled in with soil. Organic fertilizers such as manure and mulch are preferable to chemicals that may replace or destroy natural organisms in the soil.

Pruning

Pruning of ornamental trees maintains the form of the tree, removes weak or sickly branches, and rejuvenates old or unhealthy plants. If performed during a period of vigourous growth, pruning often also results in an increased production of flowers. In pruning small branches, cuts are made just above the buds that point in the direction branches are desired. When it is necessary to remove a large branch, cuts are made just in front of a swollen area at the base of the branch called the branch collar. Protective chemicals contained in the branch collar prevent insect infestation and decay from harming the tree after a large branch has been removed.

Unusual Trees

There are many types of unusual trees around the world that exhibit a variety of interesting characteristics. Among these are prehistoric relics, trees that exhibit bizarre growth patterns or formations, and trees with interesting strategies for obtaining the air, water, and nutrients necessary for growth.

Like the ginkgo, the dawn redwood is old enough to be considered a living fossil. Its fossilized remains were studied and identified in the 1800s, and scientists believed that the tree had become extinct about 20 million years ago. In 1941, however, a Chinese botanist discovered living trees in an isolated valley in central China.

Since then, the tree has been found in other places in China, and the fossil record indicates that millions of years ago it grew in Greenland and in North America as far south as California. Like other sequoias, the dawn redwood grows well from seeds, and seedlings have been planted throughout the Pacific Northwest and in Alaska. Specimen trees have also been successfully grown in many of the milder parts of the East Coast of the United States. Unlike other sequoias, the dawn redwood is deciduous and loses its leaves in the fall.

Although the banyan tree begins life with a single trunk, aerial roots grow down from its spreading limbs and take root. These roots enlarge, eventually becoming trunklike, and in old age a single tree may have the appearance of a small forest.

The largest banyan, found on the island of Sri Lanka, has 350 major trunks and several thousand smaller ones. The name of the tree comes from a Hindu word for trader, because in many regions where banyans are found, traders and merchants use the tree's shade while displaying their wares.

The baobab tree, the closely related bottle tree, and certain cactus trees have trunks with fleshy centres. These trunks store large amounts of water, enabling the trees to survive the arid conditions under which they grow. The trunk of the baobab may measure 9 m (30 ft) in diameter. The bottle tree has a bulging bottle-shaped trunk. Cacti, although frequently covered with spines, can yield water to a lost hiker even in the driest desert.

Although it is native to Africa, the sausage tree is cultivated as an ornamental in warm areas such as southern Florida and Hawaii. The sausage tree has large deep red flowers, which are replaced eventually by giant sausage-shaped fruits about 60 cm long. Both the flowers and fruits are borne on long stems hanging from the limbs of the tree.

The pencil tree, a native of Asia, is grown as an ornamental in Hawaii and elsewhere because of its odd twigs, which are swollen, pencil-like, and bright green. The twigs serve the tree in place of leaves, which are almost totally lacking. The pencil tree has strongly caustic sap. On contact with the skin the sap causes a rash, and it may even cause temporary or permanent blindness if it touches the eye.

Bald cypress trees, deciduous needle-leaf trees that grow in swampy areas, are unusual because of special breathing organs known as cypress knees. These organs are extensions from the root system that project above the usual water level and absorb oxygen from the air for use by the roots.

Strangler fig trees are an example of a parasitic method of development that occurs in several plant families. A seed is deposited by a bird, monkey, or other animal in a depression or a crotch of a limb. The seed sprouts and begins to develop, and roots eventually find their way to the ground, sometimes traveling 25 m (82 ft) or more. There the roots take hold and begin to enlarge toward each other, enclosing the trunk of the host tree. Finally, the roots join side by side to restrict the growth of the original tree, which eventually rots away, leaving the parasite standing as an independent plant.

STEM

Stem, portion of vascular plants that commonly bears leaves and buds. It usually is aerial, upright, and elongate, but may be highly modified in structure. Subterranean stems include the rhizomes of the iris and the runners of the strawberry; the potato is a portion of an underground stem. Some plants, such as the century plant, have very short stems that bear a dense cluster of leaves. Those points on the stem at which leaves or buds arise are called nodes, and the regions of the stem between the nodes are known as internodes.

The chief functions of stems are the production and support of leaves and reproductive structures, conduction of water and nutrients and food storage. In some plants, such as cactus, stems also have the specialized functions of storing water and manufacturing food.

Conducting tissues within plant stems are arranged in columns called vascular bundles. These bundles are composed of xylem, which conducts water up the stem, and of phloem, which transports sugars produced by the leaf down the stem. Vascular bundles extend into leaves, in which they are called veins. As the stem grows longer, new cells are added to the vascular system, providing conductive tissue for new leaves and branches.

The arrangement of vascular bundles differs in the stems of the two major groups of angiosperms or flowering plants: the monocotyledons and the dicotyledons. In monocotyledons, such as corn, the vascular tissue occurs in many scattered bundles throughout the cross section of the stem. In dicotyledons, such as the pea, the vascular bundles are arranged in a cylindrical ring; the remainder of the stem constitutes the fundamental tissue and is usually divided into the cortex, or portion outside the ring of vascular bundles, and the pith, the portion inside the cylindrical ring. The outer layer of the stem of herbaceous plants is called the epidermis.

In the angiosperms, only dicotyledons have true woody

growth. Gymnosperms, comprising the conifers and related plants, all have woody stems. Such stems have a thin layer of cells between the xylem and phloem, called the cambium. During the growing season, these cells divide actively, producing new cells that differentiate into xylem, or wood, toward the inner side of the cambium and phloem toward the outer side. As the cambium grows, the diameter of the stem increases, and the new phloem presses outward upon the soft tissues of the cortex, which become distorted and eventually die. A second layer of dividing cells, however, is formed either in the cortex or, in older stems, in the phloem. This layer of cells produces cork, which is the protective tissue that replaces the dead cells of the epidermis. The bark of tree trunks, thus, is a complex tissue consisting of phloem and cork.

Herbaceous stems, lacking in woody growth, may derive strength by other means. The monocotyledon bamboo which does not develop wood, is strengthened by the presence of numerous fibres in its stem. The phloem and cortex may contain fibres in addition to soft cells. Such fibres having commercial importance include linen, obtained from flax, and hemp and jute. Wood is the most important economic product of the stem.

XYLEM

Xylem, woody tissue, found in higher plants, that conducts water and inorganic salts throughout the plant and provides it with mechanical support. In leaves, flowers, and young stems, xylem is present in conjunction with phloem in the form of conducting strands called vascular bundles. In roots there is a central core of xylem. Xylem that derives from the shoot and root-growing points is called primary xylem. In addition, new xylem, called secondary xylem, may be added by the activity of the cambium, which actively divides cells situated between the xylem and phloem. This division gives rise to new xylem cells toward the centre in roots and toward the outside in most stems. Some plants have little or no secondary xylem, in contrast to woody plants in which indefinite amounts of secondary xylem is the botanical term equivalent to wood.

Xylem may contain three types of elongated cells: tracheids, vessel elements, and fibres. At maturity, when functioning in conduction, all of these cells are dead. Tracheids are elongated cells with thick walls characterized by small, sharply defined thin areas known as pits. Vessel elements are specialized tracheids in which the end walls have one or more pores; a vertical series of vessel elements forming a continuous tube is known as a vessel. Fibres, which are specialized tracheids with much-thickened walls, function only slightly in conduction, but serve to increase the strength of xylem.

The xylem of plants that are earlier than most in evolutionary development, such as ferns and conifers, consists of tracheids. In most flowering plants, the xylem also contains well-developed vessels and fibres. Because sequences in the specialization of all these tissue elements can be observed quite clearly, the study of xylem provides important clues to the evolutionary pathways of higher plants.

PHLOEM

Phloem, in higher plants, vascular tissue that conducts sugars and other synthesized food materials from the regions of manufacture in the plant to those of consumption and storage. Phloem is found in the vascular bundles, the longitudinal strands of conductive tissue, in association with the water-conducting tissue, or xylem. The vascular bundles constitute major structural units in herbaceous stems and are the veins in leaves. In the vascular cylinder traversing the centre of the buttercup root the xylem forms a star-shaped central core, and bands of phloem are present in the grooves of this core.

Typically, the xylem is on the side of the vascular bundle closest to the pith, although other arrangements are not uncommon. In the older portions of a plant the soft cells of the phloem are crushed as new phloem is formed in the growing process and pushed outward. This new phloem is formed by the action of the cambium, or growing zone, a layer of cells that separates the xylem and phloem and produces phloem cells toward the outside of the plant.

Phloem consists of two types of conducting cells, the characteristic type known as sieve-tube elements and another type called companion cells. Sieve-tube elements are elongate cells that have end walls perforated by numerous minute pores through which dissolved materials can pass. Such sieve-tube elements are connected in vertical series known as sieve tubes. Sieve-tube elements are alive at maturity, although their nuclei disintegrate before the element begins its conductive function. Companion cells, which are smaller, have nuclei at maturity and are living; they are found adjacent to the sieve-tube elements and are believed to control the process of conduction in the sieve tubes.

Phloem may contain bast fibres. These fibres are very strong and in certain plants are the source of such commercial fibres as flax and jute, used to make linen fabric and burlap and sacking.

DICOTS

Dicots, popular name for dicotyledons, one of the two large groups of flowering plants. A number of floral and vegetative features of dicots distinguish them from the more recently evolved monocotyledons, the other class of flowering plants. In dicots the embryo sprouts two cotyledons, which are seed leaves that usually do not become foliage leaves but serve to provide food for the new seedling.

Flower parts of dicots are in fours or fives, and the leaves usually have veins arranged in a *reticulate* (netlike) pattern. The vascular tissue in the stems is arranged in a ring, and true secondary growth takes place, causing stems and roots to increase in diameter. Tree forms are common. Certain woody dicot groups exhibit characteristics such as large flowers with many unfused parts that are thought to be similar to those of early flowering plants. About 170,000 species of dicots are known, including buttercups, maples, roses, and violets.

MONOCOTS

Monocots, more properly monocotyledons, one of two classes of flowering plants. They are mostly herbaceous and include such familiar plants as iris, lily, orchid, grass, and palm. Several floral and vegetative features distinguish them from dicots, the other angiosperm class. These features include flower parts in threes; one *cotyledon;* leaf veins that are usually parallel; vascular tissue in scattered bundles in the stem; and no true secondary growth.

Monocots are thought to have evolved from some early aquatic group of dicots through reduction of various flower and vegetative parts. Among living monocot groups, one order contains the most primitive monocots. About 50,000 species of monocots are known—about one-third the number of dicot species.

ANGIOSPERM

Angiosperm common name for the division or phylum comprising flowering plants, the dominant form of plant life. Members of the division are the source of most of the food on which humans and other mammals rely and of many raw materials and natural products. Included in the division are most shrubs and herbs, most familiar trees except pines and other conifers, and specialized plants such as succulents, parasites, and aquatic types.

Although about 230,000 species are known, many remain obscure. Flowering plants occupy almost every ecological situation and dominate most natural landscapes. About two-thirds occur in the Tropics, where they are rapidly being exterminated by human activities. Only about 1000 species are of major economic importance, and the bulk of the world's food supply is derived from only 15. Many hundreds more could be useful if properly investigated and developed.

Description

The characteristic feature of angiosperms is the flower, the function of which is the reproduction of the plant through the development of seeds. Flowers are highly modified shoots made up of four fundamental parts arranged in separate series, or whorls, on specialized stem tips. The outer series consists of the sepals, which are modified leaves or bracts that are usually green. The next inner series, the petals, are also modified leaves, but they are usually finer textured and more conspicuously coloured. The third series consists of the stamens, the pollen-producing male portion of the flower. The innermost series is the carpels, female structures that produce the seeds. Carpels are often fused into a structure called the pistil.

The seeds of angiosperms develop in an ovary, a part of the carpel that surrounds and protects the egg-containing ovules. Seeds develop from the ovules after pollination and fertilization of the eggs. Ovules and seeds are not exclusive to angiosperms. The "naked-seed" plants, which include the conifers, cycads, and ginkgo, have ovules that lie exposed on the surface of specialized, scalelike leaves arranged into cones. The development of seeds from ovules enclosed in an ovary, which enlarges into a fruit as the fertilized seeds grow, is a feature unique to the angiosperms.

Evolution

The unique angiosperm flower probably evolved from a now extinct gymnosperm group that had insect-pollinated cones combining male and female reproductive parts. Living gymnosperms are mostly wind-pollinated, but among certain fossil and extant groups evidence of insect pollination exists. Although insects facilitate pollination, they also eat ovules, and it is believed that the development of the ovule-enclosing carpel of the angiosperm was an adaptation to protect the ovules and developing seeds from insect predation.

The carpel also provided protection from other harmful environmental influences, such as dryness, and it allowed reduction in the size of the ovule, refinement of the process of pollination, and the development of other parts of the flower, all of which improved the chances of successful reproduction.

Angiosperms are divided into two classes, the Magnoliopsida and Liliopsida, popularly termed dicots and monocots, representing separate evolutionary lines that must have diverged early in the history of the group. The direct predecessors of angiosperms are thought to have been woody gymnosperms; certain woody groups of dicots are thought to be primitive angiosperms. Monocots are more advanced than dicots, and they evolved from a primitive dicot group.

FLOWER

Flower, reproductive organ of most seed-bearing plants. Flowers carry out the multiple roles of sexual reproduction, seed development, and fruit production. Many plants produce highly visible flowers that have a distinctive size, colour, or fragrance. Almost everyone is familiar with beautiful flowers such as the blossoms of roses, orchids, and tulips. But many plants—including oaks, beeches, maples, and grasses—have small, green or gray flowers that typically go unnoticed.

Whether eye-catching or inconspicuous, all flowers produce the male or female sex cells required for sexual reproduction. Flowers are also the site of fertilization, which is the union of a male and female sex cell to produce a fertilized egg. The fertilized egg then develops into an embryonic (immature) plant, which forms part of the developing seed. Neighbouring structures of the flower enclose the seed and mature into a fruit.

Botanists estimate that there are more than 240,000 species of flowering plants. However, flowering plants are not the only seed-producing plants. Pines, firs, and cycads are among the few hundred plants that bear their seeds on the surface of cones, rather than within a fruit. Botanists call the cone-bearing plants *gymnosperms,* which means naked seeds; they refer to flowering plants as *angiosperms,* which means enclosed seeds.

Flowering plants are more widespread than any other group of plants. They bloom on every continent, from the bogs and marshes of the Arctic tundra to the barren soils of Antarctica. Deserts, grasslands, rainforests, and other biomes display distinctive flower species. Even streams, rivers, lakes, and swamps are home to many flowering plants.

In their diverse environments, flowers have evolved to become irreplaceable participants in the complex, interdependent communities of organisms that make up ecosystems. The seeds or fruits that flowers produce are food sources for many animals, large and small. In addition, many insects, bats, hummingbirds, and small mammals feed on nectar, a sweet liquid produced by many flowers, or on flower products known as pollen grains. The animals that eat flowers, seeds, and fruits are prey for other animals—lizards, frogs, salamanders, and fish, which in turn are devoured by yet other animals, such as owls and snakes. Thus, flowers provide a bountiful feast that sustains an intricate web of predators and prey.

Flowers play diverse roles in the lives of humans. Wildflowers of every hue brighten the landscape, and the attractive shapes and colours of cultivated flowers beautify homes, parks, and roadsides. The fleshy fruits that flowers produce, such as apples, grapes, strawberries, and oranges, are eaten worldwide, as are such hard-shelled fruits as pecans and other nuts.

Flowers also produce wheat, rice, oats, and corn—the grains that are dietary mainstays throughout the world. People even eat unopened flowers, such as those of broccoli and cauliflower, which are popular vegetables. Natural dyes come from flowers, and fragrant flowers, such as jasmine and damask rose, are harvested for their oils and made into perfumes. Certain flowers, such as red clover blossoms, are collected for their medicinal properties, and edible flowers, such as nasturtiums, add colour and flavour to a variety of dishes. Flowers also are used to symbolize emotions, as is evidenced by their use from ancient times in significant rituals, such as weddings and funerals.

Parts of a Flower

Flowers typically are composed of four parts, or whorls, arranged in concentric rings attached to the tip of the stem. From innermost to outermost, these whorls are the (1) Pistil, (2) Stamens, (3) Petals, and (4) Sepals.

Pistil

The innermost whorl, located in the centre of the flower, is the female reproductive structure, or pistil. Often vase-shaped, the pistil consists of three parts: the stigma, the style, and the ovary. The stigma, a slightly flared and sticky structure at the top of the pistil, functions by trapping pollen grains, the structures that give rise to the sperm cells necessary for fertilization. The style is a narrow stalk that supports the stigma. The style rises from the ovary, a slightly swollen structure seated at the base of the flower. Depending on the species, the ovary contains one or more ovules, each of which holds one egg cell. After fertilization, the ovules develop into seeds, while the ovary enlarges into the fruit. If a flower has only one ovule, the fruit will contain one seed, as in a peach. The fruit of a flower with many ovules, such as a tomato, will have many seeds. An ovary that contains one or more ovules also is called a carpel, and a pistil may be composed of one to several carpels.

Stamens

The next whorl consists of the male reproductive structures, several to many stamens arranged around the pistil. A stamen consists of a slender stalk called the filament, which supports the anther, a tiny compartment where pollen forms. When a flower is still an immature, unopened bud, the filaments are short and serve to transport nutrients to the developing pollen. As the flower opens, the filaments lengthen and hold the anthers higher in the flower, where the pollen grains are more likely to be picked up by visiting animals, wind, or in the case of some aquatic plants, by water. The animals, wind, or water might then carry the pollen to the stigma of an appropriate flower. The placement of pollen on the stigma is called pollination. Pollination initiates the process of fertilization.

Petals

Petals, the next whorl, surround the stamens and collectively are termed the corolla. Many petals have bright colours, which attract animals that carry out pollination, collectively termed pollinators. Three groups of pigments—alone or in combination—produce a veritable rainbow of petal colours: anthocyanins yield shades of violet, blue, and red; betalains create reds; and carotenoids produce yellows and orange. Petal colour can be modified in several ways. Texture can play a role in the overall effect a smooth petal is shiny, while a rough one appears velvety. If cells inside the petal are filled with starch, they create a white layer that makes pigments appear brighter. Petals with flat air spaces between cells shimmer iridescently.

In some flowers, the pigments form distinct patterns, invisible to humans but visible to bees, who can see ultraviolet light. Like the landing strips of an airport, these patterns, called nectar guides, direct bees to the nectar within the flower. Nectar is made in specialized glands located at or near the petal's base.

Some flowers secrete copious amounts of nectar and attract big pollinators with large appetites, such as bats. Other flowers, particularly those that depend on wind or water to transport their pollen, may secrete little or no nectar. The petals of many species also are the source of the fragrances that attract pollinators. In these species, the petals house tiny glands that produce essential, or volatile, oils that vapourize easily, often releasing a distinctive aroma. One flower can make dozens of different essential oils, which mingle to yield the flower's unique fragrance.

Sepals

The sepals, the outermost whorl, together are called the calyx. In the flower bud, the sepals tightly enclose and protect the petals, stamens, and pistil from rain or insects. The sepals unfurl as the flower opens and often resemble small green leaves at the flower's base. In some flowers, the sepals are colourful and work with the petals to attract pollinators.

Variations in Structure

Like virtually all forms in nature, flowers display many variations in their structure. Most flowers have all four whorls—pistil, stamens, petals, and sepals. Botanists call these complete flowers. But some flowers are incomplete, meaning they lack one or more whorls. Incomplete flowers are most common in plants whose pollen is dispersed by the wind or water. Since these flowers do not need to attract pollinators, most have no petals, and some even lack sepals. Certain wind-pollinated flowers do have small sepals and petals that create eddies in the wind, directing pollen to swirl around and settle on the flower. In still other flowers, the petals and sepals are fused into structures called a floral tube.

Flowers that lack either stamens or a pistil are said to be imperfect. The petal-like rays on the edge of a sunflower are actually tiny, imperfect flowers that lack stamens. Imperfect flowers can still function in sexual reproduction. A flower that lacks a pistil but has stamens produces pollen, and a flower with a pistil but no stamens provides ovules and can develop into fruits and seeds. Flowers that have only stamens are termed staminate, and flowers that have only a pistil are called pistillate.

Although a single flower can be either staminate or pistillate, a plant species must have both to reproduce sexually. In some species with imperfect flowers, the staminate and pistillate flowers occur on the same plant. Such plants, known as monoecious species, include corn. The tassel at the top of the corn plant consists of hundreds of tiny staminate flowers, and the ears, which are located laterally on the stem, contain clusters of pistillate flowers. The silks of corn are very long styles leading to the ovaries, which, when ripe, form the kernels of corn. In dioecious species—such as date, willow, and hemp—staminate and pistillate flowers are found on different plants. A date tree will develop male or female flowers but not both. In dioecious species, at least two plants, one bearing staminate flowers and one bearing pistillate flowers, are needed for pollination and fertilization.

Other variations are found in the types of stems that support flowers. In some species, flowers are attached to only one main stem, called the peduncle. In others, flowers are attached to smaller stems, called pedicels, that branch from the peduncle. The peduncle and pedicels orient a flower so that its pollinator can reach it. In the morning glory pedicels hold the flowers in a horizontal position. This enables their hummingbird pollinators to feed since they do not crawl into the flower as other pollinators do, but hover near the flower and lick the nectar with their long tongues. Scientists assign specific terms to the different flower and stem arrangements to assist in the precise identification of a flower. A plant with just one flower at the tip of the peduncle a tulip is termed solitary. In a spike, such as sage, flowers are attached to the sides of the peduncle.

Sometimes flowers are grouped together in a cluster called an inflorescence. In an indeterminate inflorescence, the lower flowers bloom first, and blooming proceeds over a period of days from the bottom to the top of the peduncle or pedicels. As long as light, water, temperature, and nutrients are favourable, the tip of the peduncle or pedicel continues to add new buds. There are several types of indeterminate inflorescences. These include the raceme, formed by a series of pedicels that emerge from the peduncle, as in snapdragons and lupines; and the panicle, in which the series of pedicels branches and rebranches, as in lilac.

In determinate inflorescences, called cymes, the peduncle is capped by a flower bud, which prevents the stem from elongating and adding more flowers. However, new flower buds appear on side pedicels that form below the central flower, and the flowers bloom from the top to the bottom of the pedicels. Flowers that bloom in cymes include chickweed and phlox.

Sexual Reproduction

Sexual reproduction mixes the hereditary material from two parents, creating a population of genetically diverse offspring. Such a population can better withstand environmental changes.

Unlike animals, flowers cannot move from place to place, yet sexual reproduction requires the union of the egg from one parent with the sperm from another parent. Flowers overcome their lack of mobility through the all-important process of pollination. Pollination occurs in several ways. In most flowers pollinated by insects and other animals, the pollen escapes through pores in the anthers. As pollinators forage for food, the pollen sticks to their body and then rubs off on the flower's stigma, or on the stigma of the next flower they visit. In plants that rely on wind for pollination, the anthers burst open, releasing a cloud of yellow, powdery pollen that drifts to other flowers.

In a few aquatic plants, pollen is released into the water, where it floats to other flowers.

Pollen consists of thousands of microscopic pollen grains. A tough pollen wall surrounds each grain. In most flowers, the pollen grains released from the anthers contain two cells. If a pollen grain lands on the stigma of the same species, the pollen grain germinates—one cell within the grain emerges through the pollen wall and contacts the surface of the stigma, where it begins to elongate.

The lengthening cell grows through the stigma and style, forming a pollen tube that transports the other cell within the pollen down the style to the ovary. As the tube grows, the cell within it divides to produce two sperm cells, the male sex cells. In some species, the sperm are produced before the pollen is released from the anther.

Independently of the pollen germination and pollen tube growth, developmental changes occur within the ovary. The ovule produces several specialized structures—among them, the egg, or female sex cell.

The pollen tube grows into the ovary, crosses the ovule wall, and releases the two sperm cells into the ovule. One sperm unites with the egg, triggering hormonal changes that transform the ovule into a seed. The outer wall of the ovule develops into the seed coat, while the fertilized egg grows into an embryonic plant.

The growing embryonic plant relies on a starchy, nutrient-rich food in the seed called endosperm. Endosperm develops from the union of the second sperm with the two polar nuclei, also known as the central cell nuclei, structures also produced by the ovary.

As the seed grows, hormones are released that stimulate

the walls of the ovary to expand, and it develops into the fruit. The mature fruit often is hundreds or even thousands of times larger than the tiny ovary from which it grew, and the seeds also are quite large compared to the miniscule ovules from which they originated.

The fruits, which are unique to flowering plants, play an extremely important role in dispersing seeds. Animals eat fruits, such as berries and grains. The seeds pass through the digestive tract of the animal unharmed and are deposited in a wide variety of locations, where they germinate to produce the next generation of flowering plants, thus continuing the species. Other fruits are dispersed far and wide by wind or water; the fruit of maple trees has a winglike structure that catches the wind.

Flowering and the Life Cycle

The life cycle of a flowering plant begins when the seed germinates. It progresses through the growth of roots, stems, and leaves; formation of flower buds; pollination and fertilization; and seed and fruit development. The life cycle ends with senescence, or old age, and death. Depending on the species, the life cycle of a plant may last one, two, or many years. Plants called annuals carry out their life cycle within one year.

Biennial plants live for two years: The first year they produce leaves, and in the second year they produce flowers and fruits and then die. Perennial plants live for more than one year. Some perennials bloom every year, while others, like agave, live for years without flowering and then in a few weeks produce thousands of flowers, fruits, and seeds before dying.

Whatever the life cycle, most plants flower in response to certain cues. A number of factors influence the timing of flowering. The age of the plant is critical—most plants must be at least one or two weeks old before they bloom; presumably they need this time to accumulate the energy reserves required for flowering.

The number of hours of darkness is another factor that influences flowering. Many species bloom only when the night is just the right length—a phenomenon called photoperiodism.

Poinsettias flower in winter when the nights are long, while spinach blooms when the nights are short—late spring through late summer. Temperature, light intensity, and moisture also affect the time of flowering. In the desert heavy rains that follow a long dry period often trigger flowers to bloom.

Evolution of Flowers

Flowering plants are thought to have evolved around 135 million years ago from cone-bearing gymnosperms. Scientists had long proposed that the first flower most likely resembled today's magnolias or water lilies, two types of flowers that lack some of the specialized structures found in most modern flowers. But in the late 1990s scientists compared the genetic material deoxyribonucleic acid (DNA) of different plants to determine their evolutionary relationships. From these studies, scientists identified a small, cream-coloured flower from the genus *Amborella* as the only living relative to the first flowering plant. This rare plant is found only on the South Pacific island of New Caledonia.

The evolution of flowers dramatically changed the face of earth. On a planet where algae, ferns, and cycads tinged the earth with a monochromatic green hue, flowers emerged to paint the earth with vivid shades of red, pink, orange, yellow, blue, violet, and white. Flowering plants spread rapidly, in part because their fruits so effectively disperse seeds. Today, flowering plants occupy virtually all areas of the planet, with about 240,000 species known.

Many flowers and pollinators coevolved—that is, they influenced each other's traits during the process of evolution. Any population of flowers displays a range of colour, fragrance, size, and shape—hereditary traits that can be passed from one generation to the next. Certain traits or combinations of traits appeal more to pollinators, so pollinators are more likely to visit these attractive plants. The appealing plants have a greater chance of being pollinated than others and, thus, are likely to produce more seeds.

The seeds develop into plants that display the inherited appealing traits. Similarly, in a population of pollinators, there are variations in hereditary traits, such as wing size and shape, length and shape of tongue, ability to detect fragrance, and so on. Pollinators whose bodies are small enough to reach inside certain flowers gather pollen and nectar more efficiently than larger-sized members of their species.

These efficient, well-fed pollinators have more energy for reproduction. Their offspring inherit the traits that enable them to forage successfully in flowers, and from generation to generation, these traits are preserved. The pollinator preference seen today for certain flower colours, fragrances, and shapes often represents hundreds of thousands of years of coevolution.

Coevolution often results in exquisite adaptations between flower and pollinator. These adaptations can minimize competition for nectar and pollen among pollinators and also can minimize competition among flowers for pollinators. Comet orchids have narrow flowers almost a foot and a half long. These flowers are pollinated only by a species of hawk moth that has a narrow tongue just the length of the flowers. The flower shape prevents other pollinators from consuming the nectar, guarantees the moths a meal, and ensures the likelihood of pollination and fertilization.

Most flowers and pollinators, however, are not as precisely matched to ach other, but adaptation still plays a significant role in their interactions. Hummingbirds are particularly attracted to the colour red.

Hummingbird-pollinated flowers typically are red, and they often are narrow, an adaptation that suits the long tongues of hummingbirds. Bats are large pollinators that require relatively more energy than other pollinators. They visit big flowers like those of saguaro cactus, which supply plenty of nectar or pollen. Bats avoid little flowers that do not offer enough reward.

Other examples of coevolution are seen in the bromeliads and orchids that grow in dark forests. These plants often have bright red, purple, or white sepals or petals, which make them visible to pollinators. Night-flying pollinators, such as moths and bats, detect white flowers most easily, and flowers that bloom at sunset, such as yucca, datura, and cereus, usually are white.

The often delightful and varied fragrances of flowers also reveal the hand of coevolution. In some cases, insects detect fragrance before colour. They follow faint aromas to flowers that are too far away to be seen, recognizing petal shape and colour only when they are very close to the flower. Some night-blooming flowers emit sweet fragrances that attract night-flying moths. At the other extreme, carrion flowers, flowers pollinated by flies, give off the odor of rotting meat to attract their pollinators.

Flowers and their pollinators also coevolved to influence each other's life cycles. Among species that flower in response to a dark period, some measure the critical night length so accurately that all species of the region flower in the same week or two.

This enables related plants to interbreed, and provides pollinators with enough pollen and nectar to live on so that they too can reproduce. The process of coevolution also has resulted in synchronization of floral and insect life cycles. Sometimes flowering occurs the week that insect pollinators hatch or emerge from dormancy, or bird pollinators return from winter migration, so that they feed on and pollinate the flowers. Flowering also is timed so that fruits and seeds are produced when animals are present to feed on the fruits and disperse the seeds.

Flowers and Extinction

Like the amphibians, reptiles, insects, birds, and mammals that are experiencing alarming extinction rates, a number of wildflower species also are endangered. The greatest threat lies in the furious pace at which land is cleared for new houses, industries, and shopping malls to accommodate rapid population growth.

Such clearings are making the meadow, forest, and wetland homes of wildflowers ever more scarce. Among the flowers so endangered is the rosy periwinkle of Madagascar, a plant whose compounds have greatly reduced the death rates from childhood leukemia and Hodgkin's disease.

Flowering plants, many with other medicinal properties, also are threatened by global warming from increased combustion of fossil fuels; increased ultraviolet light from ozone layer breakdown; and acid rain from industrial emissions. Flowering plants native to a certain region also may be threatened by introduced species. Yellow toadflax a garden plant brought to the United States and Canada from Europe, has become a notorious weed, spreading to many habitats and preventing the growth of native species. In some cases, unusual wildflowers such as orchids are placed at risk when they are collected extensively to be sold.

Many of the threats that endanger flowering plants also place their pollinators at risk. When a species of flower or pollinator is threatened, the coevolution of pollinators and flowers may prove to be disadvantageous.

If a flower species dies out, its pollinators will lack food and may also die out, and the predators that depend on the pollinators also become threatened. In cases where pollinators are adapted to only one or a few types of flowers, the loss of those plants can disrupt an entire ecosystem. Likewise, if pollinators are damaged by ecological changes, plants that depend on them will not be pollinated, seeds will not be formed, and new generations of plants cannot grow. The fruits that these flowers produce may become scarce, affecting the food supply of humans and other animals that depend on them.

Worldwide, more than 300 species of flowering plants are endangered, or at immediate risk of extinction. Another two dozen or so are considered threatened, or likely to become extinct in the near future. Of these species, fewer than 50 were the focus of preservation plans in the late 1990s. Various regional, national, and international organizations have marshaled their resources in response to the critical need for protecting flowering plants and their habitats. In the United States, native plant societies work to conserve regional plants in every state.

The United States Fish and Wildlife Endangered Species Programmeme protects habitats for threatened and endangered species throughout the United States, as do the Canadian Wildlife Service in Canada, the Ministry for Social Development in Mexico, and similar agencies in other countries. At the international level, the International Plant Conservation Programmememe at Cambridge, England, collects information and provides education worldwide on plant species at risk, and the United Nations Environmental Programmememe supports a variety of efforts that address the worldwide crisis of endangered species.

EDIBLE FLOWERS

Edible Flowers, flower blossoms or buds that can be eaten. Edible flowers are used in a variety of dishes to add flavours ranging from sweet and floral to pungent and spicy. Flowers are typically floated on soups or sprinkled on salads for colour and flavour. When stuffed with spiced ricotta or cottage cheese they make a flavourful and unusual side dish. Stir-fried or deep-fried flowers are used for tasty hors d'oeuvres. Flowers often are candied or crystallized—brushed with egg white and dusted with granulated sugar and then air dried—to make sweets or to decorate desserts. Edible flowers are also used to enhance beverages, jams and jellies, butters, vinegars, and water. Most edible flowers are used in small amounts and, because they are used lightly, contribute little to a dish's nutritional value.

The culinary use of flowers dates back thousands of years to the ancient civilizations of China, Greece, and Rome. Edible flowers were also grown in American colonial gardens. In the United States and Europe their popularity waned after the Victorian era in the early 20th century, but the popularity of edible flowers has grown with recent interest in Asian and Indian cooking.

Sample Edible Flowers

A variety of flower blossoms are used to enhance cuisines. Calendula, also called pot marigold, is a daisy-like flower with yellow petals that impart a tangy flavour to tea, butters, soups, egg dishes, and rice. Since Roman times, calendula has been used as an affordable substitute for saffron, an expensive spice made from crocus flowers.

Day Lily, with its large, trumpet-shaped petals in a wide range of colours, is chopped and added to salads and soups. The dried buds, called golden needles, are mentioned in early Chinese writing and are still used in Asian dishes.

The orange, white, or red flowers of nasturtium have a peppery flavour and are used to enhance salads or sandwiches. The round, lobed leaves are also edible. Nasturtium's use as a food has been credited to the ancient Persians and Peruvians.

Rose flowers have edible petals and seedpods, or hips. Both were commonly used in the Victorian era and are still popular in Asian and Indian cooking. Rose hips are rich in vitamin C and are often steeped for tea or made into jellies. The petals are used to make fragrant rose water and rose syrup, brewed into a tea, or crystallized.

Violet has been eaten since the days of the Roman Empire. The small, sweet, delicate purple or white blossoms are ideal for decorating desserts and punches and are well suited to being crystallized. The large trumpet-shaped white or yellow flowers of zucchini taste like cucumber.

In France and Italy, cooks stuff the blossoms with a soft cheese, such as ricotta, flavoured with herbs, or dip them in batter and deep-fry them to make a fritter, a small sweet cake. In Mexico the blossoms are sautéed and used to fill tortillas.

Cooking with Flowers

Before using flower blossoms for cooking, consider their source. Flowers picked from roadsides may contain dangerous levels of lead from car exhaust. And flowers sold by a florist may have been treated with chemicals that keep the blooms lasting longer.

To avoid unsafe chemical residues, use only organically grown flowers, and wash all flowers thoroughly before use. Fully opened flowers should be picked in the morning, when their moisture content is highest; buds can be picked at any time.

When eating flowers for the first time, start with only a few. Until your digestive system is accustomed to flowers, eating too many may cause a stomachache. Usually just the flower petals are eaten, not the pollen-bearing stamens, which often have an unpleasant flavour. For some flowers, such as roses and marigolds, the bitter white base of the petal is removed.

BIOME

Biome, also known as life zones, all plants, animals, and other organisms, as well as the physical environment in a particular area. A biome is characterized by its plant life, the types of which are determined by a location's climatic conditions, latitude, and altitude. Northern coniferous forests exist in subarctic portions of North America and Asia, the conditions are simply too harsh and the season too brief for trees to grow. Instead of trees, the short vegetation of the tundra thrives in these areas. The same phenomenon occurs with altitude, as trees give way to short alpine vegetation in high mountainous regions.

A biome is composed of many ecosystems—smaller communities of plants and animals and their habitats (the physical parts of their environment that affect them). Whereas the boundaries of a biome are determined by climate, the boundaries of ecosystems are physical features, such as ridges or riverbanks, that separate one community from another. The ecosystems of a particular biome tend to have plants with similar growth forms and animals with similar feeding habits.

Major terrestrial biomes include tropical rain forest, northern coniferous forest, tundra, desert, grassland, savanna, and chaparral. Although not necessarily associated with marine environments, the term biome is sometimes used by ecologists to describe marine life zones such as the littoral zone, found in shallow water; the pelagic zone in the open ocean; and the benthic zone on the ocean floor.

The tropical rain forest is the most complex biome in the world. This biome is found at low elevations in the tropics where it is perpetually warm and wet. Rain forests are characterized by a dense tree canopy—tree top branches and leaves that overlap with each other, creating a shaded forest interior. These canopies may reach up to 50 m (160 ft) high. The thick canopy allows little sunlight to penetrate, so rain forest floors have sparse ground cover. The soils are nutrient-poor, and most plants are able to store what few nutrients they can absorb.

The northern coniferous forest, also known as the taiga in Russia, is found in a broad subarctic band across Alaska, Canada, Scandinavia, Russia, and China, where the winters are long and cold. Conifers, such as spruce, larch, and fir, are the dominant plants, but lichens and mosses are abundant too. Muskegs, or bogs, occur throughout the region.

The tundra is the treeless plain that lies north of the northern coniferous forests and on the Antarctic Peninsula in the southern hemisphere. Trees cannot survive in this biome because of the cold temperatures, high winds, and heavy snowfall, as well as the permafrost, a layer of permanently frozen subsoil. Plant life tends to grow low to the ground. In the summer, large numbers of birds migrate to the tundra to feed on insects.

Other animals found in this area include reindeer, wolves, fox, voles, and lemmings. A similar biome, called the alpine biome, is found in high mountain areas around the world. Similar harsh conditions cause vegetation to grow low to the ground in alpine meadows.

Desert biomes are characterized by less than 254 mm (10 in) of annual precipitation and high temperatures. To combat this lack of moisture, desert plants have developed water-conserving features, such as leaves that are light-coloured, small, thick, or waxy. Animals that live in the desert are often light-coloured, blend in well with their surroundings, and are usually more active at night to avoid the blazing heat during the day.

Grassland biomes are found on every continent except Antarctica, accounting for about one quarter of the Earth's land surface. Typically found on flat or rolling terrain, grasslands tend to occur in the interior of continents where precipitation is lower. Periodic droughts occur in most grasslands, accompanied by searing heat that scorches most vegetation in the area. Grasslands are covered with grasses, sedges, and other low-growing, perennial plants. Drought, fire, and grazing by herbivores, such as bison and deer, restrict tree growth. Most grasslands have been extensively cultivated and are now regions where major crops of wheat, corn, and other grains are grown.

Tropical savannas are expansive grasslands dotted with trees. The world's largest and best-known savanna is the African savanna, which covers much of the continent south of the Sahara desert. In the African savanna, herds of animals graze on the tall grass, and giraffes browse on the trees. Other tropical savannas are found in South America, India, and Australia.

The chaparral biome is dominated by dense thickets of mostly small-leafed evergreen shrubs. It is characterized by hot, dry summers and cool, wet winters. This biome can be found in the foothills of California and Mediterranean climate regions. Chaparral plants have adapted to the frequent fires that result from lightning and dry conditions.

FOREST

Forest, plant community, predominantly of trees or other woody vegetation, occupying an extensive area of land. In its natural state, a forest remains in a relatively fixed, self-regulated condition over a long period of time.

Climate, soil, and the topography of the region determine the characteristic trees of a forest. In local environments, dominant species of trees are characteristically associated with certain shrubs and herbs.

The type of vegetation on the forest floor is influenced by the larger and taller plants, but because low vegetation affects the organic composition of the soil, the influence is reciprocal. Disturbances such as a forest fire or timber harvesting may result in a shift to another forest type. Left undisturbed, ecological succession will eventually result in a climax forest community. Human intervention is practiced to maintain some desirable forest types.

Classification

Forests may be divided into the following eight general types on the basis of leaf characteristics and climate.

- Deciduous forests of the temperate regions are the typical formation of the eastern United States. Two subtypes exist; forests of the same latitude in the northern and southern hemispheres are radically different, probably due to the continental climate of the northern hemisphere and the oceanic climate of the southern.
- Deciduous monsoon forests are characteristic of Bengal and Myanmar (formerly known as Burma) and common throughout Southeast Asia and India; they are also found along the Pacific coastal regions of Mexico and Central America. The climate is characterized by heavy daily rainfall, seasonally relieved by dry periods during which the trees shed their leaves.
- Tropical savanna forests are found in regions such as the campos of Brazil, where forest and grassland meet. Savannas, which occur widely in Africa and South America, are dominated by grasses and sedges, with open stands of widely spaced trees that are frequently thorny. Some savannas are created by fire or by grazing and browsing mammals.
- Northern coniferous forests form a worldwide belt in subarctic and alpine regions of the northern hemisphere. Gnarled scrub trees dominate at the northern tree line and on mountaintops. Spruce and fir trees are characteristic of the more northerly forests; pine, larch, and hemlock dominate farther south. These forests usually occupy formerly glaciated regions and occur in association with lakes, bogs, and rivers.
- Tropical rain forests are characteristic of central Africa and the Amazon watershed. Plant growth is profuse, and because the fall and regrowth of leaves

occur gradually throughout each year, the forest is always active. Tree species are highly diverse but usually have smooth, straight trunks and large, simple leaves. Large vines are common, but the tangled growth of a jungle occurs only where the normal forest area has been abused or at a river's edge.

- Temperate evergreen forests are found in the subtropical regions of North America and the Caribbean islands that have a warm maritime climate. The type is best developed along the Gulf Coast and in the Florida Everglades. The characteristic trees are live oak, magnolia, palms, and bromeliads.
- Temperate rain forests, with broad-leaved evergreen trees, are common on Mediterranean coasts. Rainfall may be low, but the ocean-cooled air is moisture laden, and fogs are frequent. In the United States the temperate West Coast rain forests are dominated by hemlock, cedar, spruce, fir, and redwood.
- Tropical scrub forests occur in regions of slight rainfall, bordering wetter forests.

United States Forests

The western forests of the Rocky Mountains and the Pacific coast are coniferous and contain Douglas fir, ponderosa pine, western white pine, Engelmann spruce, and white fir. More than half of the softwood lumber yield of the United States comes from the productive Douglas fir forests of the Pacific Northwest.

The South Atlantic and Gulf states account for most of the remaining softwood lumber, chiefly from longleaf, shortleaf, loblolly, and slash pines. Hardwoods, yielding about one-fourth of the total production, are found in the eastern half of the United States, with particularly dense stands in the area surrounding the Mississippi and Ohio river valleys. Among the many hardwood species are oaks, black walnut, yellow poplar, and sugar maple.

More than one-fourth of the forest area of the United States is under the administration of the Forest Service. Beginning in 1891 with a single area in Wyoming, the National Forest System had by the late 1980s expanded to more than 77 million hectares (191 million acres) in 44 states, Puerto Rico, and the Virgin Islands.

The earliest national forests, called forest reserves, were established through reservation of public lands. Present national forests, whose boundaries are established by Congress, cover areas that include about 17 percent privately held land, which the federal government is acquiring gradually. Almost every state has a state forester, whose duties involve administration and protection of state forestlands.

Canadian Forests

The forestlands of Canada stretch across the continent in a belt varying from about 800 to 950 km (about 500 to 590 mi) in width. Forests producing usable timber cover about 3 million sq km (about 1.2 million sq mi).

Coniferous trees make up four-fifths of the total, and deciduous trees the rest. The belt of conifers that extends from the Atlantic coast westward and northwest to Alaska includes spruce, balsam, fir, and pine, with poplar and white birch the principal deciduous species represented.

South of this coniferous belt are the mixed forests of the Great Lakes, St. Lawrence, and Acadian regions. Here the major conifers are eastern white and red pine, eastern hemlock, spruce, cedar, and fir. Also present are deciduous yellow birch, maple, oak, and basswood trees. On the western coast, in British Columbia, the large coniferous species provide more than one-fourth of all wood cut in Canada annually. Most important are cedar, hemlock, spruce, fir, and Douglas fir.

More than 90 percent of productive forestland is publicly owned. Its administration and protection is largely vested in the various provincial governments, which lease the forests to private industry.

In the three Maritime provinces (Nova Scotia, New Brunswick, and Prince Edward Island), however, a sizable proportion of the forestland is privately owned. On the federal level, the Canadian Forestry Service of the Department of the Environment promotes improved management of forest resources and better products, in addition to providing advisory services to the provincial forestry administrations.

Diseases and Pests

Insects and diseases are a continuing menace to forests. Various insects, such as the gypsy moth, the tussock moth, and the spruce budworm, devastate extensive areas by defoliation. Other insects serve as carriers for the causative agents of diseases that destroy trees.

Parasitic tree diseases may be caused by bacteria, fungi, viruses, and nematodes, or by such parasitic plants as the mistletoe or dodder. Noninfectious diseases of trees include sunscald; drought injury; root drowning, or suffocation; nutritional excesses or deficiencies; winter injury; and injury from smoke, gases, and fumes.

Chapter 3

Fuel

Fuel, substance that reacts chemically with another to produce heat, or that produces heat by nuclear processes. The term *fuel* is generally limited to those substances that burn readily in air or oxygen, emitting large quantities of heat. Fuels are used for heating, for the production of steam for heating and power purposes, for powering internal-combustion engines and for a direct source of power in jet and rocket propulsion. In cases where a fuel must supply its own oxygen, as in many rockets and torpedoes, an oxidizing agent such as hydrogen peroxide or nitric acid is added to the fuel mixture.

Chemical reactions in the combustion of all ordinary fuels involve the combination of oxygen with any carbon, hydrogen, or sulfur present in the fuels. The end products are carbon dioxide, water, and sulfur dioxide. Other substances present in fuels do not contribute to the combustion but either are driven off in the form of vapour or remain after combustion in the form of ash.

Fuel efficiency or heating value of a fuel is usually measured in terms of the number of Btu that are produced when a given amount of the fuel is burned under standard conditions. Heating values for solid and liquid fuels are stated in terms of Btu per lb, and values for gases in Btu per cu ft. A distinction is sometimes made between higher heating value, the entire heat evolved during combustion, and lower heating value, the net heat evolved, with allowance for the heat lost in the vapourization of the water produced by combustion. Approximate higher heating values of common fuels are: Solid fuels (Btu per lb): coal 12,000 to 15,000; lignite 6000 to 7400;

coke 12,400; dry wood 8500. Liquid fuels: alcohol 11,000; fuel oil 19,000; gasoline 20,750; kerosene 19,800. Gaseous fuels (Btu per cu ft): acetylene 1480; blast-furnace gas 93; carbon monoxide 317; coke-oven gas or coal gas about 600; hydrogen 319; natural gas 1050 to 2220; oil gas 516; producer gas 136.

FOSSIL FUELS

Fossil Fuels, energy-rich substances that have formed from long-buried plants and microorganisms. Fossil fuels, which include petroleum, coal, and natural gas, provide most of the energy that powers modern industrial society. The gasoline that fuels our cars, the coal that powers many electrical plants, and the natural gas that heats our homes are all fossil fuels.

Chemically, fossil fuels consist largely of hydrocarbons, which are compounds composed of hydrogen and carbon. Some fossil fuels also contain smaller amounts of other compounds. Hydrocarbons form from ancient living organisms that were buried under layers of sediment millions of years ago. As accumulating sediment layers exerted increasing heat and pressure, the remains of the organisms gradually transformed into hydrocarbons.

The most commonly used fossil fuels are petroleum, coal, and natural gas. These substances are extracted from the earth's crust and, if necessary, refined into suitable fuel products, such as gasoline, heating oil, and kerosene. Some of these hydrocarbons may also be processed into plastics, chemicals, lubricants, and other nonfuel products.

Geologists have identified other types of hydrocarbon-rich deposits that can serve as fuels. Such deposits, which include oil shale, tar sands, and gas hydrates, are not widely used because they are too costly to extract and refine.

The majority of fossil fuels are used in the transportation, manufacturing, residential heating, and electric-power generation industries. Crude petroleum is refined into gasoline, diesel fuel, and jet fuel, which power the world's transportation system.

Coal is the fuel most commonly burned to generate electric power, and natural gas is used primarily in commercial and residential buildings for heating water and air, for air conditioning, and as fuel for stoves and other heating appliances.

Formation of Fossil Fuels

Fossil fuels formed from ancient organisms that died and were buried under layers of accumulating sediment. As additional sediment layers built up over these organic deposits, the material was subjected to increasing temperatures and pressures. Over millions of years, these physical conditions chemically transformed the organic material into hydrocarbons.

Most organic debris is destroyed at the earth's surface by oxidation or by consumption by microorganisms. Organic material that survives to become buried under sediments or deposited in other oxygen-poor environments begins a series of chemical and biological transformations that may ultimately result in petroleum, natural gas, or coal.

Many such deposits occur in sedimentary basins (depressed areas in the earth's crust where sediments accumulate), and along continental shelves. Sediments may accumulate to depths of several thousand feet in a basin, exerting pressures up to one hundred million pascals (tens of thousands of pounds per square inch) and temperatures of several hundred degrees on the organic material. Over millions of years, these conditions can chemically transform the organic material into petroleum, natural gas, coal, or other types of fossil fuels.

Petroleum Formation

Petroleum formed chiefly from ancient, microscopic plants and bacteria that lived in the ocean and saltwater seas. When these microorganisms died and settled to the seafloor, they mixed with sand and silt to form organic-rich mud. As layers of sediment accumulated over this organic ooze, the mud was gradually heated and slowly compressed into shale or mudstone, chemically transforming the organic material into petroleum and natural gas.

Sometimes, the petroleum and natural gas would slowly

fill the tiny holes within nearby porous rocks, which geologists call reservoir rocks. Because these porous rocks were usually filled with water, the liquid and gaseous hydrocarbons (which are less dense and lighter than water) migrated upward, through the earth's crust, sometimes for long distances. A portion of these hydrocarbons would eventually encounter an impermeable (nonporous) layer of rock in an anticline, salt dome, fault trap, or stratigraphic trap.

The impermeable rock would trap the hydrocarbons, creating a reservoir of petroleum and natural gas. Exploration geologists seek these underground formations because they often contain recoverable petroleum deposits. The fluids and gases caught in these geologic traps typically separate into three layers: water (highest density, bottom layer), petroleum (middle layer), and natural gas (low density, top layer).

Coal Formation

Coal is a solid fossil fuel formed from ancient plants—including trees, ferns, and mosses—that grew in swamps and bogs or along coastal shorelines. Generations of these plants died and were gradually buried under layers of sediment. As the sedimentary overburden increased, the organic material was subjected to increasing heat and pressure that caused the organic material to undergo a number of transitional states to form coal. The mounting pressure and temperature caused the original organic material, which was rich in carbon, hydrogen, and oxygen, to become increasingly carbon-rich and hydrogen- and oxygen-poor.

The successive stages of coal formation are peat (partially carbonized plant matter), lignite (soft brownish-black coal with low carbon content), subbituminous coal (soft coal with intermediate carbon content), bituminous coal (soft coal with higher carbon and lower moisture content than subbituminous coal), and anthracite (hard coal with highest carbon content and lowest moisture content). Because anthracite is the most carbon-rich, moisture-deficient form of coal, it has the highest heating value.

Two regions in the United States produce nearly all the

coal mined in the United States. One region covers the Appalachian region (encompassed by Alabama, Georgia, Kentucky, Maryland, Ohio, Pennsylvania, Tennessee, Virginia, and West Virginia) plus the Illinois Basin (encompassed by Illinois, Indiana, and western Kentucky). The other area covers parts of Montana and Wyoming.

Natural Gas Formation

Most natural gas is formed from plankton—tiny water-dwelling organisms, including algae and protozoans—that accumulated on the ocean floor as they died. These organisms were slowly buried and compressed under layers of sediment. Over millions of years, the pressure and heat generated by overlying sediments converted this organic material into natural gas. Natural gas is composed primarily of methane and other light hydrocarbons.

Natural gas frequently migrates through porous and fractured reservoir rock with petroleum and subsequently accumulates in underground reservoirs. Because of its light density relative to petroleum, natural gas forms a layer over the petroleum. Natural gas may also form in coal deposits, where it is often found dispersed throughout the pores and fractures of the coal bed.

Other Fossil Fuels

Geologists have identified immense deposits of other hydrocarbons, including gas hydrates (methane and water), tar sands, and oil shale. Vast deposits of gas hydrates are contained in ocean sediments and in shallow polar soils. In these marine and polar environments, methane molecules are encased in a crystalline structure with water molecules. This crystalline solid is known as gas hydrate.

Because technology for the commercial extraction of gas hydrates has not yet been developed, this type of fossil fuel is not included in most world energy resource estimates. However, in February 2007 the U.S. Department of Energy completed the drilling of a well to retrieve core samples of gas hydrates found in the Prudhoe Bay region of Alaska's

North Slope. By identifying the nature of these gas hydrates, the Energy Department hoped to evaluate the potential of natural gas production from this region.

Tar sands are heavy, asphaltlike hydrocarbons found in sandstone. Tar sands form where petroleum migrates upward into deposits of sand or consolidated sandstone. When the petroleum is exposed to water and bacteria present in the sandstone, the hydrocarbons often degrade over time into heavier, asphaltlike bitumen.

Oil shale is a fine-grained rock containing high concentrations of a waxy organic material known as kerogen. Oil shale forms on lake and ocean bottoms where dead algae, spores, and other microorganisms died millions of years ago and accumulated in mud and silt. The increasing pressure and temperature from the buildup of overlying sediments transformed the organic material into kerogen and compacted the mud and silt into oil shale. However, this pressure and heat was insufficient to chemically break down the kerogen into petroleum. Because the hydrocarbons contained in tar sand and oil shale are not fluids, these hydrocarbons are more difficult and costly to recover than liquid petroleum.

Removing and Refining Fossil Fuels

Geologists use a variety of sophisticated instruments to locate underground petroleum, natural gas, and coal deposits. These instruments allow scientists to interpret the geologic composition, history, and structure of sedimentary basins in the earth's crust. Once located, petroleum and natural gas deposits are removed by wells drilled down into the deposit, while coal is removed by excavation.

Petroleum and Natural Gas

To locate deposits of petroleum and natural gas, exploration geologists search for geologic regions containing the ingredients necessary for petroleum formation: organic-rich source rock, burial temperatures sufficiently high to generate petroleum from organic material, and petroleum-trapping rock formations.

When potentially petroleum-rich geologic formations are identified, wells are drilled into the sedimentary basin. If a well intersects porous reservoir rock containing significant petroleum and natural gas deposits, pressure inside the trap may force the liquid hydrocarbons spontaneously to the surface. However, pressure inside the trap typically declines to the point where the petroleum must be pumped to the surface.

While domestic petroleum exploration continues on land, oil companies are also exploring promising offshore locations along the continental margins.

Once petroleum has been extracted from the ground, it is transported by pipeline, truck, or tanker to a refinery to be separated into liquid and gas components. Raw petroleum is heated to distill hydrocarbons by molecular weight. Lighter molecules are separated and refined into gasoline and other fuels, while heavier molecules are processed into engine lubricants, asphalt, waxes, and other products.

Because demand for fuel far exceeds demand for the products made from the heavier hydrocarbons, refiners often break apart the heavy molecules into lighter ones that can be refined into gasoline. They do so by means of processes called thermal cracking and catalytic cracking.

Coal

Because of their enormity, the world's most extensive coal beds have already been identified. Currently, scientists and engineers are working on finding the most economically efficient means of removing the coal. Coal mining underwent a complete transformation in the United States during the 20th century, evolving from a labour-intensive, hand-mining industry to a modern mechanized industry. The modern coal mining industry uses some of the largest, most sophisticated excavating equipment ever developed.

Modern underground mining commonly employs machines called longwall miners to remove coal. These machines use rotating drums studded with picks to rip coal from seams in large chunks.

Surface-mine operators use mammoth earth-moving shovels to mine coal. These shovels first remove overlying soil and rock so the coal beds can be blasted apart. The blasted coal is scooped up and loaded into the beds of huge trucks for transport.

Consumption of Fossil Fuels

In 2003, the most recent year for which data are available, the world consumed 29 billion barrels of petroleum, 5 billion metric tons of coal, and 2.7 trillion cubic meters (96 trillion cubic feet) of natural gas. Overall, the United States accounts for approximately 25 percent of worldwide energy consumption, while it has less than 5 percent of the world's population.

Commercial Uses

Once fossil fuel has been extracted and processed, it can be burned for direct uses, such as to power cars or heat homes, or it can be combusted for the generation of electrical power.

Direct Combustion

Fossil fuels are primarily burned to produce energy. This energy is used to power automobiles, trucks, airplanes, trains, and ships around the world; to fuel industrial manufacturing processes; and to provide heat, light, air conditioning, and energy for homes and businesses. About two-fifths of all energy consumed in the United States is used by industry, one-third by homes and businesses, and about one-fourth by transportation.

To provide fuel for transportation, petroleum is refined into gasoline, diesel fuel, jet fuel, and other derivatives used in most of the world's automobiles, trucks, trains, aircraft, and ships. In the United States, transportation accounts for about two-thirds of total petroleum consumption—more than two-thirds of which is burned as automobile gasoline.

Demand for natural gas, historically considered a waste by-product of petroleum and coal mining, is growing in business and industry because it is a cleaner-burning fuel than petroleum or coal. Natural gas, which can be piped directly to commercial plants or individual residences and used on demand, is used for heating and for air conditioning. Residential uses of natural gas also include fuel for stoves and other heating appliances.

Electricity Generation

In addition to direct combustion for commercial uses, fossil fuels are also burned to generate most of the world's electric power. Fossil fuel–fired power plants produced 65 percent of the world's electrical power, down from 71 percent in the late 1970s. The world's remaining electricity supply was generated primarily by hydroelectric power (17 percent) and nuclear fission (16 percent), with solar, geothermal, and other sources accounting for a relatively small amount.

Environmental Effects of Using Fossil Fuels

Acid rain and global warming are two of the most serious environmental issues related to large-scale fossil fuel combustion. Other environmental problems, such as land reclamation and oil spills, are also associated with the mining and transporting of fossil fuels.

Acid Rain

When fossil fuels are burned, sulfur, nitrogen, and carbon combine with oxygen to form compounds known as oxides. When these oxides are released into the air, they react chemically with atmospheric water vapour, forming sulfuric acid, nitric acid, and carbonic acid, respectively. These acid-containing water vapours—commonly known as acid rain—enter the water cycle and can subsequently harm the biological quality of forests, soils, lakes, and streams.

The U.S. Clean Air Act has significantly reduced emissions of acid-producing oxides. The legally mandated removal of sulfur-bearing compounds from coal prior to burning has significantly reduced atmospheric levels of sulfur dioxide. Environmental laws also require use of pollution-trapping equipment, such as air scrubbers. Scrubbers—devices installed inside the smokestacks at a coal-burning plant—filter out sulfur-dioxide vapours and other compounds before these pollutants enter the atmosphere.

Ash Particles

Combustion of fossil fuels produces unburned fuel particles, known as ash. In the past, coal-fired power plants have emitted large amounts of ash into the atmosphere. However, government regulations also require that emissions containing ash be scrubbed or that particles otherwise be trapped to reduce this source of air pollution. While petroleum and natural gas generate less ash than coal, air pollution from fuel ash produced by automobiles may be a problem in cities where diesel and gasoline vehicles are concentrated.

Global Warming

Carbon dioxide is a major by-product of fossil fuel combustion, and it is what scientists call a greenhouse gas. Greenhouse gases absorb solar heat radiated from the earth's surface and retain this heat, keeping the earth warm and habitable for living organisms. Rapid industrialization through the 19th and 20th centuries, however, has resulted in increasing fossil fuel emissions, raising the percentage of carbon dioxide in the atmosphere by about 28 percent. This dramatic increase in carbon dioxide has led some scientists to predict a global warming scenario that could cause numerous environmental problems, including disrupted weather patterns and polar ice cap melting.

Although it is extremely difficult to attribute observed global temperature changes directly to fossil fuel combustion, some countries are working together to lower emissions of carbon dioxide from fossil fuels. One proposal is to establish a system requiring companies to pay to emit carbon dioxide above a specified level.

This payment could take several forms, including: (1) purchasing the rights to pollute from a company whose carbon dioxide emissions fall below the specified level; (2) purchasing and then preserving forests, which absorb carbon dioxide; and (3) paying to upgrade a carbon dioxide emitting plant in a lesser-developed country, lowering the upgraded plant's carbon dioxide emissions.

Petroleum Recovery and Transportation

Environmental problems are created by drilling oil wells and extracting fluids because the petroleum pumped up from deep reservoir rocks is often accompanied by large volumes of salt water. This brine contains numerous impurities, so it must either be injected back into the reservoir rocks or treated for safe surface disposal.

Petroleum usually must also be transported long distances by tanker or pipeline to reach a refinery. Transport of petroleum occasionally leads to accidental spills. Oil spills, especially in large volumes, can be detrimental to wildlife and habitat.

Coal Mining

Surface coal mining operations, often called strip mines, use massive shovels to remove soil and rock overlying the coal, disrupting the natural landscape. However, new land reclamation methods, driven by stringent laws and regulations, now require mining companies to restore strip-mined landscapes to nearly premined conditions.

Another environmental problem associated with coal mining occurs when freshly excavated coal beds are exposed to air. Sulfur-bearing compounds in the coal oxidize in the presence of water to form sulfuric acid. When this sulfuric acid solution, known as *acid mine drainage,* enters surface water and groundwater, it can be detrimental to water quality and aquatic life. Efforts are currently underway to remove sulfuric acid from mine drainage before it reaches rivers, lakes, and streams. Scientists are studying whether artificial wetlands have the ability to neutralize acid mine drainage.

World Fossil Fuel Supply

Because the global economy is powered by fossil fuels, it is critical to know how long world reserves will last. However, estimating the world's remaining fossil fuel reserves requires extensive information, including comprehensive geological maps of the world's sedimentary basins, models of energy production systems, and data showing world energy consumption patterns and trends.

Reserves and Resources

When estimating the world's fossil fuel supply, experts distinguish between *reserves* and *resources*. Reserves are fossil fuel deposits that have already been discovered and are immediately available.

Resources are fossil fuel deposits that geologists believe are located in certain sedimentary basins, but have not yet been discovered. Because geologists base fossil fuel resource estimates on the location, extent, and formation of deposits recovered in geologically similar basins, resource estimates are less certain than reserve estimates. Both reserve and resource estimates are revised as data about new and existing deposits become available.

Fossil fuel reserves can be further divided into *proved reserves* and *inferred reserves*. Proved reserves are deposits that have been measured, sampled, and evaluated for production quality. Inferred reserves have been discovered but have not been measured or evaluated.

The definition of fossil fuel resources can be narrowed to *technically recoverable resources*. This definition does not consider whether a deposit can be extracted economically, but only whether the fossil fuel can be recovered using existing technology. By definition, the world fossil fuel supply increases as technological advances are made allowing previously unrecoverable resources to be extracted and processed.

World Energy Data

Worldwide deposits of fossil fuels are finite. Some experts use data on world energy deposits to estimate how many years world energy supplies will last at current and projected consumption rates.

At the beginning of the 21st century, the world reserves of petroleum were estimated to be roughly 1.3 trillion barrels. Worldwide consumption of petroleum totaled 29 billion barrels a year. The world's natural gas reserves were estimated to be roughly 170 trillion cubic meters (6,000 trillion cubic feet). Worldwide consumption of natural gas by 2003 totaled 2.7 trillion cubic meters (96 trillion cubic feet) a year. At the beginning of the 21st century the world coal reserves were estimated to be roughly 1 trillion metric tons, and by 2003 worldwide consumption of coal totaled 5 billion metric tons a year. Total worldwide energy consumption is expected to grow at about 2.2 percent per year until 2015.

Theoretical models can be developed to estimate how many years the world fossil fuel supply will last. However, these models are complicated by technological advances in the energy production industry, unexpected discoveries of new fossil fuel deposits, and political, social, and economic factors that influence energy production and consumption.

Because fossil fuels are being consumed at much faster rates than they are produced in the earth's crust, humankind will eventually deplete these nonrenewable resources. While it is unclear how far in the future this will happen, there is evidence that some regions are becoming depleted in certain types of fossil fuels. Production of crude petroleum peaked in 1970.

Alternative Energy Source

The prospect of reducing the world's dependence on fossil fuels is problematic. Alternative energy industries, such as nuclear energy, hydroelectric energy, solar energy, wind energy, and geothermal energy exist, but these energy sources currently only account for a combined 14 percent of energy consumed worldwide.

To date, alternative energy sources have been hindered by technological and environmental difficulties. For instance, although the uranium that fuels nuclear power is abundant, the risk of nuclear accidents and the difficulty associated with safe disposal of radioactive waste have led to the decline of the nuclear power industry. Conversely, solar and wind power seem environmentally safe, but they are unreliable as steady sources of energy. As global energy consumption grows each year, development of certain alternative energy sources becomes increasingly important.

PETROLEUM

Petroleum, or crude oil, naturally occurring oily,

bituminous liquid composed of various organic chemicals. It is found in large quantities below the surface of Earth and is used as a fuel and as a raw material in the chemical industry. Modern industrial societies use it primarily to achieve a degree of mobility—on land, at sea, and in the air—that was barely imaginable less than 100 years ago. In addition, petroleum and its derivatives are used in the manufacture of medicines and fertilizers, foodstuffs, plastics, building materials, paints, and cloth and to generate electricity.

In fact, modern industrial civilization depends on petroleum and its products; the physical structure and way of life of the suburban communities that surround the great cities are the result of an ample and inexpensive supply of petroleum. In addition, the goals of developing countries—to exploit their natural resources and to supply foodstuffs for the burgeoning populations—are based on the assumption of petroleum availability. In recent years, however, the worldwide availability of petroleum has steadily declined and its relative cost has increased. Many experts forecast that petroleum will no longer be a common commercial material by the mid-21st century. World Energy Supply.

Characteristics

The chemical composition of all petroleum is principally hydrocarbons, although a few sulfur-containing and oxygen-containing compounds are usually present; the sulfur content varies from about 0.1 to 5 percent. Petroleum contains gaseous, liquid, and solid elements. The consistency of petroleum varies from liquid as thin as gasoline to liquid so thick that it will barely pour. Small quantities of gaseous compounds are usually dissolved in the liquid; when larger quantities of these compounds are present, the petroleum deposit is associated with a deposit of natural gas.

Three broad classes of crude petroleum exist: the paraffin types, the asphaltic types, and the mixed-base types. The paraffin types are composed of molecules in which the number of hydrogen atoms is always two more than twice the number of carbon atoms. The characteristic molecules in the asphaltic types are naphthenes, composed of twice as many hydrogen atoms as carbon atoms. In the mixed-base group are both paraffin hydrocarbons and naphthenes.

Formation

Petroleum is formed under Earth's surface by the decomposition of marine organisms. The remains of tiny organisms that live in the sea—and, to a lesser extent, those of land organisms that are carried down to the sea in rivers and of plants that grow on the ocean bottoms—are enmeshed with the fine sands and silts that settle to the bottom in quiet sea basins.

Such deposits, which are rich in organic materials, become the source rocks for the generation of crude oil. The process began many millions of years ago with the development of abundant life, and it continues to this day.

The sediments grow thicker and sink into the seafloor under their own weight. As additional deposits pile up, the pressure on the ones below increases several thousand times, and the temperature rises by several hundred degrees. The mud and sand harden into shale and sandstone; carbonate precipitates and skeletal shells harden into limestone; and the remains of the dead organisms are transformed into crude oil and natural gas.

Once the petroleum forms, it flows upward in Earth's crust because it has a lower density than the brines that saturate the interstices of the shales, sands, and carbonate rocks that constitute the crust of Earth. The crude oil and natural gas rise into the microscopic pores of the coarser sediments lying above. Frequently, the rising material encounters an impermeable shale or dense layer of rock that prevents further migration; the oil has become trapped, and a reservoir of petroleum is formed.

A significant amount of the upward-migrating oil, however, does not encounter impermeable rock but instead flows out at the surface of Earth or onto the ocean floor. Surface deposits also include bituminous lakes and escaping natural gas.

Historical Development

These surface deposits of crude oil have been known to humans for thousands of years. In the areas where they occurred, they were long used for limited purposes, such as caulking boats, waterproofing cloth, and fueling torches. By the time the Renaissance began in the 14th century, some surface deposits were being distilled to obtain lubricants and medicinal products, but the real exploitation of crude oil did not begin until the 19th century.

The Industrial Revolution had by then brought about a search for new fuels, and the social changes it effected had produced a need for good, cheap oil for lamps; people wished to be able to work and read after dark. Whale oil, however, was available only to the rich, tallow candles had an unpleasant odor, and gas jets were available only in then-modern houses and apartments in metropolitan areas.

The search for a better lamp fuel led to a great demand for "rock oil"—that is, crude oil—and various scientists in the mid-19th century were developing processes to make commercial use of it. Thus British entrepreneur James Young, with others, began to manufacture various products from crude oil, but he later turned to coal distillation and the exploitation of oil shales. In 1852 Canadian physician and geologist Abraham Gessner obtained a patent for producing from crude oil a relatively clean-burning, affordable lamp fuel called kerosene.

Thus the quest for greater supplies of crude oil began. For several years people had known that wells drilled for water and salt were occasionally infiltrated by petroleum, so the concept of drilling for crude oil itself soon followed. The first such wells were dug in Germany from 1857 to 1859, but the event that gained world fame was the drilling of an oil well near Oil Creek, Pennsylvania, by "Colonel" Edwin L. Drake in 1859. Drake, contracted by the American industrialist George H. Bissell—who had also supplied Silliman with rock-oil samples for producing his report—drilled to find the supposed "mother pool" from which the oil seeps of western Pennsylvania were assumed to be emanating. The reservoir

Drake tapped was shallow—only 21.2 m (69.5 ft) deep—and the petroleum was a paraffin type that flowed readily and was easy to distill.

Drake's success marked the beginning of the rapid growth of the modern petroleum industry. Soon petroleum received the attention of the scientific community, and coherent hypotheses were developed for its formation, migration upward through the earth, and entrapment. With the invention of the automobile and the energy needs brought on by World War I (1914-1918), the petroleum industry became one of the foundations of industrial society.

Exploration

In order to find crude oil underground, geologists must search for a sedimentary basin in which shales rich in organic material have been buried for a sufficiently long time for petroleum to have formed. The petroleum must also have had an opportunity to migrate into porous traps that are capable of holding large amounts of fluid. The occurrence of crude oil in Earth's crust is limited both by these conditions, which must be met simultaneously, and by the time span cf tens of millions to a hundred million years required for the oil's formation.

Petroleum geologists and geophysicists have many tools at their disposal to assist in identifying potential areas for drilling. Thus, surface mapping of outcrops of sedimentary beds makes possible the interpretation of subsurface features, which can then be supplemented with information obtained by drilling into the crust and retrieving cores or samples of the rock layers encountered. In addition, increasingly sophisticated seismic techniques—the reflection and refraction of sound waves propagated through Earth—reveal details of the structure and interrelationship of various layers in the subsurface.

Ultimately, however, the only way to prove that oil is present in the subsurface is to drill a well. In fact, most of the oil provinces in the world have initially been identified by the presence of surface seeps, and most of the actual reservoirs have been discovered by so-called wildcatters who relied perhaps as much on intuition as on science. (The term wildcatter comes from West Texas, where in the early 1920s drilling crews encountered many wildcats as they cleared locations for exploratory wells. Shot wildcats were hung on the oil derricks, and the wells became known as wildcat wells.)

An oil field, once found, may comprise more than one reservoir—that is, more than one single, continuous, bounded accumulation of oil. Several reservoirs may be stacked one above the other, isolated by intervening shales and impervious rock strata. Such reservoirs may vary in size from a few tens of hectares to tens of square kilometres, and from a few meters in thickness to several hundred or more. Most of the oil that has been discovered and exploited in the world has been found in a relatively few large reservoirs.

Primary Production

Most oil wells in the United States are drilled by the rotary method that was first described in a British patent in 1844 assigned to R. Beart. In rotary drilling, the drill string, a series of connected pipes, is supported by a derrick. The string is rotated by being coupled to the rotating table on the derrick floor. The drill bit at the end of the string is generally designed with three cone-shaped wheels tipped with hardened teeth. Drill cuttings are lifted continually to the surface by a circulating-fluid system driven by a pump.

Trapped crude oil is under pressure; were it not trapped by impermeable rock it would have continued to migrate upward, because of the pressure differential caused by its buoyancy, until it escaped at the surface of Earth. When a well bore is drilled into this pressured accumulation of oil, the oil expands into the low-pressure sink created by the well bore in communication with Earth's surface. As the well fills up with fluid, however, a back pressure is exerted on the reservoir, and the flow of additional fluid into the well bore would soon stop, were no other conditions involved.

Most crude oils, however, contain a significant amount of natural gas in solution, and this gas is kept in solution by the high pressure in the reservoir. The gas comes out of solution when the low pressure in the well bore is encountered, and the gas, once liberated, immediately begins to expand. This expansion, together with the dilution of the column of oil by the less dense gas, results in the propulsion of oil up to Earth's surface.

Nevertheless, as fluid withdrawal continues from the reservoir, the pressure within the reservoir gradually decreases, and the amount of gas in solution decreases. As a result, the flow rate of fluid into the well bore decreases, and less gas is liberated. The fluid may not reach the surface, so a pump (artificial lift) must be installed in the well bore to continue producing the crude oil.

Eventually, the flow rate of the crude oil becomes so small, and the cost of lifting the oil to the surface becomes so great, that the well costs more to operate than the revenues that can be gained from selling the crude oil (after discounting the price for operating costs, taxes, insurance, and return on capital). The well's economic limit has then been reached and it is abandoned.

Enhanced Oil Recovery

In primary production, no extraneous energy is added to the reservoir other than that required for lifting fluids from the producing wells. Most reservoirs are developed by numerous wells; and as primary production approaches its economic limit, perhaps only a few percent and no more than about 25 percent of the crude oil has been withdrawn from a given reservoir.

The oil industry has developed methods for supplementing the production of crude oil that can be obtained mostly by taking advantage of the natural reservoir energy. These supplementary methods, collectively known as enhanced oil recovery technology, can increase the recovery of crude oil, but only at the additional cost of supplying extraneous energy to the reservoir. In this way, the recovery of crude oil has been increased to an overall average of 33 percent of the original oil. Two successful supplementary methods are in use at this time: water injection and steam injection.

Water Injection

In a completely developed oil field, the wells may be drilled anywhere from 60 to 600 m (200 to 2,000 ft) from one another, depending on the nature of the reservoir. If water is pumped into alternate wells in such a field, the pressure in the reservoir as a whole can be maintained or even increased. In this way the rate of production of the crude oil also can be increased; in addition, the water physically displaces the oil, thus increasing the recovery efficiency.

In some reservoirs with a high degree of uniformity and little clay content, water flooding may increase the recovery efficiency to as much as 60 percent or more of the original oil in place. Water flooding was first introduced in the Pennsylvania oil fields, more or less accidentally, in the late 19th century, and it has since spread throughout the world.

Steam Injection

Steam injection is used in reservoirs that contain very viscous oils, those that are thick and flow slowly. The steam not only provides a source of energy to displace the oil, but also causes a marked reduction in viscosity (by raising the temperature of the reservoir), so that the crude oil flows faster under any given pressure differential.

This scheme has been used extensively in California and in the state of Zulia in Venezuela, where large reservoirs contain viscous oil. This technology is also being used to recover some of the vast accumulations of viscous crude oil, known as bitumen, along the Athabasca River in north central Alberta, Canada, and along the Orinoco River in eastern Venezuela.

Bitumen must be converted into a form of petroleum known as synthetic crude and is considered an unconventional crude oil. In Canada the steam technique most often used to extract bitumen is called steam-assisted gravity drainage (SAGD). This procedure requires a significant amount of energy and consequently is considered cost-efficient only when the price of conventional crude oil is high.

Offshore Drilling

Another method to increase oil-field production has been the construction and operation of offshore drilling rigs. The drilling rigs are installed, operated, and serviced on an offshore platform in water up to a depth of several hundred meters; the platform may either float or sit on legs planted on the ocean floor, where it is capable of resisting waves, wind, and—in Arctic regions—ice floes.

As in traditional rigs, the derrick is basically a device for suspending and rotating the drill pipe, to the end of which is attached the drill bit. Additional lengths of drill pipe are added to the drill string as the bit penetrates farther and farther into Earth's crust. The force required for cutting into the earth comes from the weight of the drill pipe itself.

To facilitate the removal of the cuttings, mud is constantly circulated down through the drill pipe, out through nozzles in the drill bit, and then up to the surface through the space between the drill pipe and the bore through the earth (the diameter of the bit is somewhat greater than that of the pipe). Successful bore holes have been drilled right on target, in this way, to depths of more than 6.4 km (more than 4 mi) from the surface of the ocean. Offshore drilling has resulted in the development of a significant additional reserve of petroleum—in the United States, about 5 percent of the total reserves.

Refining

Once oil has been produced from an oil field, it is treated with chemicals and heat to remove water and solids, and the natural gas is separated. The oil is then stored in a tank, or battery of tanks, and later transported to a refinery by truck, railroad tank car, barge, or pipeline. Large oil fields all have direct outlets to major, common-carrier pipelines.

Basic Distillation

The basic refining tool is the distillation unit. In the United States after the Civil War (1861-1865), more than 100 still refineries were already in operation. Crude oil begins to vapourize at a temperature somewhat less than that required to boil water. Hydrocarbons with the lowest molecular weight vapourize at the lowest temperatures, whereas successively higher temperatures are required to distill larger molecules. The first material to be distilled from crude oil is the gasoline fraction, followed in turn by naphtha and then by kerosene. The residue in the kettle, in the old still refineries, was then treated with caustic and sulfuric acid, and finally steam distilled thereafter. Lubricants and distillate fuel oils were obtained from the upper regions and waxes and asphalt from the lower regions of the distillation apparatus.

In the late 19th century the gasoline and naphtha fractions were actually considered a nuisance because little need for them existed. The demand for kerosene also began to decline because of the growing production of electricity and the use of electric lights. With the introduction of the automobile, however, the demand for gasoline suddenly burgeoned, and the need for greater supplies of crude oil increased accordingly.

Thermal Cracking

In an effort to increase the yield from distillation, the thermal cracking process was developed. In this process, the heavier portions of the crude oil were heated under pressure and at higher temperatures.

This resulted in the large hydrocarbon molecules being split into smaller ones, so that the yield of gasoline from a barrel of crude oil was increased. The efficiency of the process was limited, however, because at the high temperatures and pressures that were used, a large amount of coke was deposited in the reactors. This in turn required the use of still higher temperatures and pressures to crack the crude oil. A coking process was then invented in which fluids were recirculated; the process ran for a much longer time, with far less buildup of coke. Many refiners quickly adopted the process of thermal cracking.

Alkylation and Catalytic Cracking

Two additional basic processes, alkylation and catalytic cracking, were introduced in early 1930s and increased the gasoline yield from a barrel of crude oil. In alkylation small molecules produced by thermal cracking are recombined in the presence of a catalyst. This produces branched molecules in the gasoline boiling range that have superior properties higher antiknock ratings as a fuel for high-powered engines such as those used in today's commercial airplanes.

In the catalytic-cracking process, the crude oil is cracked in the presence of a finely divided catalyst.

This permits the refiner to produce many diverse hydrocarbons that can then be recombined by alkylation, isomerization, and catalytic reforming to produce high antiknock engine fuels and specialty chemicals. The production of these chemicals has given birth to the gigantic petrochemical industry, which turns out alcohols, detergents, synthetic rubber, glycerin, fertilizers, sulfur, solvents, and the feedstocks for the manufacture of drugs, nylon, plastics, paints, polyesters, food additives and supplements, explosives, dyes, and insulating materials. The petrochemical industry uses about 5 percent of the total supply of oil and gas in the United States.

Petroleum Engineering

The disciplines employed by exploration and petroleum engineers are drawn from virtually every field of science and engineering. Thus the exploration staffs include geologists who specialize in surface mapping in order to try to reconstruct the subsurface configuration of the various sedimentary strata that will afford clues to the presence of petroleum traps. Subsurface specialists then study drill cuttings and interpret data on the subsurface formations that is relayed to surface recorders from electrical, sonic, and nuclear logging devices lowered into the bore hole on a wire line.

Seismologists interpret sophisticated signals returning to the surface from sound waves that are propagated through Earth's crust. Geochemists study the transformation of organic matter and the means for detecting and predicting the occurrence of such matter in subsurface strata. In addition, physicists, chemists, biologists, and mathematicians all support the basic research and development of sophisticated exploration techniques.

Petroleum engineers are responsible for the development of discovered oil accumulations. They usually specialize in one of the important categories of production operation: drilling and surface facilities, petrophysical and geological analysis of the reservoir, reserve estimation and specification of optimal development practices, or production control and surveillance. Although many of these specialists have formal training as petroleum engineers, many others are drawn from the ranks of chemical, mechanical, electrical, and civil engineers; physicists, chemists, and mathematicians; and geologists.

The drilling engineer specifies and supervises the actual programmeme by which a well will be bored into the Earth, the kind of drilling mud to be used, the way in which the steel casing that isolates the productive strata from all other subsurface strata will be cemented, and how the productive strata will be exposed to the well bore.

The facilities-engineering specialists specify and design the surface equipment that must be installed to support the production operation, the well-head pumps, the field measurement and collection of produced fluids and gas separation systems, the storage tankage, the dehydration system for removing water from the produced oil, and the facilities for enhanced recovery programmes.

The petrophysical and geological engineer, after interpreting the data supplied by analysis of cores and by various logging devices, develops a description of the reservoir rock and its permeability, porosity, and continuity. The reservoir engineer then develops the plan for the number and location of the wells to be drilled into the reservoir, the rates of production that can be sustained for optimum recovery, and the need for supplementary recovery technology. The reservoir engineer also estimates the productivity and ultimate recovery (reserves) that can be achieved from the reservoir, in terms of time, operating costs, and value of the crude oil produced.

Finally, the production engineer monitors the performance of the wells. The engineer recommends and implements remedial tasks such as fracturing, acidizing, deepening, adjusting gas to oil and water to oil ratios, and any other measures that will improve the economic performance of the reservoir.

Production Volumes and Reserves

Crude oil is perhaps the most useful and versatile raw material that has become available for exploitation. By 2003, the United States was using 7 billion barrels of petroleum per year, and worldwide consumption of petroleum was 29.3 billion barrels per year.

Reserves

The world's technically recoverable reserves of conventional crude oil totaled about 1.3 trillion barrels in 2004, of which some 216 billion barrels were in North America. Of the known oil reserves that can be profitably extracted at current prices, about 57 percent (730 billion barrels) were in the Middle East.

However, beginning in the 21st century oil companies became more focused on exploiting unconventional crude oil reserves. Improved techniques for the extraction of unconventional crude oil, especially of bitumen in the tar sand deposits of western Canada, combined with higher conventional crude oil prices, made exploitation of unconventional reserves more cost-efficient. The reserves of bitumen in the province of Alberta were believed sufficient to yield 1.7 trillion barrels of synthetic crude oil. Only ten percent of this amount, however, was thought to be technically recoverable. Nevertheless, by 2007 Canada had become the principal foreign supplier of oil to the United States.

Projections

It is likely that some additional discoveries will be made of new reserves in coming years, and new technologies will be developed that permit the recovery efficiency from already known resources to be increased. The supply of crude oil will at any rate extend into the early decades of the 21st century.

Virtually no expectation exists among experts, however, that discoveries and inventions will extend the availability of cheap crude oil much beyond that period. The Prudhoe Bay field on the North Slope of Alaska is the largest field ever discovered in the Western Hemisphere. The ultimate recovery of crude oil from this field is anticipated to be about 10 billion barrels, which is sufficient to supply the current needs of the United States for less than two years, but only one such field was discovered in the West in more than a century of exploration.

Alternatives

In light of the reserves available and the dismal projections, it is apparent that alternative energy sources will be required to sustain the civilized societies of the world in the future. The options are indeed few, however, when the massive energy requirements of the industrial world come to be appreciated.

Although alternative energy sources, such as geothermal energy, solar energy, and nuclear energy, hold much promise, none has yet proved an economically viable replacement for petroleum products.

Environmental Effects of Using Petroleum

Adding to the urgency of finding alternatives to petroleum and other fossil fuels is the problem of global warming. Petroleum combustion releases carbon dioxide, a greenhouse gas, into the atmosphere, and most atmospheric scientists believe that rising levels of greenhouse gases are driving climate change. These changes could cause numerous environmental problems, including disrupted weather patterns and polar ice cap melting.

Disrupted weather patterns could lead to extensive drought and desertification. Polar ice cap melting could cause flooding and profound changes in ocean circulation. Many environmental organizations are urging governments and individuals to reduce greenhouse gas emissions by conserving energy with fuel-efficient technologies and by developing alternative, renewable energy sources such as wind and solar power. In the United States most environmental groups have urged the U.S. government to ratify the Kyôto Protocol, a global treaty that sets a specific timetable for reducing greenhouse gas emissions.

Drilling oil wells also creates environmental problems because the petroleum pumped up from deep reservoir rocks is often accompanied by large volumes of salt water. This brine contains numerous impurities, so it must either be injected back into the reservoir rocks or treated for safe surface disposal. The extraction of unconventional crude oil sources, such as bitumen, poses even greater environmental problems due to the large number of pollutants produced and the use of fossil fuels involved in the extraction.

Petroleum usually must also be transported long distances by tanker or pipeline to reach a refinery. Transport of petroleum occasionally leads to accidental spills. Oil spills, especially in large volumes, can be detrimental to wildlife and habitat.

FUEL GASES

Fuel Gases, any combustible gaseous mixture used as fuel to provide energy for domestic or industrial use.

Fuel gases consist principally of hydrocarbons, that is, of molecular compounds of carbon and hydrogen. The properties of the various gases depend on the number and arrangement of the carbon and hydrogen atoms within their molecules. All these gases are odorless in the pure state, and carbon monoxide is toxic.

It is therefore common practice to add sulfur compounds to manufactured gas; such sulfur compounds, which are sometimes normally present in the gas, have an unpleasant smell and serve to give warning of a leak in the supply lines or gas appliance. In addition to their combustible components most gases have varying amounts of noncombustible nitrogen and water as their end products.

The devices used to burn gas for either heat or illumination consist of a burner nozzle and some means of mixing air with the gas before it reaches the nozzle, as in the

Bunsen burner invented by British chemist and physicist Michael Faraday and improved and popularized by German chemist Robert Wilhelm Bunsen.

Fuel gases still in use are coal gas, made by the destructive distillation of coal producer gas and blast-furnace gas, made by the interaction of steam, air, and carbon; natural gas, drawn from gas deposits in the earth; and bottled gases, made from the lighter hydrocarbons.

Coal Gas

The most important coal-gasification processes aim chiefly at production of so-called pipeline quality gas, which is reasonably interchangeable with natural gas. Gas from coal, besides having pumping and heating specifications, must meet strict limits on content of carbon monoxide, sulfur, inert gases, and water. To meet these standards, most coal-gasification processes culminate with gas cleanup and methanation operations.

Various hydrogasification processes, in which hydrogen reacts directly with coal to form methane, are used today; these processes bypass the indirect step of producing synthesis gas, hydrogen and carbon monoxide, before an upgrading yields methane. Other coal-gas processes include the carbon dioxide acceptor process, employing the lime-bearing material dolomite, and the molten salt process.

These processes work indirectly to produce synthesis gas first. Other gases manufactured formerly from coal and coke, such as illumination gas and coke-oven gas, are of little or no importance today.

Producer and Blast-Furnace Gases

Producer gas is a form of water gas, a term applied to steam-process gases. It is made by burning low-grade fuel (such as lignite or bituminous coal) in a closed vessel, called a producer, while passing a continuous stream of steam and air through the producer. Because of the air present in the producer, the resulting gas is approximately 50 percent incombustible nitrogen and is low in fuel value, having only about 28 percent the heating value of coke-oven gas.

Blast-furnace gas, which results from the interaction of limestone, iron ore, and carbon in blast furnaces, has some heating value because of its carbon monoxide content but contains about 60 percent nitrogen. Enormous quantities are produced during the operation of furnaces. Most of this gas is consumed in heating the air blast and driving the compressors for the blast. The heating value of blast-furnace gas is about 16 percent of that of coke-oven gas.

Natural Gas

A certain amount of natural gas almost always occurs in connection with oil deposits and is brought to the surface together with the oil when a well is drilled. Such gas is called casing-head gas. Certain wells, however, yield only natural gas.

Natural gas contains valuable organic elements that are important raw materials of the natural-gasoline and chemical industries. Before natural gas is used as fuel, hydrocarbons such as butane, propane, and natural gasoline are extracted as liquids. The remaining gas constitutes so-called dry gas, which is piped to domestic and industrial consumers for use as fuels; dry gas, devoid of butane and propane, also occurs in nature. Composed of the lighter hydrocarbons methane and ethane, dry gas is used also in the manufacture of plastics, drugs, and dyes.

Bottled Gas

Several of the lighter hydrocarbons, such as propane, butane, pentane, and mixtures of these gases are liquefied and employed as fuels. These so-called bottled gases, which are usually stored in steel cylinders, make possible the use of appliances such as cooking stoves and heaters in localities where a centralized gas supply is not available. Such bottled gases are produced from natural gas and petroleum.

NAPHTHA

Naphtha, term applied to several volatile, flammable liquids, obtained by distillation of various organic materials and used as a solvent for fats, gums, and resins, particularly in the manufacture of varnishes and waxes and in the dry cleaning of textiles. Petroleum naphtha, or mineral naphtha, is obtained from petroleum as a crude distillate that is lighter than kerosene and has a lower boiling point. It contains a mixture of methane-type hydrocarbons.

The distillates with lower boiling points than petroleum naphtha are called ligroin. Other forms of naphtha are crude naphtha, obtained from coal tar; shale naphtha, obtained from shale; and wood naphtha, obtained from wood. Solvent naphtha, used for dissolving rubber, is a high-boiling-point fraction distilled from coal tar.

ASPHALT

Asphalt, black, cementlike material varying in consistency at room temperature from solid to semisolid. It can be poured when heated to the temperature of boiling water and is used in surfacing roads, in lining the walls of water-retaining structures such as reservoirs and swimming pools, and in manufacturing floor tiles and roofing materials. It is not to be confused with tar, a black substance derived from coal, wood, and other substances.

Asphalt is found in natural deposits, but almost all of the asphalt used commercially is now derived from petroleum. Straight-run asphalts, which are made up of the nonvolatile hydrocarbons left after petroleum has been refined into gasoline and other products, are used for paving. Air-blown asphalts, produced from petroleum residues at temperatures of from 204° to 316°C (400° to 600°F), are used to make roofing materials and similar products. A small amount of asphalt is "cracked" at temperatures of about 500°C (about 930°F) to make some insulation materials.

Natural asphalt was used extensively in ancient times. Natural deposits of asphalt occur in pits or lakes as residue from crude petroleum that has seeped up through fissures in the earth. Typical of these deposits are the La Brea tar pits in Los Angeles, in which the remains of prehistoric flora and fauna have been found. A natural asphalt pool is Pitch Lake, Trinidad. Deposits of asphalt-impregnated rock, called rock asphalt, are found throughout the world. An asphalt deposit of some commercial importance is Gilsonite, also called uintaite, found in the Uinta River Basin of Utah and used in the manufacture of paints and lacquers.

The use of asphalt for street paving in the United States began in 1870; by 1903 more than 35 million sq m (about 42 million sq yd) of U.S. streets were paved with asphalt. Today, asphalt derived from petroleum is used to surface about 90 percent of paved roads in the United States. About 75 percent of the more than 24 million metric tons of asphalt produced in the United States each year is used for this purpose.

INTERNAL-COMBUSTION ENGINE

Internal-Combustion Engine, any type of machine that obtains mechanical energy directly from the expenditure of the chemical energy of fuel burned in a combustion chamber that is an integral part of the engine. Four principal types of internal-combustion engines are in general use: the Otto-cycle engine, the diesel engine, the rotary engine, and the gas turbine. For the various types of engines employing the principle of jet propulsion.

The Otto-cycle engine, named after its inventor, the German technician Nikolaus August Otto, is the familiar gasoline engine used in automobiles and airplanes; the diesel engine, named after the French-born German engineer Rudolf Christian Karl Diesel, operates on a different principle and usually uses oil as a fuel. It is employed in electric-generating and marine-power plants, in trucks and buses, and in some automobiles. Both Otto-cycle and diesel engines are manufactured in two-stroke and four-stroke cycle models.

Components of Engines

The essential parts of Otto-cycle and diesel engines are the same. The combustion chamber consists of a cylinder, usually fixed, that is closed at one end and in which a close-fitting piston slides. The in-and-out motion of the piston varies the volume of the chamber between the inner face of the piston and the closed end of the cylinder.

The outer face of the piston is attached to a crankshaft by

a connecting rod. The crankshaft transforms the reciprocating motion of the piston into rotary motion. In multicylindered engines the crankshaft has one offset portion, called a crankpin, for each connecting rod, so that the power from each cylinder is applied to the crankshaft at the appropriate point in its rotation. Crankshafts have heavy flywheels and counterweights, which by their inertia minimize irregularity in the motion of the shaft. An engine may have from 1 to as many as 28 cylinders.

The fuel supply system of an internal-combustion engine consists of a tank, a fuel pump, and a device for vapourizing or atomizing the liquid fuel. In Otto-cycle engines this device is either a carburetor or, more recently, a fuel-injection system. In most engines with a carburetor, vapourized fuel is conveyed to the cylinders through a branched pipe called the intake manifold and, in many engines, a similar exhaust manifold is provided to carry off the gases produced by combustion.

The fuel is admitted to each cylinder and the waste gases exhausted through mechanically operated poppet valves or sleeve valves.

The valves are normally held closed by the pressure of springs and are opened at the proper time during the operating cycle by cams on a rotating camshaft that is geared to the crankshaft. By the 1980s more sophisticated fuel-injection systems, also used in diesel engines, had largely replaced this traditional method of supplying the proper mix of air and fuel. In engines with fuel injection, a mechanically or electronically controlled monitoring system injects the appropriate amount of gas directly into the cylinder or inlet valve at the appropriate time.

The gas vapourizes as it enters the cylinder. This system is more fuel efficient than the carburetor and produces less pollution. In all engines some means of igniting the fuel in the cylinder must be provided.

The ignition system of Otto-cycle engines described below consists of a source of low-voltage, direct-current electricity that is connected to the primary of a transformer called an ignition coil. The current is interrupted many times a second by an automatic switch called the timer. The pulsations of the current in the primary induce a pulsating, high-voltage current in the secondary.

The high-voltage current is led to each cylinder in turn by a rotary switch called the distributor. The actual ignition device is the spark plug, an insulated conductor set in the wall or top of each cylinder. At the inner end of the spark plug is a small gap between two wires. The high-voltage current arcs across this gap, yielding the spark that ignites the fuel mixture in the cylinder.

Because of the heat of combustion, all engines must be equipped with some type of cooling system. Some aircraft and automobile engines, small stationary engines, and outboard motors for boats are cooled by air. In this system the outside surfaces of the cylinder are shaped in a series of radiating fins with a large area of metal to radiate heat from the cylinder. Other engines are water-cooled and have their cylinders enclosed in an external water jacket. In automobiles, water is circulated through the jacket by means of a water pump and cooled by passing through the finned coils of a radiator.

Some automobile engines are also air-cooled, and in marine engines sea water is used for cooling. Unlike steam engines and turbines, internal-combustion engines develop no torque when starting, and therefore provision must be made for turning the crankshaft so that the cycle of operation can begin. Automobile engines are normally started by means of an electric motor or starter that is geared to the crankshaft with a clutch that automatically disengages the motor after the engine has started. Small engines are sometimes started manually by turning the crankshaft with a crank or by pulling a rope wound several times around the flywheel.

Methods of starting large engines include the inertia starter, which consists of a flywheel that is rotated by hand or by means of an electric motor until its kinetic energy is sufficient to turn the crankshaft, and the explosive starter, which employs the explosion of a blank cartridge to drive a turbine wheel that is coupled to the engine. The inertia and explosive starters are chiefly used to start airplane engines.

Otto-Cycle Engines

The ordinary Otto-cycle engine is a four-stroke engine; that is, in a complete power cycle, its pistons make four strokes, two toward the head (closed head) of the cylinder and two away from the head. During the first stroke of the cycle, the piston moves away from the cylinder head while simultaneously the intake valve is opened.

The motion of the piston during this stroke sucks a quantity of a fuel and air mixture into the combustion chamber. During the next stroke, the piston moves toward the cylinder head and compresses the fuel mixture in the combustion chamber. At the moment when the piston reaches the end of this stroke and the volume of the combustion chamber is at a minimum, the fuel mixture is ignited by the spark plug and burns, expanding and exerting a pressure on the piston, which is then driven away from the cylinder head in the third stroke. During the final stroke, the exhaust valve is opened and the piston moves toward the cylinder head, driving the exhaust gases out of the combustion chamber and leaving the cylinder ready to repeat the cycle.

The efficiency of a modern Otto-cycle engine is limited by a number of factors, including losses by cooling and by friction. In general, the efficiency of such engines is determined by the compression ratio of the engine. The compression ratio (the ratio between the maximum and minimum volumes of the combustion chamber) is usually about 8 to 1 or 10 to 1 in most modern Otto-cycle engines. Higher compression ratios, up to about 15 to 1, with a resulting increase of efficiency, are possible with the use of high-octane antiknock fuels. The efficiencies of good modern Otto-cycle engines range between 20 and 25 percent—in other words, only this percentage of the heat energy of the fuel is transformed into mechanical energy.

Diesel Engines

Theoretically, the diesel cycle differs from the Otto cycle in that combustion takes place at constant volume rather than at constant pressure. Most diesels are also four-stroke engines but they operate differently than the four-stroke Otto-cycle engines. The first, or suction, stroke draws air, but no fuel, into the combustion chamber through an intake valve.

On the second, or compression, stroke the air is compressed to a small fraction of its former volume and is heated to approximately 440°C (approximately 820°F) by this compression. At the end of the compression stroke, vapourized fuel is injected into the combustion chamber and burns instantly because of the high temperature of the air in the chamber. Some diesels have auxiliary electrical ignition systems to ignite the fuel when the engine starts and until it warms up. This combustion drives the piston back on the third, or power, stroke of the cycle. The fourth stroke, as in the Otto-cycle engine, is an exhaust stroke.

The efficiency of the diesel engine, which is in general governed by the same factors that control the efficiency of Otto-cycle engines, is inherently greater than that of any Otto-cycle engine and in actual engines today is slightly more than 40 percent.

Diesels are, in general, slow-speed engines with crankshaft speeds of 100 to 750 revolutions per minute (rpm) as compared to 2500 to 5000 rpm for typical Otto-cycle engines. Some types of diesel, however, have speeds up to 2000 rpm. Because diesels use compression ratios of 14 or more to 1, they are generally more heavily built than Otto-cycle engines, but this disadvantage is counterbalanced by their greater efficiency and the fact that they can be operated on less expensive fuel oils.

Two-Stroke Engines

By suitable design it is possible to operate an Otto-cycle or diesel as a two-stroke or two-cycle engine with a power stroke every other stroke of the piston instead of once every four strokes. The power of a two-stroke engine is usually double that of a four-stroke engine of comparable size.

The general principle of the two-stroke engine is to shorten the periods in which fuel is introduced to the combustion chamber and in which the spent gases are exhausted to a small fraction of the duration of a stroke instead of allowing each of these operations to occupy a full stroke. In the simplest type of two-stroke engine, the poppet valves are replaced by sleeve valves or ports (openings in the cylinder wall that are uncovered by the piston at the end of its outward travel). In the two-stroke cycle, the fuel mixture or air is introduced through the intake port when the piston is fully withdrawn from the cylinder.

The compression stroke follows, and the charge is ignited when the piston reaches the end of this stroke. The piston then moves outward on the power stroke, uncovering the exhaust port and permitting the gases to escape from the combustion chamber.

Rotary Engine

An internal-combustion engine of a radically new design, in which the piston and cylinder were replaced by a three-cornered rotor turning in a roughly oval chamber. The fuel-air mixture is drawn in through an intake port and trapped between one face of the turning rotor and the wall of the oval chamber. The turning of the rotor compresses the mixture, which is ignited by a spark plug. The exhaust gases are then expelled through an exhaust port through the action of the turning rotor.

The cycle takes place alternately at each face of the rotor, giving three power strokes for each turn of the rotor. Because of the Wankel engine's compact size and consequent lesser weight as compared with the piston engine, it appeared to be an important option for automobiles. In addition, its mechanical simplicity provided low manufacturing costs, its cooling requirements were low, and its low centre of gravity made it safer to drive.

A line of Wankel-engine cars was produced in Japan in the early 1970s, and several United States automobile manufacturers researched the idea as well. However, production of the Wankel engine was discontinued as a result of its poor fuel economy and its high pollutant emissions. Mazda, a Japanese car manufacturer, has continued to design and innovate the rotary engine, improving performance and fuel efficiency.

The Stratified Charge Engine

A modification of the conventional spark-ignition piston engine, the stratified charge engine is designed to reduce emissions without the need for an exhaust-gas recirculation system or catalytic converter. Its key feature is a dual combustion chamber for each cylinder, with a prechamber that receives a rich fuel-air mixture while the main chamber is charged with a very lean mixture. The spark ignites the rich mixture that in turn ignites the lean main mixture. The resulting peak temperature is low enough to inhibit the formation of nitrogen oxides, and the mean temperature is sufficiently high to limit emissions of carbon monoxide and hydrocarbon.Research on modifications of conventional engines as well as alternatives to conventional engines continues. Some of these options include a modified version of the two-stroke engine, the twin engine (a combination of an internal-combustion engine and an electric engine), and the Stirling engine.

Chapter 4

Smoking Materials

COCAINE

Cocaine, alkaloid obtained from leaves of the coca plant and used medically as a local anesthetic. It is also widely abused as a drug. Native Americans of the Inca Empire chewed coca leaves to obtain mild euphoria, stimulation, and alertness. The drug was first isolated in 1855 and came to be used widely as a local anesthetic in minor surgery. At present, local anesthetics with less abuse potential, such as lidocaine, are commonly used instead. Cocaine has long been known as a drug of abuse, but it came into particular prominence in the late 1970s and the 1980s. Cocaine hydrochloride, a water-soluble salt, is a dry white powder (known on the street as "snow") that is usually inhaled through a thin tube inserted into the nostril. More rarely, cocaine is injected into a vein.

The drug may also be smoked in a purified form through a water pipe ("freebasing") or in a concentrated form ("crack") shaped into pellets and placed in special smoking gear. Users experience euphoria, exhilaration, and a decreased appetite. The drug also increases heart rate, elevates blood pressure, and dilates the pupils. Chronic use can lead to skin abscesses, perforation of the septum of the nose, weight loss, and damage to the nervous system. Negative mental effects include extreme restlessness, anxiety, irritability, and, occasionally, paranoid psychosis. Death from even a small dose can occur, and is usually caused by seizures or heart attacks. Cocaine is classified as a narcotic for legal purposes by the United States government. It causes strong psychological dependence.

ALKALOIDS

Alkaloids, group of mildly alkaline compounds, mostly of plant origin and of moderate molecular complexity. Even in very small amounts, the alkaloids produce strong physiological effects on the body. All contain nitrogen atoms that are structurally related to those of ammonia.

Nearly 3000 alkaloids have been recorded; the first to be prepared synthetically (1886) was one of the simplest, called coniine, or 2-propyl piperidine, $C_5H_{10}NC_3H_7$. It is highly poisonous; less than 0.2 g (0.007 oz) is fatal. Coniine, obtained from seeds of the hemlock, was the poison used in the execution of Socrates. Some 30 of the known alkaloids are used in medicine. Atropine, obtained from belladonna, causes dilation of the pupils; morphine is a painkiller; quinine is a specific remedy for malaria; nicotine is a potent insecticide; and reserpine is a valuable tranquilizer.

COCA

Coca, common name for any of several related South American shrubs. Of particular importance is a species the leaves of which are used by the inhabitants of Peru and Bolivia as a stimulant. The dried leaves, which contain cocaine and several other derivatives, are mixed with unslaked lime or wood ash and chewed. The shrub is cultivated in Colombia, Peru, and Bolivia. It is about 1 to 2 m (about 3 to 6 ft) high, with straight branches and leaves that resemble tea leaves.

POISON HEMLOCK

Poison Hemlock, common name for poisonous herbs belonging to two different genera of the parsley family. Hemlock, or poison hemlock, is a large, coarse, unpleasant-smelling plant, all parts of which are poisonous and may be fatal if eaten. It is the poison hemlock that was used to put Socrates to death. Native to Europe, the plant is now naturalized in the United States and occurs as a luxuriant weed, up to 3 m (10 ft) tall, along roadsides and in abandoned fields. The dark-green leaves are divided and redivided into small, ovate, toothed segments. The hollow stems are characteristically blotched with purple. The small white flowers are grouped into flat-topped clusters called umbels. The poisonous principles in hemlock are alkaloids that affect the nervous system and induce trembling, loss of coordination, and paralysis of respiration.

The second type of poison hemlock are the water hemlocks, such as musquash root, related botanically to poison hemlock but toxicologically entirely different. The roots and, to a much lesser extent, the foliage contain a complex unsaturated alcohol that brings on convulsions. The roots grow in clusters of dahlialike tubers that are about 5 cm (about 2 in) long. The amount of root that must be eaten to cause death is very small. The plant grows in swamps, along streams, and in other moist locations. The foliage, which arises in early spring in a cluster from the roots, is divided and redivided into leaflets with regularly pointed and notched edges. A central vein runs the length of each leaflet. From it, secondary veins run toward the edge, ending in or near the notches of the leaf rather than in the points.

PARSLEY

Parsley, common name for a large family of herbaceous flowering plants, containing many important foods and flavourings, and for one of its genera. This family of dicots contains about 3,000 species and is nearly cosmopolitan in distribution, although most common in temperate areas. The family is well known for its characteristic inflorescence (flower cluster), called an umbel.

The individual pedicels (flower stalks) arise from the same point on the peduncle (one of the inflorescence stalks) and are of such lengths that all the flowers are raised to the same height above their point of common attachment; thus the umbel is flat-topped. The basically five-parted flowers are rather uniform throughout the family. The fruits, however, which develop from the two-parted ovary, which is inferior (borne below and fused to the other flower parts), vary remarkably.

Members of the family have many uses. The carrot and parsnip are important root crops; celery is the petioles (leafstalks) of one species. Parsley, dill, fennel, caraway, anise, and coriander are flavouring herbs. Some species are poisonous, whereas others are used medicinally and a few are used horticulturally.

PARSNIP (PLANT)

Parsnip (plant), common name for a plant genus of the parsley family. Plants of the genus are annual, biennial, and perennial herbs with carrotlike fleshy roots and pinnate, feathery leaves. The common parsnip, native to Europe and northern Asia, has stems up to 91 cm (3 ft) tall and ovate leaflets. The edible white roots are aromatic, moist, and sweet, but slightly acrid. The plant thrives in an open rich soil, but also grows in clay soils.

DILL

Dill, common name for an annual or biennial herb of the parsley family. It grows wild in grainfields of southern Europe, the British Isles, and the United States and is also cultivated as an herb. Dill has a strong, aromatic taste; its leaves are used for flavouring pickles and sauces.

BELLADONNA

Belladonna, also deadly nightshade, common name for an Old World herb, and for a crude drug obtained from the plant. Belladonna is a biennial or annual plant with large simple leaves and bell-shaped flowers. The flower tube is five-pointed, dull purple or red-purple, and surrounded by five green sepals. The fruit is a single green berry that becomes purple to black with maturity.

Belladonna is occasionally grown in gardens in North America but rarely becomes naturalized. It does not normally persist without cultivation. Other members of the nightshade family are sometimes erroneously called belladonna. All parts of the true belladonna are poisonous and narcotic. The leaves and root contain alkaloids; one, atropine, is used to dilate the pupils of the eyes, to facilitate eye examinations and as an antispasmodic in the treatment of asthma. In earlier times in

Italy, extracts of belladonna were used by women for the cosmetic value of this dilating effect; such use explains the origin of the common name (Italian, "beautiful woman").

NIGHTSHADE

Nightshade, common name for both a family of plants, and for a genus of mostly weedy plants. The family has about 90 genera and 2600 species and includes crop and garden plants—such as potato, tomato, petunia, tobacco, and eggplant—as well as many poisonous plants. The poisonous nightshades contain alkaloids of three major types: tropane, found in belladonna, jimsonweed, and henbane; pyridine, in tobacco; and steroid, in some members of the nightshade genus.

Included in the nightshade genus are such common weeds as horse nettle, a spiny, perennial herb of the south-central to eastern United States; European bittersweet; silverleaf nightshade, a whitish herb of prairies of the southwestern states and Mexico; black nightshade, an annual, self-seeding herb found in disturbed soils of eastern and central North America; and buffalo bur, a spiny weed of the Great Plains and eastward. Also in this genus are the common potato, eggplant, and Jerusalem cherry.

Plants in the nightshade family bear flowers with five sepals, five petals, five stamens, and a solitary pistil that in most species ripens into a berry. In horse nettle, the flowers are white or pale violet, and the berry, yellow; in European bittersweet, the flowers are blue or purple, and the berry, red; in silverleaf nightshade, the flowers are violet or blue and yellow, and the berry, orange; and in black nightshade, the flowers are white, and the berry, black. Buffalo bur has yellow flowers and a spiny fruit or bur resulting from the persistence of the spiny calyx about the berry as it ripens.

The foliage and unripe fruit of most nightshades contain dangerous levels of a steroid alkaloid, solanine. The ripe berries are the least toxic part of these plants but may be deadly under some circumstances. Solanine is also found in potato sprouts and the green spots of some potatoes. A toxic dose of any of these will usually result in severe digestive upset. This may be accompanied by trembling, weakness, difficulty in breathing, or paralysis. Potato sprouts should be removed before using the tubers for food. Potato vines, sprouts, and rotten potatoes should not be used as forage for livestock. The members of the nightshade family are placed in a medium-size order that includes many attractive spring and summer garden plants. The order is widely distributed, with concentrations of species in the Americas. It contains 8 families and nearly 5000 species. Plants of the order vary greatly in habit, from herbs to trees, and some of them are parasites. The flowers are basically five-parted. The petals are fused into a tube, on the inside of which are borne the stamens.

The morning glory family, with about 1650 species, is a well-known member of the order and contains important food, drug, and horticultural plants. The sweet potato, a member of the morning glory family, is cultivated worldwide; its nutritious tuberous root has been used as a food source since prehistoric times. Other members of the same genus have chemicals similar to LSD. Still other species of this and other genera provide garden ornamentals, such as the morning glory. The phlox family, which contains about 300 species, provides such ornamentals as Jacob's ladder and the common annual phlox, native to Texas. The mostly herbaceous waterleaf family also contains about 250 species.

QUININE

Quinine, drug that reduces fever in the treatment of malaria. Although quinine kills certain forms of the parasite that causes malaria, it cannot kill the parasite in all stages of its life cycle. Quinine, therefore, is not a true cure for malaria, but is useful in suppressing and controlling the recurring attacks of fever that characterize the disease. In many areas, quinine has been largely replaced by synthetic antimalarial drugs that produce fewer side effects and are more effective. However, quinine is still used in areas of the world where the synthetic drugs are not available, are not effective against particular strains of malaria, or are too expensive. Quinine is also used as a muscle relaxant to treat nighttime leg cramps.

Quinine is found in the root, bark, and branches of cinchonas and other trees native to the Andes mountains in South America. As early as 1633, Calancha, an Augustinian monk living in Peru, described how the Indians ground cinchona bark into a fine powder that was used to treat fever. By 1640, use of the so-called fever bark had spread to Europe. During the next two centuries, cinchona trees were so indiscriminately stripped of bark that they began to die out, and by the middle of the 19th century the bark commanded excessively high prices. To combat the rising price, cinchona trees were introduced to other parts of the world. The trees are now cultivated in Java, India, and Sri Lanka.

In 1820, a new method was developed to isolate quinine and cinchonine, another drug from the cinchona tree, from cinchona bark. These drugs were then used to combat malaria instead of the bark itself. In the 1930s the first synthetic antimalarial drugs were developed. However, quinine remained in wider use than its synthetic counterparts until World War II (1939-1945), when the supply of quinine from countries in the South Pacific was cut off by Japanese military conquest. In response, several new antimalarial drugs such as chloroquine and primaquine were developed and are still used today.

NICOTINE

Nicotine, an oily liquid substance found in tobacco leaves that acts as a stimulant and also contributes to smoking addiction. When extracted from the leaves, nicotine is colourless, but quickly turns brown when exposed to air. It has an acrid, burning taste. Nicotine is a very powerful poison, and it forms the base of many insecticides.

Cigarette tobacco contains only a small amount of nicotine and most of this nicotine is destroyed by the heat of burning so that the actual concentration of nicotine in smoke is low. However, even a small amount of nicotine is sufficient to be addictive. The amount of nicotine absorbed by the body from inhaling smoke depends on many factors including the type of tobacco, whether the smoke is inhaled, and whether a filter is used.

Tobacco smokers absorb small amounts of nicotine by

inhaling smoke from cigars, cigarettes, or pipes. Nicotine is drawn into the lungs, where it enters the bloodstream and is pumped by the heart to the brain. It takes only seven seconds for nicotine to enter the brain after being inhaled.

Nicotine has various effects on the body. In small doses nicotine serves as a nerve stimulant, entering the bloodstream and promoting the flow of adrenaline, a stimulating hormone. It speeds up the heartbeat and may cause it to become irregular. It also raises the blood pressure and reduces the appetite, and it may cause nausea and vomiting.

Most of the known health risks associated with cigarette smoking, such as damage to the lungs and lung cancer, are caused by other components of cigarettes such as tars and other byproducts of smoking, and by the irritating effects of smoke on the lung tissue. Addiction to smoking is caused by nicotine itself. Stopping smoking produces withdrawal symptoms within 24 to 48 hours, which commonly include irritability, headaches, and anxiety, in addition to the strong desire to smoke.

TOBACCO

Tobacco, plant grown commercially for its leaves and stems, which are rolled into cigars, shredded for use in cigarettes and pipes, processed for chewing, or ground into snuff, a fine powder that is inhaled through the nose. Tobacco is the source of nicotine, an addictive drug that is also the basis for many insecticides.

Tobacco is a member of the nightshade family. There are more than 70 species of tobacco, of which 45 are native to the Americas. The two cultivated species, common tobacco and wild tobacco, are annuals—they live only one growing season. Common tobacco is 1 to 3 m (3 to 10 ft) tall and has a thick, woody stem with few side branches.

One plant typically produces 10 to 20 broad leaves that branch alternately from the central stalk. The leaf size depends on the strain. The narrow, trumpet-shaped flowers are dark pink to almost white. Wild tobacco is about 0.6 m (2 ft) tall and has a stem that is more slender and less woody than common tobacco. The leaves have a short stalk that attaches to the stem. The flowers are pale yellow with five separate lobes.

Growing and Harvesting

Tobacco grows in tropical and temperate regions, and it can be grown as far north as Canada and Norway. It thrives best in areas with a frost-free growing season of 120 to 170 days, depending on the type of tobacco. Good-quality tobacco requires fertile, well-drained, moist soil and warm temperatures.

Most types of tobacco are grown in full sun. Environmental factors influence the plant's characteristics. Soil can affect leaf size, texture, and colour. Sandy soils tend to produce a relatively large leaf that is light in colour and body, fine in texture, and burns with a weak aroma. Heavier soils, which contain silt and clay, tend to produce a small, dark leaf with a heavy body and a strong aroma when burned.

Several strains of common tobacco are grown for use primarily in different tobacco products. In the United States, Virginia tobacco is the main tobacco used in cigarettes; most of it is grown in North Carolina, Georgia, and Virginia. Burley tobacco, which is grown mostly in Kentucky and Tennessee, is used in cigarettes and pipes. Several countries, including the United States, Turkey, and Cuba, grow cigar tobacco.

Tobacco plants are susceptible to attack from a wide range of insects and bacterial, fungal, and viral diseases. To counteract these problems, tobacco farmers grow strains of tobacco that resist diseases and insects. By rotating crops (planting tobacco one year and a different crop in the same field the next year), farmers keep the population of tobacco pests in check by depriving them of tobacco plants on alternate years. Before planting, farmers may work a fungicide into the soil to control fungal diseases, such as blue mold and damping-off. They may also fumigate the soil to control nematodes—microscopic worms that infest the roots. Growers also use herbicides to control weeds and insecticides to control insects.

The annual tobacco cultivation cycle begins with the

planting of seeds. In the United States, seed planting begins in March in southern states and June in northern states. Tobacco seeds are extremely small: one million seeds (the potential yield of a single mature plant) weigh about 80 g (about 3 oz). Tobacco seeds are so tiny that they need special care to keep them from drying out once they begin sprouting. To keep young plants watered and weeded, growers sow the seeds in specially prepared seedbeds of fertile, loose soil, rather than directly in the field.

One to two months after planting, the growers transplant the seedlings into the field—a labour-intensive process called setting the tobacco. As flowers form on the plants, growers remove them in a process called topping, which encourages more leaf growth.

Tobacco is harvested 70 to 130 days after setting. The harvesting method used depends on the type of tobacco. For some tobaccos, farmers cut whole plants off at the ground and spear them onto a stick about 1 m (3 ft) long, called a tobacco stick. Each stick holds about six plants. For other tobaccos, farmers remove the mature leaves and string them on wires, leaving the rest of the plant to continue growing.

Curing and Aging

After tobacco is harvested, it is cured (dried), and then aged to improve its flavour. There are four common methods of curing tobacco: air curing, fire curing, flue curing, and sun curing. The curing method used depends on the type of tobacco and its intended use.

Air-cured tobacco is sheltered from wind and sun in a well-ventilated barn, where it air dries for six to eight weeks. Air-cured tobacco is low in sugar, which gives the tobacco smoke a light, sweet flavour, and high in nicotine. Cigar and burley tobaccos are air cured.

In fire curing, smoke from a low-burning fire on the barn floor permeates the leaves. This gives the leaves a distinctive smoky aroma and flavour. Fire curing takes three to ten weeks and produces a tobacco low in sugar and high in nicotine. Pipe tobacco, chewing tobacco, and snuff are fire cured.

Flue-cured tobacco is kept in an enclosed barn heated by flues (pipes) of hot air, but the tobacco is not directly exposed to smoke. This method produces cigarette tobacco that is high in sugar and has medium to high levels of nicotine. It is the fastest method of curing, requiring about a week. Virginia tobacco that has been flue cured is also called bright tobacco, because flue curing turns its leaves gold, orange, or yellow.

Sun-cured tobacco dries uncovered in the sun. This method is used in Greece, Turkey, and other Mediterranean countries to produce oriental tobacco. Sun-cured tobacco is low in sugar and nicotine and is used in cigarettes.

Once the tobacco is cured, workers tie it into small bundles of about 20 leaves, called hands, or use a machine to make large blocks, called bales. The hands or bales are carefully aged for one to three years to improve flavour and reduce bitterness.

Preparation of Tobacco Products

Tobacco products include cigarettes, cigars, and pipe tobacco, which are smoked; snuff, which is inhaled into the nose; and chewing tobacco, which is chewed but not swallowed. Tobacco is also used for nicotine products, such as insecticides and medicines to help people quit smoking. The nitrogen-rich stalks left after harvesting are used as a fertilizer in tobacco-growing regions.

In the first stages of processing, the stems and veins are removed and the leaves are cut into strips. Various tobacco strains are then blended in rotating drums. Blends of bright, burley, and oriental tobaccos are used in cigarettes. Moisture-holding substances, such as apple juice or glycerin, and flavourings, such as honey, licorice, or mint, are sometimes added to the blends. The blended tobaccos are then chopped into small shreds.

The tobacco used in cigarettes and cigars needs to be rolled. Cigarette machines roll tobacco in a special paper that burns slowly and evenly. A filter is often added to collect impurities and make the smoke less harsh to inhale. Cigars consist of three types of tobacco. The filler, or core, consists of small pieces of leaves, or small whole leaves. The binder holds the filler in place and is, in turn, covered by the wrapper, which is wound spirally, starting at the end that is to be lighted. Although some high-quality cigars are made entirely by hand, most cigars are manufactured by machine.

Chewing tobaccos are generally made from thick grades of leaves to which binders and flavourings are added. Chewing tobacco is formed by pressing the tobacco into blocks known as plugs. Snuff is made by grinding tobacco into fine powder, which is then allowed to ferment for a long period of time. Frequently, snuff is scented with spices, such as jasmine or cloves.

Tobacco Industry

Over 6 million tons of commercial tobacco are grown each year. Leading tobacco-growing countries are China, Brazil, India, the United States, Zimbabwe, and Turkey. Tobacco is an economically important crop for many nations—more than 2 million tons of tobacco leaf, at a value of more than $6 billion, are exported each year worldwide. Brazil exports the most tobacco leaf. Some countries that grow and export tobacco also import foreign tobacco. For instance, the United States imports the same amount of tobacco as it exports. The United States exports the most cigarettes and manufactured tobacco products, accounting for nearly 20 percent of the world total. Japan is the largest importer of tobacco products.

Cigarette consumption, which accounts for most tobacco use in the United States, reached a high of 4,345 cigarettes per person per year in 1963. This number has dropped steadily since 1964, when a special report by the U.S. surgeon general linked cigarette smoking with lung cancer, coronary artery disease, and other ailments. As smoking became less popular in the United States and Europe, cigarette manufacturers have found new markets in eastern Europe, Asia, Africa, and the former Soviet Union. Due to the aggressive marketing efforts of the international tobacco industry, tobacco consumption in these areas is expected to rise by almost 3 percent annually.

Since the Great Depression, the federal government has run price support programmes for a variety of agricultural products, including rice, peanuts, and tobacco. The tobacco price support programmeme stabilizes prices and ensures tobacco growers a fairly steady income. Farmers registered in the programmeme belong to a cooperative association that sells their tobacco at auction. The cooperative buys, at a price set each year, any tobacco that the grower cannot sell. Although the federal government sponsors the cooperative association, it does not fund the purchase of unsold tobacco; that money comes from tobacco sales and association membership fees. The cooperative stores unsold tobacco and sells it the next year.

History

As early as 2,000 years ago, natives of the Americas used tobacco as a medicine, as a hallucinogen in religious ceremonies, and as offerings to the spirits they worshiped. When Italian Spanish explorer Christopher Columbus traveled to the Americas in 1492, he observed the Arawak people of the Caribbean smoking tobacco loosely rolled in a large tobacco leaf. They also smoked tobacco through a tube they called a *tobago,* from which the name tobacco originated. Columbus's crew introduced tobacco growing and use to Spain. During the next 50 years, sailors, explorers, and diplomats helped spread pipe and cigar smoking throughout Europe. At first, it was used medicinally as a purported treatment for diseases and disorders such as bubonic plague, migraines, labour pains, asthma, and cancer. Within 100 years, however, smoking for pleasure became common.

Growing wild tobacco and exporting it to England. They soon switched to common tobacco, the milder kind grown in the West Indies and in demand in Europe. It quickly became the main crop grown in the colonies and was so profitable that without it, historians agree, the English colonies in North America would have failed.

As tobacco farming expanded through the colonies, growers brought British prisoners and debtors to work the fields. These indentured servants earned their freedom after 5 to 12 years of labour. Growers soon found it more profitable to bring in African slaves, since they never had to be given their freedom. Slavery enabled growers to farm larger areas, making giant plantations possible. Tobacco farming expanded from Virginia south to North Carolina and west as far as Missouri. An Ohio farmer happened upon a chlorophyll-deficient strain of tobacco called white burley, which became a main ingredient of American blended tobaccos.

Cigarettes were invented by beggars in Seville, Spain, a centre for cigar production. The beggars collected scrap tobacco and rolled it in paper. However, snuff, cigars, and pipes remained the most popular means of using tobacco until the 19th century. Cigarette popularity rose when British soldiers fighting in the Crimean War (1853-1856) found the cigarettes of their Turkish allies to be more convenient than pipes or cigars. Cigarettes grew in popularity in the United States after the Civil War (1861-1865) but were relatively expensive because they were hand-rolled.

Cigarette prices fell after American inventor James A. Bonsack patented a machine to roll cigarettes in 1880; the machines could produce more than 10,000 cigarettes in an hour. Cigarettes were more popular than cigars. Smoking continued to grow in popularity until the 1960s and 1970s, when awareness of its health risks grew.

Health Effects

Tobacco contains nicotine, an addictive drug. Tobacco smoke also contains more than 4,000 chemical compounds, including at least 43 cancer-causing compounds. Forms of tobacco that are smoked—cigarettes, pipes, and cigars—cause lung cancer, emphysema, and other respiratory diseases. Smoking also contributes to coronary heart disease and, in pregnant women who smoke, low birth weight of newborns. Chewing tobacco and inhaling snuff causes cancer of the mouth, nose, and throat and can lead to nicotine addiction.

Cigarette smoking causes nearly 90 percent of all lung cancer cases. Inhaled tobacco smoke, from cigars and pipes as well as from cigarettes, also comes into direct contact with the tissues of the mouth, throat, and larynx, or voice box. Several studies have estimated that smokers are four to five times more likely to develop oral and laryngeal cancer than are nonsmokers. Studies have also linked smoking with the development of cancer in distant organs—that is, in organs not directly exposed to the smoke, such as the bladder, pancreas, kidney, stomach, liver, and uterus. Smoking also causes health problems in nonsmokers. Each year about 3,000 nonsmoking adults die of lung cancer as a result of breathing the secondhand smoke from others' cigarettes.

Emphysema, the chronic narrowing and clogging of the airway passages in the lung, is the most common chronic lung disease. Its victims are almost exclusively smokers; it very seldom occurs in nonsmokers. However, not all smokers are susceptible to this disease; only 20 percent of heavy smokers will develop it.

Antismoking Actions in the United States

In light of the disease risks associated with tobacco products and their associated high health-care costs, many individuals and health organizations have lobbied for public policy changes that would change the way tobacco products are regulated, manufactured, marketed, and sold in the United States.

In November 1998 the tobacco industry and the attorneys general of 46 states, along with representatives of the public health field and lawyers representing smokers, announced an agreement that bans outdoor cigarette advertising and the use of cartoon characters in advertising, a practice that may attract young people to smoking. The agreement also requires tobacco companies to pay $206 billion during the next 25 years to fund antismoking public education programmes, smoking cessation programmes, tobacco-related medical research, and reimbursement to states for some of the health-care costs associated with treating smokers.

Although the tobacco settlement provides tobacco companies with some protection against suits brought by states, it leaves open the possibility of lawsuits brought by individual smokers and their families for smoking-related health problems or deaths. Such suits have had mixed results in the United States. In several cases, juries relieved the tobacco companies of all responsibility, while in others, juries awarded individual smokers and their families millions of dollars in compensation for their losses.

Representatives of the tobacco industry have long denied that smoking is addictive or a serious health risk. But in late 1999 Philip Morris (now known as Altria), the nation's largest cigarette maker, publicly acknowledged that smoking is addictive and causes life-threatening health problems. This action was considered a move to protect the company from future lawsuits by people who started smoking in recent years but claim they were unaware of the risks.

SMOKING

Smoking, inhalation and exhalation of the fumes of burning tobacco. Leaves of the tobacco plant are smoked in various ways. After a drying and curing process, they may be rolled into cigars or shredded for insertion into smoking pipes. Cigarettes, the most popular method of smoking, consist of finely shredded tobacco rolled in lightweight paper. About 46 million people in the United States smoke an estimated 420 billion cigarettes each year.

Until the 1940s smoking was considered harmless, but labouratory and clinical research has since confirmed that tobacco smoke presents a hazard to health. Smoke from the average cigarette contains around 4,000 chemicals, some of which are highly toxic and at least 43 of which cause cancer. Nicotine, a major constituent of tobacco smoke, is both poisonous and highly addictive. According to the American Cancer Society, smoking is the most preventable cause of death in America today.

History

European explorers who arrived in the Western Hemisphere in the 1500s observed Native Americans smoking tobacco plant leaves in pipes. The colonists who followed them grew tobacco plants as a cash crop for export, and smoking became part of European culture by the 1600s. Most tobacco was consumed in pipes and cigars or as *snuff* (finely pulverized tobacco inhaled into the nostrils). This pattern changed by the early 20th century, by which time smokers consumed more than 1,000 cigarettes per capita each year in the United States and some European countries. The general attitude of society was that smoking relieved tension and produced no ill effects. During World War II (1939-1945) American physicians endorsed sending soldiers tobacco, and cigarettes were included in the field ration kits of U.S. armed forces personnel until 1975.

Some scientists noticed, however, that lung cancer, which was rare before the 20th century, had increased dramatically since about 1930. The American Cancer Society and other organizations initiated studies comparing deaths among smokers and nonsmokers over a period of several years. All such studies found increased mortality among smokers, both from cancer and other causes. In addition, experimental studies in animals showed that many of the chemicals contained in cigarette smoke are carcinogenic.

In 1962 the U.S. government appointed a panel of ten scientists to study the available evidence concerning the health effects of smoking. Their conclusions were included in the 1964 surgeon general's report, which stated that "cigarette smoking is a health hazard of sufficient importance in the United States to warrant appropriate remedial action." Smoking in adults, measured as an average number of cigarettes smoked per year, began to decline steadily after the 1964 report and has fallen more than 40 percent since 1965.

Health Effects of Smoking

About 442,000 people in the United States die each year from illnesses caused by cigarette smoking. Smoking accounts for nearly 90 percent of lung cancer deaths. Additionally, smokers are at increased risk for cancer of the larynx, oral cavity, esophagus, bladder, kidney, and pancreas. While some negative health effects of smoking manifest slowly over time, others can be measured almost immediately. Sticky brown tar leaves yellow stains on fingers and teeth.

Some of the inhaled tar is absorbed by lung cells, causing them to die. Tar also damages the cilia in the upper airways that protect against infection. Nicotine causes arteries to constrict, lowering skin temperature and reducing blood flow to the hands and feet. Carbon monoxide deprives the body of oxygen, binding to red blood cells in place of the oxygen molecule and forcing the heart to pump more blood through the body.

One-third of smoking-related deaths are caused by coronary heart disease or chronic airway obstruction. The nicotine in tobacco combines with carbon monoxide in tobacco smoke to damage the lining of blood vessels and make blood platelets stickier. Platelets form part of the damaging plaque buildup in artery walls.

These effects in combination contribute to the development of heart disease. Smoking also increases the risk of stroke by 50 percent—40 percent among men and 60 percent among women. Other research has shown that mothers who smoke give birth more frequently to premature or underweight babies, probably because of a decrease in blood flow to the placenta. Babies born to mothers who smoke during pregnancy are also at increased risk for sudden infant death syndrome.

Cigar and pipe smoke contains the same toxic and carcinogenic compounds found in cigarette smoke. A report by the National Cancer Institute concluded that the mortality rates from cancer of the mouth, throat, larynx, pharynx, and esophagus are approximately equal in users of cigarettes, cigars, and pipes. Rates of coronary heart disease, lung cancer, emphysema, and chronic bronchitis are elevated for cigar and pipe smokers and are correlated to the amount of smoking and the degree of inhalation.

Studies have found that cigarettes are addictive because an unknown component of tobacco smoke appears to destroy an important brain enzyme known as monoamine oxidase B (MAO B). The enzyme is vital for breaking down excess amounts of dopamine, a neurotransmitter that triggers pleasure-seeking behaviour. Smokers have decreased levels of

MAO B and abnormally high levels of dopamine, which may encourage the smoker to seek the pleasure of more tobacco smoke.

Even nonsmokers are at risk from smoking. Recent research has focused on the effects of environmental tobacco smoke (ETS)—that is, the effect of tobacco smoke on nonsmokers who must share the same environment with a smoker. The United States Environmental Protection Agency (EPA) estimates that exposure to ETS, which contains all the toxic agents inhaled by a smoker, causes 3,000 lung cancer deaths and an estimated 35,000 deaths from heart disease per year among nonsmokers. Secondhand smoke can aggravate asthma, pneumonia, and bronchitis, and impair blood circulation.

The smoking habit and addiction to nicotine usually begin at an early age. In the United States, more than 90 percent of adults who smoke started by age 21, and nearly half of them were regular smokers by the age of 18. Despite increasing warnings about the health hazards of smoking and widespread bans on smoking in public places, smoking remains common among teenagers and young adults. In 2001 surveys of students in grades 9 through 12 found that more than 38 percent of male students and nearly 30 percent of female students smoke. Although black teenagers have the lowest smoking rates of any racial group, cigarette smoking among black teens increased 80 percent in the late 1990s. Advertisements aimed at a young audience are largely blamed for this new generation of smokers.

Quitting Smoking

Studies of former smokers show that their risk of dying from smoking-related disease decreases with each year of abstinence. According to the World Health Organization (WHO), smokers who quit smoking before the age of 50 reduce their risk of life-threatening disease by half after just one year, compared with those who continue smoking.

Other benefits of quitting smoking include more disposable income, admission to social activities and institutions that ban smoking, and often, lower health insurance premiums. Nonetheless, to quit smoking is difficult, most likely because smokers crave the effect of the nicotine in the smoke.

The U.S. surgeon general declared nicotine an addictive drug comparable to other addictive substances, including cocaine, heroin, and alcohol, in its ability to induce dependence. Overall, tobacco smoking causes about 20 times the number of deaths in the United States than all other addictive drugs combined.

Smoking cessation methods are plentiful, and products are available to help an individual stop smoking. Many smokers turn to group help because of the support and understanding provided by other former smokers or people trying to quit. Most successful group-help techniques involve a challenge and reward system that also bolsters the self-discipline of the former smoker.

A number of nicotine replacement products are available to help a person quit smoking. Nicotine patches are small, nicotine-containing adhesive disks that must be applied to the skin. The nicotine is slowly absorbed through the skin and enters the bloodstream.

Over time, a smoker uses nicotine patches containing smaller and smaller doses of nicotine until eventually the craving for nicotine ends. Nicotine gum works in a similar manner, providing small doses of nicotine when chewed. A nicotine nasal spray is a physician-prescribed spray that relieves cravings for a cigarette by delivering nicotine to the nasal membranes. Also available by prescription, the nicotine inhaler looks like a cigarette; when puffed, the inhaler releases nicotine into the mouth.

An approach combining three different smoking cessation therapies has found remarkable success. This approach combines an antidepressant drug called bupropin, marketed under the brand name Zyban, with a nicotine replacement product and counseling. While less than 25 percent of smokers who use nicotine replacement products alone remain smoke-free for more than a year, 40 to 60 percent of smokers using this combination approach achieved this milestone.

Antismoking Action

In the United States, the first direct action to curb smoking after the U.S. surgeon general's 1964 report on smoking was the mandate of a warning on cigarette packages by the Federal Trade Commission. This warning took effect in 1964 and was strengthened in 1969 to read: "Warning: The Surgeon General Has Determined That Cigarette Smoking Is Dangerous to Your Health." A stronger sequence of four alternative warnings was developed in 1984. In 1971 all cigarette advertising was banned from radio and television, and cities and states passed laws requiring nonsmoking sections in public places and workplaces.

This trend has continued and smoking is now banned at the federal and state levels in most government buildings and in many private businesses. As of February 1990 federal law banned smoking on all domestic United States airline flights under six hours in duration. By 1998 more than 90 percent of nonstop flights between the United States and all foreign countries were also smoke free.

The tobacco industry has been increasingly criticized for its role in encouraging smoking, particularly in young people. Various lawsuits have been brought against tobacco companies to reclaim damages due to disease or death associated with smoking. The first major successful suit occurred in March 1996 when the Liggett Group, a consortium of companies, agreed to pay damages to five states. An onslaught of litigation against the tobacco industry followed.

In part to avoid potentially ruinous lawsuits filed by states, in 1998 the tobacco industry and attorneys general from 46 U.S. states agreed to settlement. The settlement, to be paid over 25 years, will be used to compensate states for the costs of treating smoking-related illness, to finance nationwide antismoking programmes, and to underwrite health care for uninsured children.

The tobacco industry must also contend with a barrage of lawsuits filed by individual smokers and their families seeking damages for smoking-related health problems and deaths. Across the United States, such lawsuits have had mixed results. In several cases, juries have cleared the tobacco companies of all responsibility.

While several other cases have resulted in large awards for the plaintiffs, few hold up under the appeals process. Tobacco industry representatives long denied that nicotine is addictive and that there is a link between smoking and poor health. In recent years, however, cigarette makers have faced increased pressure from smoking-related lawsuits and federal regulators to accept prevailing scientific opinions about the health risks of smoking. In late 1999 Philip Morris, now known as Altria, the nation's largest cigarette maker, publicly acknowledged that smoking is addictive and causes serious health problems.

This latest admission was considered a way to make it more difficult for those who have recently started smoking to claim they were unaware of the dangers if they choose to sue cigarette companies. In 2003 an Illinois judge ordered Philip Morris to pay $10.1 billion in damages for using misleading advertising campaigns suggesting that cigarette brands marketed as "low tar" or "light" are safer than regular brands. Numerous scientific studies prove that the use of low-tar cigarettes does not reduce the risk of developing smoking-related disease, and the judge found that Philip Morris intentionally disregarded consumer rights by spreading disinformation.

INCENSE

Incense, material, usually consisting of aromatic gums and spices, that produces a fragrant smoke when burned. The term is also used to describe the fragrant smoke itself. The ingredients are usually frankincense, styrax, benzoin, and cascarilla bark, combined in various proportions. Other substances often used in incense include balsam, cinnamon, myrrh, sandalwood, and musk.

The burning of incense has been a feature of sacrificial religious ceremonies since ancient times. It is mentioned on an inscribed tablet that was placed on the Sphinx at Giza, Egypt, in about 1530 BC. Incense was used in the early Jewish religion and, later, by the Romans, both in religious ceremonies and on state occasions.

MUSK

Musk, substance with a strong, persistent odor from an abdominal gland on the male of the musk deer found in high Asian mountains. The long-lasting odor of musk has made it an important ingredient in perfumes throughout history. Musk also delays evapouration of more volatile scents in a perfume, and is used as a fixative in blends where other scents are dominant.

In Asia it is sought as an aphrodisiac, and it is believed to be medically beneficial as a stimulant. Fresh musk is viscous but dries to a grainy powder and a tincture of this powder is used in perfumes. The basic oil that is the source of the odor has been identified and called muskone.

SANDALWOOD

Sandalwood, common name for a family of flowering plants mostly parasitic on the roots and stems of other plants, and for its representative genus. The family contains about 400 tropical and subtropical species of mostly root parasites. Members of the family can manufacture their own food through photosynthesis but depend on their hosts for water and minerals. True sandalwood is a medium-size tree widely cultivated in southern India.

Sandalwood for carving and carpentry comes from its sapwood, and the sandal oil distilled from its roots and heartwood is used in soap, perfume, and ointments and for Eastern religious ceremonies. Because true sandalwood is rare and expensive, substitutes are often made from other plants.

The order to which sandalwood belongs contains about 10 families with a total of about 2000 species. The mistletoe family contains about 300 species. Several species are parasitic on economically important trees in Europe and North America; other species are pests on such tropical trees as rubber and cacao. The largest family in the order contains about 900 species, some of which are also commonly called mistletoe.

Members of the order characteristically attach themselves to their host by means of a haustorium (a specialized structure through which water and nutrients are absorbed). In many members of the order, the leaves are reduced to minute scales; those with full-size leaves are commonly evergreen.

MISTLETOE

Mistletoe, common name for various parasitic plants belonging to the mistletoe family. The common European mistletoe grows on various trees, usually apples and junipers. It is an evergreen plant with small, greenish flowers and white berries. A similar mistletoe, American mistletoe, found in the United States, grows on deciduous trees, particularly red maple and elm, from eastern Texas to Florida and northward to Missouri and New Jersey.

The leafless flowering dwarf mistletoes depend entirely on the host tree for nourishment. These scrubs are lethal parasites of conifers, such as pine, spruce, fir, and hemlock. The plant leaves and berries contain toxic chemicals that can be poisonous and the plant should be kept out of reach of young children who may be tempted to eat the berries.

The common mistletoe figured significantly in the folklore and religions of pre-Christian Europe. Reputedly endowed with magical powers, it was used as a remedy for evil. It is used as a Christmas and New Year's decoration, and kissing under a branch of mistletoe is still customary.

STYRAX

Styrax, genus of deciduous or evergreen shrubs and small trees of the ebony family. The genus, which contains about 100 species, is native to tropical, subtropical, and warm temperate regions throughout the world and is cultivated widely as an ornamental plant in the eastern United States.

The showy white flowers, arranged in drooping racemes, have a five-toothed outer floral envelope, five petals, ten stamens, and a solitary pistil. The several-seeded fruit is often dehiscent—that is, it splits to release the seeds. Species of styrax include a deciduous shrub that is found along the Atlantic coast from Virginia to Florida and reaches a height of 3.7 m (12 ft). The hardiest species of styrax, the Japanese snowbell, is a deciduous shrub or small tree, 9 m (30 ft) high, native to Japan and China. An important resinous substance called storax is obtained as an exudate from an Asian and European species. A species native to Borneo, Java, and the Malay Peninsula yields the important balsamic resin that is called benzoin.

EBONY (PLANT)

Ebony (plant), common name for a family of flowering plants and for trees of its representative genus. Because of its wood and fruits, the ebony family, with close to 500 species, is probably the best-known and most important member of its order. Several tropical species in the representative order are exploited for their hard, dense wood. Ebony wood varies in colour from species to species but has the common characteristics of being derived from the heartwood of the trees and of being capable of taking a beautiful polish. Other Temperate Zone species of the same genus produce persimmons.

These include the common persimmon, native to the United States, and the kaki, originally from China but now widely grown elsewhere.The order to which the ebony family belongs comprises 5 families and about 2000 species. Leaves are simple and entire. Flowers are bisexual with many stamens and superior ovaries. Many members of the order, primarily in the Tropics, produce latex; other characteristics vary considerably. Useful products include wood, latex derivatives, and edible fruits.The snowbell family contains 12 genera and about 180 species. In tropical areas, trees of this family are tapped to extract saplike materials containing benzoin, used in medicine and incense, and storax, useful as an antiseptic. Snowbell and silverbell are useful ornamentals in temperate areas.

FRANKINCENSE

Frankincense, name applied to various gum resins, containing volatile oils, that diffuse a strong fragrance in burning. Oriental frankincense, also known as olibanum, was esteemed by ancient peoples for use in embalming and as incense and is still the most important incense resin. It is obtained from several Oriental trees that grow in northeastern Africa and Arabia. The hardened, semitransparent yellowish material is still used widely as ceremonial incense. Common frankincense is obtained from the bark of the Norway spruce. When boiled in water and strained, the resin becomes Burgundy pitch, formerly used in making medicinal plasters.

EMBALMING

Embalming, mortuary custom, the art of preserving bodies after death, generally by the use of chemical substances. It is believed to have originated among the Egyptians, probably before 4000 BC, and was used by them for more than 30 centuries. Much evidence demonstrates that embalming is religious in origin, conceived as a means of preparing the dead for the life after death.

From the Egyptians, the practice of embalming spread to other ancient peoples, including the Assyrians, Jews, Persians, and Scythians. Ancient embalming methods consisted of removal of the brains and viscera, and the filling of bodily cavities with a mixture of balsamic herbs and other substances. The Egyptians immersed the body in carbonate of soda, injected the arteries and veins with balsams, filled the cavities of the torso with bituminous and aromatic substances and salt, and wound cloths saturated with similar materials around the body. The Assyrians used honey in embalming, the Persians used wax, and the Jews used spices and aloes. Alexander the Great was embalmed with honey and wax.

The Egyptians were particularly adept at embalming; the soles of the feet of mummies, when unwrapped after as much as 3000 years, are often still soft and elastic. Historians estimate that by AD 700, when the practice had died out among them, the Egyptians had embalmed approximately 730 million bodies. Although many were destroyed or disintegrated in the tropical heat of northern Africa, a large number of mummies were preserved; archaeologists estimate that several million are still preserved in undiscovered tombs and burial places.

From the ancient peoples of Africa and Asia, embalming spread to Europe, where, in time, it became a widespread practice. Descriptions of methods used in Europe for almost 1200 years, from about AD 500, have been preserved in the writings of contemporary physicians. Embalming during the Middle Ages included evisceration, immersion of the body in alcohol, insertion of preservative herbs into incisions previously made in the fleshy parts of the body, and wrapping the body in tarred or waxed sheets.

The Danish king of England, Canute II, was embalmed by the above, or similar methods, as were the English monarchs William the Conqueror and Edward I. William's body was found well preserved in the French city of Caen in the 16th century; Edward's was also found to be well preserved when it was disinterred in Westminster Abbey in 1700; and Canute's body was still in a state of good preservation when it was discovered in Winchester Cathedral in 1776.

The first man to embalm by injecting a prepared preservative chemical solution into the blood vessels is believed to be the Dutch anatomist Fredrik Ruysch, but his technique is unknown. During the 19th century, French and Italian scientists perfected such techniques, thereby enabling them to reach every part of the cadaver. Modern embalming is believed to have begun in the U.S. during the American Civil War.

The essential purposes of modern embalming are preservation of the body to permit burial without unseemly haste and prevention of the spread of infection both before and after burial. Cosmetic work is used to restore injured facial features or for aesthetic reasons. Embalming methods now consist essentially of the removal of all blood and gases from the body and the insertion of a disinfecting fluid; sometimes the viscera are removed and immersed in an embalming fluid and are then replaced in the body, in which they are surrounded with a preservative powder. Most corpses in the United States and Canada are embalmed, and the practice is widespread in other countries.

Chapter 5

Oil Yielding Plants

AVOCADO

Avocado, also alligator pear, common name for a tree native to tropical America, and for the fruit of this tree. The fruit is a greenish, thick-skinned drupe, similar in size and shape to a large pear. When ripe, the flesh has the consistency of firm butter and a faint nutlike flavour. It has a high fat content, containing 10 to 20 percent oil, and is rich in protein. In the United States avocado is popular as a salad vegetable, and in the tropics it is often used in soup. The tree is extensively cultivated in the southern United States and California.

LAUREL (PLANT)

Laurel (plant), common name for a flowering plant family, widespread in tropical and subtropical regions, and for its representative genus. The laurel family contains between 30 and 50 genera and at least 2000 species. Several well-known and important genera of the family also occur in temperate areas camphor, cinnamon, avocado, and spice-bush. The laurel, or bay, also called bay laurel and bayberry, is a large evergreen shrub native to the Mediterranean region; it has been important since classical times and is now widely cultivated in warm temperate areas as an ornamental and for its aromatic leaves, which are used in cooking. California bay yields a valuable wood.

The order to which the family belongs contains 8 families with about 2500 species distributed mostly in tropical and subtropical regions. Many species exhibit botanically interesting structures, and some are of economic value because of the useful products derived from them.

Although a great diversity of form occurs in the order, several features are common to most of its members and distinguish the order from others. All members are woody trees, shrubs, or vines, and all produce aromatic oils in their tissues. The stamens (male floral structures) have appendages that produce nectar, and the pistil (female floral part) often consists of a single carpel (ovary receptacle).

The members of the order are believed to resemble the earliest flowering plants in their woody nature, floral characteristics, and details of anatomy and pollen structure. In addition, the order has a long fossil history, with specimens similar to plants of several living genera having been found in rocks more than 65 million years old. Members of the order to which laurels belong, however, are considered more advanced than another primitive group of woody flowering plants, which have stamens and carpels that more closely resemble leaves.

Of the remaining 7 families in the order, one, the Monimia family, has about 450 species, and the rest have a total of fewer than 100, with 3 having only one species each. They are mostly of restricted distribution and little economic importance.

Unrelated plants also called laurel include the mountain laurel and several other members of its genus, along with several members of the cherry genus.

CAMPHOR

Camphor, volatile, white, crystalline compound, $C_{10}H_{16}O$, with a characteristic aromatic odor. Ordinary camphor is obtained from the camphor tree, *Cinnamomum camphora,* which grows in Asia and Brazil. The camphor is distilled by steaming chips of the root, stem, or bark. The leaves of certain plants, such as tansy and feverfew, contain a second form of camphor, which is not used commercially.

A racemic form is present in the oil of an Asian chrysanthemum and is also produced synthetically for most commercial uses. Camphor is used in the manufacture of celluloid and explosives and medicinally in liniments and other preparations for its mild antiseptic and anesthetic qualities. It is poisonous if ingested in large amounts.

CASTOR BEAN

Castor Bean, also castor-oil plant, common name for a plant of the spurge family. Native to tropical Africa, where it grows to 12 m (40 ft) or more, it is widely planted in temperate areas as an annual ornamental for its large, lobed, fanlike leaves. It rarely exceeds 4.5 m (15 ft) in height in cooler climates. The bean-shaped seeds, castor beans, contain the castor oil of commerce; in Brazil, India, and Thailand the plant is an important crop. The orange flowers are without petals and are clustered in long panicles; the fruit is covered with soft, orange-brown spines. All parts of the plant are poisonous to humans and animals; the seeds are extremely poisonous.

CASTOR OIL

Castor Oil, colourless or yellow to yellowish-brown, thick, oily liquid obtained from the seeds of the castor-oil plant. Although it has a disagreeable taste, it is practically odorless. It is insoluble in water, but soluble in organic solvents. The medicinal oil is prepared from husked seeds. Unhusked seeds, the source of industrial castor oil, yield from 45 to 55 percent oil. The oil is pressed from the seeds, purified, and then bleached.

In addition to its use as a simple purgative, castor oil is used as a plasticizer in nitrocellulose compositions, in cosmetics, and in insulation products. It is also used in the manufacture of waterproof lacquers and paints.

CANDLENUT

Candlenut, common name for an evergreen tree (a tree that keeps its foliage year-round) native to Malaysia and the Pacific Islands but now widespread throughout the tropics. The seeds, or "nuts," are rich in oil and can be used as candles—hence the tree's common name. Polynesians who settled the Hawaiian Islands about 1500 years ago brought candlenut seeds with them. Known there as the kukui, which means "light" or "lamp," it is now the official tree of the state of Hawaii, and its nuts are commonly polished and made into leis, garlands worn around the neck.

Candlenut trees grow to heights of 18 m (60 ft). The tree is easy to recognize because the young leaves have a frosted appearance—almost as if they had been dusted with flour. Separate male and female flowers are produced in the same clusters, with the male flowers at the top of the clusters and the female flowers below. The flowers give rise to clusters of olive-green fruits, each containing one or more large black seeds with white kernels.

In the past, people would dry the nuts and string them on a sliver of bamboo or on the stiff midrib of a palm leaf, much like meat is placed on a spike for shish kebab. When the top nut was lighted, it would burn for several minutes; the "candle" was then inverted and the nut at the opposite end was lighted. A more efficient system was to crush the nuts to release the oil. The oil was then poured into a cup or hollowed-out stone and a cloth wick was added. This type of lamp was known to burn for hours.

Candlenut trees have numerous other uses. The oil can also be used in paints, varnishes, soap, and other products. The roots and the shell of the fruit yield a black dye. The bark is rich in tannins, organic acids that can be used for tanning hides. When baked, the kernels are edible, but when raw they are a potent laxative.

CANOLA

Canola, specially named variety of the rape plant. Also called rapeseed, the common rape plant is a member of the mustard family. Rape is grown both as feed for livestock and for its seeds, which are used as birdfeed. The seeds are also processed into an oil, which has been used in China and India for cooking and as lamp oil for 4,000 years. In the 1930s, rape plants were introduced into cultivation in Canada, where the climate is especially suitable for their growth.

During World War II, rapeseed oil was used as a marine

lubricant. When European sources were cut off, growers in western Canada increased their production of rapeseed. Early researchers physically crossbred plants to identify strains that were cold hardy and produced higher yields of oil. Following the end of the war, the market for rapeseed oil plummeted, and rapeseed growers needed other uses for their crop. This situation stimulated the research that led to the development of canola.

One problem faced by the producers of rapeseed oil from the common rape plant was its high erucic acid content, which animal studies suggested to be a health hazard. In addition, the meal produced after extracting the oil in rapeseed contained large amounts of glucosinolates (sulfur compounds responsible for the hotness in mustard). These sulfur compounds can react with other seed components to produce toxic substances that render the crushed seed residue unfit for use as animal feed.

Different varieties of rape were crossed to find plant strains low in these chemicals. In 1968, Agriculture Canada developed Oro, the first cultivar with low erucic acid content in the oil. In 1974, the University of Manitoba released a strain called Tower, which was low in both erucic acid and glucosinolates. The term *Canola,* a contraction of "Canadian oil," was registered later that same year to differentiate these new varieties. Canola plants are indistinguishable in appearance from the related rape plants. The plants have short, branching stems, bluish green leaves, and yellow flowers. However, the oil produced from the canola plant is low in saturated fats and high in essential fatty acids. It can be used as a salad oil, in cooking, and in such commercial preparations as margarine and shortening.

By the 1990s, over 5 million hectares (over 13 million acres) of Canadian soil were dedicated to canola production. Growers faced problems of disease and weed control, and researchers wished to alter the levels of other chemicals in the oil. To solve these problems, researchers use recombinant DNA techniques, in which a desirable gene from a bacterium or other plant is inserted into the genetic makeup of the host plant. Using this technology, researchers have developed varieties of canola that are resistant to the specific herbicides used to combat weeds growing in canola fields. Another transgenic variety of canola includes an enzyme from the seed of the California Bay tree. Including this enzyme produces a variety of canola that is high in lauric acid, which is a key ingredient in soaps and body lotions. Research is also being conducted in the United States to develop canola varieties suitable for the climate and soils of the United States.

MUSTARD

Mustard, common name for a large family of pungent-juiced herbs, important for the many food plants and other crops it produces, and for its representative genus. The family contains about 390 genera and 3,000 species. It is cosmopolitan in distribution, with centres of diversity in the Mediterranean region and southwestern and Central Asia, where about two-thirds of the species occur.

Most members of the mustard family are annual or perennial herbs; a few are shrubs or climbers. The flowers are characteristic and distinctive. Four petals are arranged opposite one another in the form of a cross. Six stamens are arranged in pairs. The filaments of the outer pair are short, whereas those of the two inner pairs are longer. The fruit is typically a capsule with two chambers divided by a false septum; at maturity, it splits in two from the bottom. Many variations on this basic fruit type are found in the family, and characteristics of the fruits are heavily used in distinguishing and classifying the various members.

The mustard family contains a great variety of food plants, but they do not form important parts of staple diets. Best known are the salad and vegetable crops, such as cabbage, cauliflower, brussels sprouts, broccoli, and kohlrabi, all of which are varieties of the wild cabbage native to coastal Britain and southern Europe. Table mustard is prepared from powdered seeds of two other species, black mustard and white mustard. Black mustard is a shaggy, many-branched plant, growing to about 1 m (about 3 ft) high, with dark-green lyre-shaped and lanceolate leaves, small yellow flowers, and short seedpods pressed against the stems. It is common along roadsides and in wastelands throughout the United States. White mustard is a somewhat smaller plant, with similar leaves, larger flowers, and bristly pods. Another important species, curled mustard or mustard greens, has large cleft leaves and is used as a vegetable. Turnip, radish, cress, and watercress are other vegetable members of this family.

CARAWAY

Caraway, common name for a plant that has long been cultivated in temperate zones for its aromatic fruit, called caraway seeds. These seeds are used in cookery, confectionery, and medicine. The caraway plant is a biennial herb; it grows up to 61 cm (up to 2 ft) high and has finely divided leaves and clusters of white flowers. The large oil glands of the seed contain caraway oil, which is used to flavour the liqueur aquavit. This oil is also used in perfumery and in pharmacy as an aromatic stimulant and as a flavouring agent.

CASHEW

Cashew, common name for a tropical evergreen tree, for its edible nuts, and for the family to which the tree belongs. The family also includes poison ivy, poison oak, poison sumac, and the mango, the pistachio, and the smoke tree.

The cashew tree, native to the Americas, is now widely cultivated in Asia (especially India) and Africa for its nuts and other products. It grows as high as 12 m (40 ft) and has leathery, oval leaves.

The fragrant, reddish flowers grow in clusters, and the pear-shaped fruits, called cashew apples, are reddish or yellowish. At the end of each fruit is a kidney-shaped ovary, the nut, with a hard double shell.

Between the shells is a caustic, black oil that has to be removed by a difficult roasting process; the oil is used in the plastics and varnish industries.

Another roasting removes the second shell, freeing the nut. The trunk of the tree yields a milky gum also used to make varnish. The sour fruits can be eaten after processing and are used in making condiments.

POISON IVY, POISON OAK, AND POISON SUMAC

Poison Ivy, Poison Oak, and Poison Sumac, common names applied to three plants of a genus in the cashew family, capable of producing an allergic reaction in people who have become sensitized to them. Poison ivy and poison oak are variants of a single plant (sometimes treated as separate species by botanists), different mainly in the shape of their leaflets. Both are woody perennial plants of roadsides, thickets, hedgerows, and open woods, and one or the other is found throughout the United States and southern Canada.

They may take the form of vines climbing up tree trunks to considerable height, shrubs or subshrubs standing erect by themselves, or vines trailing on the forest floor, sometimes also trailing out into meadows from hedgerows. Distinguishing characteristics include the regular grouping of three leaflets in each leaf, and stiff clusters of small, yellowish or white berries that appear in summer and fall. Other characteristics vary considerably, especially size of leaflet, notching, whether the surface is shiny or dull, or colour.

Poison sumac is a tall, smooth-stemmed shrub that grows in swamps throughout the eastern United States and Canada. It bears pinnately compound leaves with about 7 to 13 leaflets, including one at the tip. The fruits are white or yellowish berries in clusters similar to those of poison ivy. Poison ivy, poison oak, and poison sumac contain a lacquerlike resin in their sap. The resin is composed of active substances that provoke a sensitizing reaction in most, if not all, persons the first time effective contact occurs. Contact may be made by brushing past the leaves or the bare stems. Contact with exposed pets, clothing, or garden tools many induce a reaction. Smoke from burning ivy plants may carry the resin and affect all uncovered parts of the body.

After a person has become sensitized, subsequent contact with the resin produces the typical allergic reaction of ivy poisoning. The effects do not become apparent for some hours.

First, the skin reddens and begins to itch. Small watery blisters soon appear, often in lines indicating the point of contact with the plant, and the itching becomes intense.

Finally, in severe cases, large watery swellings appear and coalesce. The condition is self-limiting, and recovery takes place in one to four weeks, even without treatment. A physician should be consulted in severe cases or if sensitive parts of the body, such as the eyelids, become involved.

Scratching slows healing, invites infection, and may spread the resin from one location to another; the watery fluid in the blisters does not spread the reaction. Boric acid solution or calamine lotion are commonly used to relieve itching. Some or all of the resin may be removed by prompt and vigourous scrubbing with strong soap. Persons whose occupation exposes them to poison ivy, poison oak, or poison sumac should consider desensitization.

SUMAC

Sumac, common name for any of a genus of deciduous or evergreen shrubs and trees of the cashew family. The genus contains about 200 species native to temperate and subtropical regions throughout the eastern and western hemispheres. The foliage and bark of most sumacs are rich in tannins, used widely for tanning leathers. Several sumacs are cultivated widely in the United States for ornamental purposes.

The staghorn sumac is a tall North American plant grown extensively as an ornamental for its brilliant autumn colour. The greenish, clustered flowers of the staghorn produce red fruits that persist throughout winter.

Smooth sumac, common in the southwestern United States, is also widely cultivated because of its large, dense, green flowers and finely cut, brilliantly coloured leaves. Another popular ornamental native to eastern North America is the dwarf sumac, which has glossy foliage that turns scarlet in the fall. The Sicilian sumac, a shrub native to the Mediterranean region and western Asia, is a principal source of tannin. The poison sumac which was formerly placed in the genus, is poisonous to the touch.

TANNINS

Tannins, also tannic acid, common name applied to a group of vegetable products, both amorphous and crystalline, obtained from various plants, and important commercially in the tanning of leather. Tannins have variable composition. Some, called condensed tannins, are phenols of moderately complex structure, and others are esters of glucose or some other sugar with one or more trihydroxybenzoic acids.

The empirical formula, $C_{14}H_{14}O_{11}$, often given for common tannin, is only an average. Tannins occur in many trees, and the best sources include oak galls and the bark of sumac. Extraction with water, or water and alcohol, is the first step in the preparation of tannin. Settling, followed by evapouration at a low temperature, yields the commercial product.

Tannins have a yellow-white to brown colour and a faint, characteristic odor. Exposure to light deepens the colour. They all taste bitter and are astringent. Water, acetone, and alcohol dissolve tannins readily, but benzene, ether, and chloroform do not. Heating to 210° C (410° F) causes decomposition, accompanied by formation of pyrogallol and carbon dioxide.

The chemical property that provides the basis for most uses of tannins is its ready formation of precipitates with albumin, with gelatin, and with many alkaloidal and metallic salts. The ability of tannins to transform proteins into insoluble products resistant to decomposition leads to their use as tanning agents. Ferric salts react with tannins to give bluish-black products that are useful as inks.

Tannins are used as mordants for dyeing cloth, as sizes for paper or silk, and as coagulants for rubber. The precipitating properties of tannins are used in clarifying, or cleaning, wines and beer. Tannic acid is valuable as an external medicine because it is astringent and styptic.

GALL

Gall, also cecidium, swelling or excrescence of plant tissues caused by the action of parasites. Such swellings, which may occur on any part of a plant but are usually found in regions of active cell division and growth, are initiated by the chemical action of secretions of infesting organisms, usually insects or fungi.

Galls assume a great variety of forms; each form is characteristic of the parasite that causes it, and usually each species of gall-forming parasite infects a specific organ of a specific plant.

The growth of the gall may result either from a tremendous swelling of the individual cells or from the rapid division of cells near the point of attack by the parasite. The gall provides a protective capsule for the parasite while it feeds on the plant.

The most striking galls are caused by insects that begin their invasion by laying eggs in plant tissues. The resultant enlargement of surrounding tissue is caused either by growth-promoting stimulation furnished by the eggs or by secretions of the larvae. The gall wasps, a family of small hymenopterous insects, Cynipidae, include the greatest number of species of gall-forming insects.

These species restrict their attacks to about 20 genera of plants included in 6 families, especially the oaks; various species produce galls on roots, trunks, leaves, buds, flowers, or acorns. Several cynipids of the genera *Amphibolips* and *Dipolepis* stimulate production of galls known as oak apples. Specialization of function is so great in the cynipids that reproduction in some has been altered. *Plagiotrochus punctatus* produces in the summer a normal generation, the larvae of which cause blister galls on oak leaves.

A second generation, entirely female, is produced in the spring; its larvae cause irregular swellings on oak twigs. The unfertilized eggs of the second generation produce gall wasps of both sexes, which repeat the cycle.

Several galls caused by members of the genus Cynips are important sources of tannic acid.The commercial gallnut which infests several Eurasian oaks, contains about 65 percent tannic acid. These gall nuts may be harvested and sold to leather-tanning or ink-manufacturing industries.

LEATHER

Leather, animal skin that has been chemically modified to produce a strong, flexible material that resists decay. Almost all the world output of leather is produced from cattle hides and calfskins, goatskins and kidskins, and sheepskins and lambskins. Other hides and skins used include those of the horse, pig, kangaroo, deer, reptile, seal, and walrus. Leather is used for a wide range of products. The variety of skins and the way they are processed can produce leather as soft as cloth or as hard as a shoe sole. Cattle hides, the major raw material for leather production, range from being lightweight and supple to tough and strong.

Tough hides are used in the production of the durable leather required for soles of shoes, machine belting, engine gaskets, and harnesses. Calfskin is lighter and finer grained, and is used for making fine leather suitable for such articles as shoe uppers. Sheepskin is soft and supple; it yields the type of leather suitable for gloves, jackets, and other apparel. Since ancient times, human beings have used animal skins and learned to make leather. The process of using chemicals to turn skins into leather is called tanning.

Curing

The raw materials used by the leather industry originate largely as by-products of the meat-packing industry. Before entering the tanning process, the raw skins are "cured" by salting or drying them promptly after being removed from the slaughtered animal. The more common methods used in curing require the use of salt (sodium chloride) in one of two ways: wet-salting or brine-curing.

In wet-salting, the skins are liberally salted and piled on top of one another until they form a pack. They are left in the pack for about 30 days to allow the salt to thoroughly penetrate the skin. Brine-curing is a much quicker method. In agitated brine-curing, the method most commonly used, skins are placed in large vats called raceways that contain a disinfectant and brine maintained close to full salt saturation. After about 16 hours in the raceway, the skins are completely penetrated by the salt.

Soaking and Unhairing

The cured skins are soaked in pure water to eliminate salt, blood, and dirt, and also to replace moisture lost in the curing process. After the skins have soaked for a period varying from two hours to seven days, the flesh is removed mechanically from the inner surface.

To loosen the hair, the skins are then immersed for one to nine days in a solution of lime and water containing a small amount of sodium sulfide. Following this operation the hair is easily removed by a dehairing machine, and the distinctive pattern known as the grain can be distinguished on the outer surface of the skin. To ensure clear, clean surfaces, any remaining flesh and hair is scraped off, usually by hand with a dull knife, by a process called scudding.

Deliming and Bating

The next operation involves deliming the skins by soaking them in a weak solution of acid, which reduces the swelling caused by the lime. Simultaneously, most types of skins are treated with a "bating" material consisting of enzymes to give a smoother grain and render the skin soft and flexible.

The amount of bating varies greatly, from none at all for sole leather to a concentrated treatment for leather to be used in kidskin gloves. After the deliming and bating operations, the stock can be tanned.Each type of skin may be treated by several tanning processes. The process is chosen according to the use for which the leather is intended.

The two principal tanning processes are mineral, or chrome, tanning, and vegetable tanning. Chrome tanning often can be completed in a single day, whereas vegetable tanning requires many weeks or months. Vegetable tanning results in a firmer leather with greater water and stretch resistance. Chrome tanning shrinks the stock and produces a longer-wearing leather with greater resistance to heat. The processes are sometimes combined to derive some of the advantages of each.

Vegetable Tanning

In this process the tanning agent, which renders the skin

immune to decay and prevents shrinkage, is a substance known as tannin. Tannin is extracted from the bark, wood, fruit, and leaves of trees. Chestnut wood, oak bark, and hemlock bark are the major domestic sources of the tannin used by the United States leather industry.

Foreign sources, which provide more than 80 percent of the tannin supply, include the wood of the quebracho tree of South America, mangrove bark from the island of Borneo, wattle bark from South Africa, and myrobalan fruit from India.

In vegetable tanning the hides are suspended from rocking frames in a series of vats containing increasingly stronger tannin solutions, called liquors.

After several weeks the hides are transferred to a "layaway" section, which consists of larger vats containing still stronger liquors. Each week more tannin is added to the liquor, until the hides have absorbed enough tannin to complete the process. The last stages of the process may be accelerated by the use of warm liquors. Flexible vegetable-tanned leathers to be used for belting, luggage, upholstery, or harnesses are less heavily tanned than the leather intended for shoe soles.

Mineral Tanning

The mineral tanning process is known as chrome tanning because the tanning agent used most frequently is a salt compound of chromium. Chrome-tanned leathers, which stretch more than vegetable-tanned leathers, are suitable for handbags, shoe uppers, gloves, and garments.

To prepare the stock for chrome tanning, the bated skins are pickled in a solution of salt and acid. The skins are then immersed in a basic chromium-sulfate solution within a large revolving drum that tumbles the skins. This type of liquor penetrates the skins so rapidly that tannage is accomplished in less than a day. The chrome process originally involved the use of two different liquors, both solutions of compounds of chromium, and required substantially more time. Known as the two-bath process, it is still used for some varieties of leather. Aluminum or zirconium compounds may be used in place of chromium in the production of white leather. Alum, formaldehyde, gluteraldehyde, and synthetic tannins (Syntans) are also used to impart special characteristics.

In the production of combination-tanned leather, the skin is first chrome-tanned and then retanned with vegetable tannins. The modified applications of both processes produce leather with some of the advantages of each type.

Lubrication and Dyeing

After tanning, all types of leather undergo various operations that differ according to the use of the desired product. Vegetable-tanned leather for shoe soles is first bleached a lighter colour. Next, it is infused with such materials as epsom salts, oils, and glucose, and then lubricated with hot emulsions of soap, greases, and sometimes wax. Finally, the stock is run through rolling machines to give the leather a desired degree of firmness and a high gloss.

Chrome-tanned leather intended for shoe uppers is split and shaved to the desired uniform thickness. It is then placed in a rotating drum for the dyeing process, which usually involves the use of several types of colouring materials to achieve colour fastness and durability. Before or after dyeing, the leather is rolled in a "fat liquor," which contains emulsified oils and greases. More than 100 leather colours exist, ranging from traditional tans and browns to such exotic shades as fuchsia and turquoise.

After dyeing and fat-liquoring, the stock is stretched for drying. Workers paste the stock on frames made of glass or ceramics or "toggle" it on perforated metal frames. The frames are then conveyed through drying tunnels with controlled heat and humidity.

Finishing

Heavy leathers are finished by coating the grain surface with a finishing compound, and finally by brushing it under a revolving, brush-covered cylinder. The grain surface of light leathers is buffed, or sandpapered, to correct imperfections in the skin. Buffing the flesh side of leather raises the nap and produces the popular leather known as suede. For smooth finishes, most light leather is seasoned, or treated with a mixture of such materials as waxes, shellac or emulsified synthetic resins, dyes, and pigments. Pigments are used sparingly to avoid a painted look. Glazing gives the grain a highly polished surface. Several coats of thick, oily varnish are required to give patent leather its characteristic high gloss.

Leather Substitutes

Today, many artificial substances are produced and sold as "leather goods." These modern synthetics include such plastics as polyvinyl chloride and nonwoven fibres impregnated with binders. These materials lack leather's porous quality, pliable nature, and resilience. However, the artificial materials cost less to produce than leather and have come to command a large share of the leather market, particularly in shoe soles.

COCONUT

Coconut, common name for the fruit of a tree of the palm family, widely distributed in tropical regions. The tree, called coconut palm, has a cylindrical trunk about 45 cm (about 18 in) in diameter and can grow up to 30 m (100 ft) high, with many rings marking the places of former leaves. At the summit it bears a crown of about 20 pinnate leaves that generally curve downward, each of which is about 3 to 4.5 m (about 10 to 15ft) long.

The fruit grow in clusters of 10 to 20 or more nuts; and 10 or 12 of these clusters, in different stages, may be seen at once on a tree.The mature coconut, about 30 cm (about 12 in) long, is oval shaped and has a thick, fibrous outer husk and a hard inner shell. The lining, or kernel, of the inner shell is a white, oily meat that is dried to produce the commercially valuable copra. Copra yields an oil used in the manufacture of soaps and candles.

Within the kernel is a sweet-tasting, milky fluid.The meat of coconuts, either raw or prepared, is an important food in the Tropics. The terminal bud, known as palm cabbage, is considered a delicacy, and trees are often cut down for the sake of it; the central part of the young stem is also succulent and edible. The sap, or toddy, like that of some other palms, is a favourite beverage in tropical countries, either in the natural state or after fermentation, which takes place in a few hours. Palm wine, or arrack, also a spirituous liquor, is obtained by distillation of fermented sap. The tree root possesses narcotic properties and is sometimes chewed.The dried leaves of the coconut palm are used for thatch and, by plaiting the leaflets, mats, screens, and baskets are made. Coir, the fibre of the nut's husk, is used to make rope.

PALM (PLANT)

Palm (plant), common name for a family of woody flowering plants widespread in the tropics. They are of great economic importance because of the food, fibre, and oil they provide, and because of their ornamental uses. The family is the only member of its order and contains about 2,600 species, making it the fourth largest among the monocots, after the grasses, lilies, and orchids.

Palms have a characteristic growth form: a single, unbranched trunk topped with a tuft of fanlike or featherlike leaves. The flowers are borne in axillary clusters (inflorescences), and a large, interwoven mass of roots occurs at the trunk base.

The trunks of palms, like those of other monocots, have no secondary growth; thus, the diameter of the trunk does not increase with the age of the tree, as in dicots. The growing tip of the trunk instead is built up into a large mass in the seedling stage, and maintains that broad width as the trunk matures. Bundles of vascular tissue are scattered throughout the trunks. The leaves of palms, often large, are formed a few at a time at the stem tips. They have large, sheathing bases that may leave semicircular scars on the stems when they fall off. The leaf blades are folded in a distinctive fashion called plicate.

Flowers of palms are usually individually inconspicuous but are often borne in great masses, some containing as many as 250,000 flowers. Flower parts are in threes, with three sepals (outer floral whorls) and petals (inner floral whorls) and six stamens (male flower parts). The pistil (female flower part), which usually consists of three separate or fused carpels (egg-bearing structures), matures into a single-seeded fruit that may be either a berry (a seed surrounded by a fleshy covering) or a drupe (a seed with a stony layer surrounded by a fleshy covering).

Palms are overwhelmingly tropical in distribution. They occur there in habitats that range from lowland rain forests to high mountains, and from deserts to mangrove swamps. Their distribution in the tropical zones, however, is uneven. About 1,400 species occur in tropical Asia, whereas only about 120 occur in Africa. Another 130 species occur on Madagascar and other nearby islands in the western Indian Ocean near Africa, and about 950 species occur in the American tropics.

Palms are important sources of foods such as dates, coconuts, and sago. Copra and coir, which are useful fibres, raffia, and rattan fibre also come from palms. The oil palm, native to West Africa but widely cultivated, has become a source of the vegetable oil used in making margarine and soap and in cooking. Palms are grown as ornamentals in tropical and subtropical regions, and many smaller species are usea as houseplants.

ORCHID

Orchid, common name for a family comprising one of the largest groups of flowering plants. The family is worldwide in distribution, being absent only from Antarctica and some of the most arid desert zones of Eurasia. The greatest diversity of genera and species occurs in tropical regions that remain poorly explored. For this reason, and because of the complexity of the family, estimates of the number of orchid species vary from 15,000 to 25,000, and the number of genera from 400 to 800.

Orchids are distinguished from other orders of flowering plants by a combination of floral characteristics rather than by a single characteristic unique to the group. Orchid flowers are borne on stalks called pedicels, as are other flowers. During the growth and development of the flower, however, the pedicel rotates 180°, so that the mature orchid flower is borne upside down.

Of the flower's three sepals (outer floral whorls) and three petals (inner floral whorls), all the sepals and the two lateral petals are usually similar to one another in colour and shape. The remaining petal, always distinct from them, is called the labellum, or lip; it is usually larger and different in colour and shape, often being lobed or cupped. The labellum, which often acts as a landing platform for the orchid pollinator, may attract the pollinator to the flower through particular colour patterns and shapes to which the pollinator responds in particular ways.

The sexual organs (pistil and stamens) of the orchid flower are fused together into a structure called the column, which lies opposite the lip. Orchids have only one stamen (male floral organ), and in most orchids it bears only one anther (pollen-producing structure); in a few orchids, however, two anthers are produced.

The pollen is not granular, as it is in most flowering plants, but is aggregated together in a number of masses, or sacs, that vary in texture from mealy to horny. Three stigmatic lobes (pollen-receptive areas) are usually present and located near the anther, although usually only two are functional.

The ovary is below the other flower parts and is surrounded by pedicel tissue. Tripartite, it contains numerous ovules (egg-bearing structures) that mature into seeds. The seeds are small, with only an undifferentiated embryo. As many as 2 million seeds may be produced from a single orchid seedpod. Unlike most other flowering plants, orchids have no food-storage tissue.

Orchid flowers are pollinated by a great variety of flying animals, and their great diversity in floral structure has resulted from adaptations to various pollinators. About half the orchid species are pollinated by bees; moths, butterflies, flies, birds, and other agents pollinate the rest.

Many orchid flowers are adapted for pollination by a single species of insect. Orchids do not vary as much vegetatively as they do in floral structure, but a great variety of forms exists, reflecting the wide range of habitats they occupy. About half are epiphytic, growing on other plants for support only, but some are parasitic and others saprophytic (living on decaying vegetation). A few Australian species complete their life cycles entirely underground.

Apart from their phenomenal popularity as ornamental flowers, orchids have little economic importance, although vanilla flavouring is obtained from fruits of one tropical orchid species, the Mexican vanilla. Growers have produced thousands of new forms of orchids through hybridization.

SUNFLOWER

Sunflower, common name for annual and perennial herbs of a genus of the family of composite flowers. The genus, which contains about 67 species, is thought to be native to South America originally, although sunflowers are now distributed almost worldwide. Some of the tall-growing forms may attain a height of 3 m (12 ft). The large, solitary blossom, sometimes as large as a meter in diameter, is composed of yellow ray flowers and a central disk of either yellow, brown, or purple flowers, depending on the species.

The daily orientation of the flower to the sun is a direct result of differential growth of the stem. A plant-growth regulator, or auxin, accumulates on the shaded side of a plant when conditions of unequal light prevail. Because of this accumulation, the darker side grows faster than the sunlit side. Thus, the stem bends toward the sun.

The plants are cultivated for their seeds. Refined sunflower-seed oil is edible and considered by many equal in quality to olive oil. Cruder sunflower oil is used for making soap and candles. The oil cakes (solid residues after oil is expressed) are used as cattle feed. The raw seeds are used in poultry mixes and are consumed by humans as well. The roots of one species, also called Jerusalem artichoke may be eaten boiled, stewed, or baked in pies.

COMPOSITE FLOWERS

Composite Flowers, common name for one of the largest families of flowering plants, with more than 20,000 species. The common name refers to the clustering of the flowers into compact heads so that an entire cluster resembles a single flower, as in the familiar aster or dandelion.

The composite family is worldwide in distribution except for Antarctica, where two species of grasses are the only flowering plants known. Composites are particularly well adapted to semiarid parts of tropical and subtropical regions, to arctic and alpine tundra, and to temperate regions. They are poorly represented only in tropical rain forests.

Although the composite family contains nearly 10 percent of all the flowering plants, its direct economic importance is relatively small. Lettuce is the most important crop; other notable food plants are artichoke, endive, salsify, chicory, and tarragon. Sunflower and safflower are important sources of vegetable oils, and some members such as guayule have been studied as potential sources of rubber.

Weedy members of the family include dandelion, thistle, cocklebur, and ragweed, which is a major source of the airborne pollen that affects hay fever sufferers. Horticulturally important members of the composite family include marigold, dahlia, zinnia, daisy, cosmos, chrysanthemum, tansy, and aster.

Structure

The flowers are always grouped into an *inflorescence* (flower cluster) called the head, or capitulum, which resembles and functions as a single flower. In more than half the species, the flowers at the margin of the head have outwardly extended corollas, called ray florets, that resemble numerous petals and make the flower head more conspicuous to pollinators. The flowers within the head are called disk florets. Both types are surrounded by *bracts* (specialized leaves) at the base.

The *calyx* (floral envelope, or pappus) that surrounds the individual flowers in a head consists of scales or bristles, which often aid in distribution of seeds. In the common dandelion the pappus consists of fine bristles that enable the fruit to float through the air. In the beggar-ticks it is barbed, causing the fruit to stick to passersby. The petals of the florets are fused along the base, forming a somewhat tubular corolla.

The *anthers* (pollen-producing flower parts) are joined to form a tube through which the *style* (part of the female flower part) extends. The anthers release the pollen into the tube, and as the style elongates, it pushes the pollen upward out of the tube, making it available to insect pollinators or to wind dispersal. The *stigmatic* (pollen-receiving) areas of the style are located on two branches of the style tip, and these branches separate after elongation. Thus, self-pollination is usually avoided, although in some cases the stigmatic branches recurve backward into the pollen-bearing anther tube.

The *pistil* (female flower part), which has a single ovary, bears the other flower parts on its apex. After fertilization it matures into a hard-coated fruit that bears a single seed.

Flower Types

Although the flowering heads of composites are fundamentally similar, variation in their structure, particularly in the corolla, accounts for much diversity. The simplest head is the discoid, consisting of all disk florets with tubular corollas. Both stamens and pistils are functional. Thistle, eupatorium, and ageratum have heads solely of disk florets.

A second type of head is the radiate, which has disk florets in the centre and ray florets at the margin. The corollas of the marginal florets are tubular at the base but flatten and elongate as they grow outward. Ray florets are usually *pistillate* (with functional pistils but nonfunctioning anthers) or sterile. Such familiar flowers as sunflowers, black-eyed Susans, and daisies have radiate heads.

A third common head is the ligulate, in which all the florets resemble ray florets but have both pistil and stamens functioning. The flowering heads of dandelions and chicory are ligulate. Other kinds of heads also occur in the family.

SOYBEAN

Soybean, also soy and soya bean, common name for an annual leguminous plant and its seeds. The soybean probably originated in eastern China and is widely cultivated as a farm crop. It is an erect, hairy plant from 0 6 to 1.5 m (2 to 5 ft) in height, with large trifoliate leaves, small white or purple flowers, and short pods with one to four seeds. On maturity, which is reached from 100 to 150 days after planting, depending on variety, location, and weather, the leaves turn yellow and drop, and the pods rapidly become brown and dry. The seeds, which are almost spherical in shape, are usually light yellow, but some rare varieties are black, brown, or green. They have a black, brown, or yellow hilum and contain about 20 percent oil and 40 percent protein. In the United States, soybeans are grown as a row crop, planted in May or June, and harvested with a grain combine in the fall.

The soybean, an ancient food crop in China, Japan, and Korea, was introduced into the United States in the early 1800s and was grown as a minor forage crop for many years. The development of a soybean-processing industry in the early 1920s gave soybean cultivation a great impetus, and today the soybean is a leading crop in the United States, ranking only behind corn and wheat. The United States produces about 60 percent of the world's soybeans, compared to 14 percent produced by Brazil, 10 percent by China, and lesser percentages by Argentina, Taiwan, Canada, and India. Production in the United States is located chiefly in the Midwest and the lower Mississippi Valley; more than 30 percent of the United States production is exported.

The two basic products of the soybean are protein meal and oil. In the United States, more than 90 percent of the oil is consumed as margarine, shortening, mayonnaise, salad oils, and other edible products; the rest is used in industrial products such as paint, varnish, linoleum, and rubber fabrics. Soybean meal is the major source of the protein supplement used in livestock feeds, which utilize 98 percent of the total meal produced. In the protein-short areas of the world and elsewhere, soybean meal is finding increasing use in human food products.

OIL SEEDS

Oil Seeds, varieties of oil-rich seeds, nuts, fruits, and cereals that are used in vegetable oils and fats for cooking, food manufacture, soap making, specialized lubricating oils, and cosmetics.

Primary sources of vegetable oils are: coconut, corn, cotton seed, oil palm, olive, peanut (groundnut or arachis oil), safflower, soybean, sunflower seed, and rape seed. A number of other seeds are used as oil sources in seasoning or salad dressing, including almond, grape pip (a byproduct of winemaking), poppy seed, pumpkin, sesame, and walnut. Some oil seed plants are grown solely for their oil, while others are primarily grown for food crops or textile fibres, in which oil production is a secondary byproduct.

Oil seed production is an important part of the agricultural economy of many countries; some oil seed plants grow only in tropical regions (coconut and oil palm), others in Mediterranean regions (olive), while still others grow in temperate regions (maize, rape, sunflowers, and soybeans).

Vegetable oil is obtained by pressing the seeds and then extracting the oil with steam or water; the high protein residue that remains after oil extraction (oil cake or oil seed cake) is a valuable feedstuff for livestock. In olive oil, virgin or extra-virgin olive oil is removed during the first pressing of the ripe fruit and is not refined. Lower grades of olive oil come from subsequent pressings of the fruit, and usually must be refined to remove the bitter flavour in the oil that is extracted after the first pressing.

OLIVE

Olive, common name for a plant family, and for its representative genus, and for the fruit of the olive tree. The family contains about 900 species, placed in 24 genera. It comprises a small group of woody flowering plants, of almost cosmopolitan distribution, that contains several plants of horticultural and economic importance. In addition to the olive, familiar members of the family include ash, lilac, privet, jasmine, forsythia, and the fringe tree.

Most members of this family of dicots are shrubs or small trees, although a few are climbers. Nearly all have opposite leaves, which may be simple, as in lilacs and forsythias, or compound (composed of several separate leaflets), as in ashes.

Flower structure is rather uniform in the family, but some variation occurs.

Typically, flowers have four sepals (outer floral whorls) and four petals (inner floral whorls), two stamens (male flower parts) attached to the inner surface of the petals, and a single ovary (female flower part), which is superior (borne above and free from other flower parts). The fruits, which develop from the ovary after fertilization, vary considerably but usually contain a single seed. Examples of distinctive fruits include those of the olive, which are technically drupes (hard seeds surrounded by fleshy material); those of the ashes, which are indehiscent (remain closed at maturity) and winged and are technically known as samaras; and those of the lilacs, which are dry and dehiscent (splitting at maturity).

The olive genus contains about 20 species and is widespread in Eurasia. A few species produce good timber the black ironwood, of southern Africa. The cultivated olive is originally native to the eastern Mediterranean region but now widely cultivated throughout that area and in other parts of the world that have Mediterranean-type climates. The olive is cultivated for its fruits, which yield an edible oil and are also pickled for eating.

Olive oil, which is derived from fresh, ripe fruits that contain about 20 percent oil, is used in cooking, in canning, and as a table oil. Olives for eating are picked either when unripe or when ripe. Unripe olives are green and remain so during pickling. Ripe olives are dark bluish when fresh and turn blackish during pickling. The seed, or stone, of the olive is often removed and the cavity stuffed with spicy materials such as sweet red pepper. The wood of the cultivated olive, being hard and variegated, is valued in cabinetry.

ALMOND

Almond, common name for a small tree of the rose family, and for the kernel of its fruit. The tree is characterized by the coarsely furrowed and wrinkled shell of the drupe and by the young leaves that have their sides folded along the central vein. It grows up to 9 m (30 ft) high. A native of western Asia, it now grows wild throughout southern Europe and is cultivated in the United States.

The wood is hard, of reddish colour, and is used by cabinetmakers. The almond is valued chiefly for its nut, which is an important article of commerce. Varieties are classified as either sweet or bitter. Sweet almonds contain a large quantity of a bland, fixed oil and emulsin, gum, and mucilage sugar; they have an agreeable taste and are nutritious. Bitter almonds contain the same substances and, in addition, a crystalline glucoside called amygdalin. The long almonds of Málaga, Spain, known as Jordan almonds, and the broad almonds of Valencia, Spain, are the most valued.

The dwarf almond tree, a low shrub, is similar to the common almond, with smaller fruit. It is common in the plains of Central Asia and is frequently planted as an ornamental shrub in England. Flowering almonds—shrubs or small trees—are cultivated extensively in the United States for their profusion of showy, white to rose blossoms.

POPPY

Poppy, common name for a small family of herbaceous flowering plants occurring principally in the North Temperate Zone, and for its representative genus. The family contains about 23 genera and 210 species; many are important as ornamentals, and one species is the source of opium. Members of the family occupy varied habitats, but they are more common in open, well-drained areas. This preference helps explain why several members of the family, especially poppies, are bothersome weeds in cultivated fields.

The representative genus contains about 50 species. The Oriental poppy is widely cultivated as an ornamental, and many colour forms have been developed. The opium poppy produces several useful products. Its tiny seeds, produced in huge quantities in each of the plant's dry fruits, or capsules, are used in baking and produce an important drying oil. Opium is the dried sap, or latex, that is harvested from the capsules while they are still young. It contains many alkaloids, including morphine and codeine, that are useful in medicine.

Heroin is synthesized from the morphine purified from the complex mixture of alkaloids in opium.

The family shares its order with the fumitory family. This family contains about 16 genera and 400 species, also mostly found in the North Temperate Zone, with a few species located in mountainous regions of tropical Africa and South Africa. The most familiar member of the family is the bleeding heart; others are of minor ornamental importance.

The leaves are usually deeply divided and arranged in a rosette around the base of the short stem. The flowers have two to four sepals (outer floral whorls) and twice as many petals (inner floral whorls). The stamens (male floral organs) vary in number from six to many more, and the ovary (female floral organ) is superior (borne above and free from the other flower parts). The order characteristically has sap that is rich in alkaloids. The sap is clear and watery in the fumitory family, milky in the poppy family.

OPIUM

Opium, narcotic drug produced from the drying resin of unripe capsules of the opium poppy, *Papaver somniferum*. Opium is grown mainly in Myanmar (formerly Burma) and Afghanistan. The legitimate world demand for opium amounts to about 680 metric tons a year, but many times that amount is distributed illegally.

In its commercial form, opium is a chestnut-coloured globular mass, sticky and rather soft, but hardening from within as it ages. It is processed into the alkaloid morphine which has long served as the chief painkiller in medical practice, although synthetic substitutes such as meperidine (trade name Demerol) are now available. Heroin, a derivative of morphine, is about three times more potent. Codeine is another important opium alkaloid.

The molecules of opiates have painkilling properties similar to those of compounds called endorphins or enkephalins produced in the body. Being of similar structure, the opiate molecules occupy many of the same nerve-receptor sites and bring on the same analgesic effect as the body's natural painkillers. Opiates first produce a feeling of pleasure and euphoria, but with their continued use the body demands larger amounts to reach the same sense of well-being. Withdrawal is extremely uncomfortable, and addicts typically continue taking the drug to avoid pain rather than to attain the initial state of euphoria. Malnutrition, respiratory complications, and low blood pressure are some of the illnesses associated with addiction.

As long ago as 100 AD, opium had been used as a folk medicine, taken with a beverage or swallowed as a solid. Only toward the middle of the 17th century, when opium smoking was introduced into China, did any serious addiction problems arise. In the 18th century opium addiction was so serious there that the Chinese made many attempts to prohibit opium cultivation and opium trade with Western countries. At the same time opium made its way to Europe and North America, where addiction grew out of its prevalent use as a painkiller.

CODEINE

Codeine, alkaloid, $C_{18}H_{21}NO_3H_2O$, derivative of opium. It is a white crystalline solid, slightly soluble in water and soluble in organic solvents. When heated, it first loses water and then melts at 157° C (315° F). Chemically a methyl ether of morphine, codeine has similar physiological effects but to a lesser degree, particularly because it is less habit-forming. It is used to reduce pain and to suppress coughing.

ETHER

Ether (chemistry), more specifically ethyl ether or diethyl ether, colourless, liquid compound, $(C_2H_5)_2O$, that boils at 34.6° C (94.3° F). Extremely volatile and flammable, with a powerful, characteristic odor and a burning, sweetish taste, ether is only slightly soluble in water, but mixes in all proportions with most organic liquids, such as alcohol and carbon disulfide. Ether itself is one of the most important organic solvents and is widely used in the labouratory as a solvent for fats, oils, resins, and alkaloids. A mixture of ether vapour with air is violently explosive; moreover, on long standing, ether may be partly oxidized to an explosive peroxide compound. Ether must therefore be stored and used with great care. Its principal uses are as a solvent, as a starting material for manufacture of chemical products, and as an anesthetic.

Discovered probably as far back as the 13th century, ether is still prepared by one of the oldest known organic reactions, that is, the heating of ethyl alcohol with strong sulfuric acid. The temperature is carefully controlled so as to be between 130° and 150° C (266° and 302° F), because at higher temperatures the ether reacts, yielding ethylene gas. The crude ether is purified by shaking with limewater (to remove acidic contaminants) and then with anhydrous calcium chloride (to remove unreacted alcohol and most of the water), and redistilling. Although containing small amounts of water, this ether is suitable for most purposes, including surgical use. If subsequent redistillation is made in the presence of phosphorous pentoxide or metallic sodium, the final product, absolute ether, is free of water and alcohol.

PISTACHIO

Pistachio, common name for a plant genus of the cashew family, which have dioecious flowers without petals, and a dry drupe with a bonelike stone. The pistachio, or pistacia, tree is a small tree about 6 m (about 20 ft) high. Native to Iran and Syria, it is now cultivated in all parts of southern Europe and northern Africa and in many other places. Pistachio nuts are much esteemed as food and also yield an oil used for cooking. The turpentine tree yields the turpentine known in commerce as Cyprus turpentine. It has a greenish-yellow colour, an agreeable odor, and a mild taste; in its properties it resembles the turpentine obtained from conifers.

TURPENTINE

Turpentine, name applied to numerous semifluid, yellow or brownish oleoresins obtained from various coniferous trees in Asia, Europe, and America. In the U.S. the principal sources of turpentine are the longleaf pine, *Pinus palustris,* and the slash pine, *P. caribaea,* of the southeastern U.S. In France the exudate known as Bordeaux turpentine is obtained from the cluster pine, *P. pinaster*.

The substance obtained from these and other species of trees consists of 75 to 90 percent resin and 10 to 25 percent oil. Upon distillation, it yields oil of turpentine, $C_{10}H_{16}$. It has a specific gravity of 0.86 to 0.88 and boils at 155° C (311° F). This is a colourless oily liquid consisting of a mixture of terpenes and essential oils. The liquid is insoluble in water, slightly soluble in aqueous alcohol, and insoluble in absolute alcohol and ether. Oil of turpentine is the principal product of turpentine, and it is widely used as a solvent and thinner for various oil paints and varnishes, to which it gives consistency and drying properties. Medically, oil of turpentine acts as a powerful stimulant and is often used as an antispasmodic and astringent. It is also capable of destroying various intestinal parasites and exhibits powerful diuretic properties. Crude commercial turpentine is valuable mainly as a source of resins.

ESSENTIAL OILS

Essential Oils, any of several chemicals that form the odoriferous essences of a number of plants. The term *essential oil* is also applied to similar synthetic substances prepared from coal tar chemicals, and semisynthetic substances prepared from natural essential oils.

Sources

Essential oils come from the flowers, fruits, leaves, roots, seeds, and bark of many plants. Oil of lavender is derived from a flower, oil of patchouli from a leaf, and oil of orange from a fruit. The oils are formed in the green (chlorophyll-bearing) parts of the plant, and with plant maturity are transported to other tissues, particularly to the flowering shoots. The exact function of an essential oil in a plant is unknown; it may be to attract insects for pollination, or to repel harmful insects, or it may be simply a metabolic intermediate.

The essential oils are volatile liquids, mostly insoluble in water, but freely soluble in alcohol, ether, and vegetable and mineral oils. They are usually not oily to the touch. They may be grouped into five classes, according to their chemical structure: alcohols, esters, aldehydes, ketones, and lactones and oxides.

Production and Uses

Essential oils are obtained by one of four methods: steam distillation, extraction by volatile solvents, expression by hand or machine, and enfleurage, a process in which fat is used as a solvent. In modern practice, essential oils, synthesized or obtained from natural sources by any one of the above four methods, are often purified by vacuum distillation.

Essential oils are used to impart flavour and delicate aroma to coffee, tea, wines, and distilled liquors. They are the basic ingredients in the manufacture of perfumes, and are also used in soaps, disinfectants, and similar products. Essential oils have an important use in medicine, either for their flavouring qualities or for their pain-relieving and physiological value. See articles on many of the specific essential oils mentioned.

FLAX

Flax, common name for a family of plants, and for plants of a genus within that family. One species is grown extensively for its fibre and seed. The fibre products include linen threads and fabrics, and the seed is the source of linseed oil and meal. Other species are cultivated as ornamental plants or for pharmaceuticals.

Flax plants range in height from 30 to 100 cm (12 to 40 in) and have shallow taproots. Because the stems contain the fibre, the taller varieties, which are sparsely branched, are used for fibre production. The seed-producing varieties have shorter stems and are more heavily branched. Both fibre and seed flaxes have narrow, alternate, lancelike leaves. The flowers are completely symmetrical, with five sepals, five petals, ten stamens, and up to ten seeds. The seeds are borne in five double-celled carpels, which are part of the pistil. The flowers of most cultivated varieties range in colour from deep to pale shades of blue. Some varieties, which may have white, violet, pink, or red blossoms, make effective ornamental plants. Flaxseeds are shiny and may be dark brown, yellow, or mottled in colour.

Origin

The use of flax fibre for cloth originated almost 10,000 years ago. Remnants of linen fishing nets and clothing and unworked flax have been found in Switzerland in the remains of Stone Age lake dwellings. The ancient Egyptians used linen shrouds, some of which are still preserved on mummies, and pictures of flax cultivation adorn the walls of various Egyptian tombs. Passages in the Bible refer to the manufacture of linen. Annual flax, which was cultivated in Mesopotamia, Assyria, and Egypt for about 5000 years, still grows wild in the regions around the Persian Gulf, the Caspian Sea, and the Black Sea.

In North America flax was grown as early as 1626, and linen was the most important textile fibre until the beginning of the Industrial Revolution. With the invention of the cotton gin in 1793, cotton became an extremely cheap raw material, and it largely displaced flax as a fibre source. Subsequently flax has been cultivated in the United States mainly for its seed.

Fibre Flax

Primarily a temperate-region plant, flax grows under a wide range of temperature and moisture conditions. High temperatures and high precipitation are, however, unfavourable for production of either flax or seed. Moderately fertile silt or clay loams are most satisfactory for cultivation.

Fibre flax is harvested by uprooting the plants, which then are piled in the fields to dry. The seed is removed to be used for feed or oilseed or to be retained for planting. The straw is retted, a process that promotes partial decomposition of the stem to permit separation of the fibre from the woody portions. In retting, the straw is spread on the ground in order to subject it to the action of rain, dew, and microorganisms, and to cyclic wetting, drying, freezing, and thawing. Another process, called water-retting, which is used in some countries, consists of immersing the straw in ponds, streams, or special tanks in which water and microorganisms promote decomposition.

The retted stems are crushed and broken and the fibre is separated from the woody fragments, called shives. This process yields relatively long and straight fibres, known as line fibres, and short, damaged or tangled fibres, called tow. Flax tow is used primarily in upholstery. Having high tensile strength, line fibres are used in the manufacture of various threads employed in the bookbinding and shoe industries and in such products as twine, fishnets, and laces. Flax fibres are also used extensively in various types of linen cloth and other fabrics.

France and Belgium produce high-quality fibre. Flax fibre is also produced in eastern Europe, and on a limited scale in Ireland and Canada. Small amounts of fibre flax have been cultivated in the United States, primarily in Michigan and Oregon, but little commercial production of flax fibre has taken place since 1950. The Soviet Union cultivated flax extensively; despite a large total yield, however, the quality of the fibre usually was inferior to that obtained from western Europe.

Seed Flax

Flax for seed is produced and harvested in about the same manner as wheat and other small grains. The crop is most productive on loamy soils with moderate to high fertility. In California, India, and Argentina, seed flax is planted in the fall and matures in about 150 days. In the northern United States and in Canada and the northern latitudes in Europe, the crop is seeded in the spring and matures in 100 to 120 days. Yields and quality are best in relatively cool climates. High temperatures and drought during the time the seed is developing often reduce the crop yield and oil content.

Seed flax does not compete well with weeds. It is planted on clean firm seedbeds, usually on acreage previously planted with corn or a similar intertilled crop, in which weeds have been killed by cultivation. The inability of seed flax to compete with weeds or other plants has made it valuable as a so-called nurse crop, or companion crop, for plantings of alfalfa, clovers, and other forage legumes. Weeds in flax crops may be controlled by use of herbicide sprays.

Flax seed yields from 30 to 40 percent linseed oil by weight. The oil is used in the manufacture of paints, varnishes, linoleum, oilcloth, printing inks, soaps, and many other products. Since 1959 it also has been used as a coating for concrete pavements and bridge decks to prevent scaling and surface deterioration from heavy traffic, freeze-thaw cycles, and applications of salt or calcium chloride for snow and ice control. The oil cake, or linseed meal, which remains after the oil has been expressed, contains 30 to 40 percent crude protein and is a valuable feed for livestock.

Chapter 6

Fibre Yielding Plants

FIBRE

Fibre, fine hairlike structure, of animal, vegetable, mineral, or synthetic origin. Commercially available fibres have diameters ranging from less than 0.004 mm (0.00015 in) to 0.2 mm (0.008 in) and they come in several different forms: short fibres (known as staple, or chopped), continuous single fibres (monofilament), untwisted bundles of continuous filaments (tow), and twisted bundles of continuous filaments (yarn). Fibres are classified according to their origin, chemical structure, or both.

They can be braided into ropes and cordage, made into felts (also called nonwovens), woven or knitted into textile fabrics, or, in the case of high-strength fibres, used as reinforcements in composites—that is, products made of two or more different materials.

Animal Fibres

All animal fibres are complex proteins. They are resistant to most organic acids and to certain powerful mineral acids such as sulfuric acid (H_2SO_4). However, protein fibres are damaged by mild alkalies (basic substances) and may be dissolved by strong alkalies such as sodium hydroxide (NaOH). They can also be damaged by chlorine-based bleaches, and undiluted liquid hypochloride bleach will dissolve wool or silk.

The principal component of silk is the protein fibroin. Silk is exuded in continuous filaments from the abdomens of various insects and spiders. It is the only natural filament that commonly reaches a length of more than 1000 m (more than 3300 ft). The only silk used in commercial textiles is produced from the cocoons of the silkworm. Several silk filaments can be gathered to produce textile yarn. However, silk is often produced and used in staple form to manufacture spun yarns.

The principal component of hair, wool, and fur is the protein keratin. Individual hairs may be as long as 91 cm (36 in) but are usually no more than 41 cm (16 in). Thus, fibres of hair and wool are not continuous and must be spun into yarn if they are to be woven or knitted into textile fabrics, or they must be made into felt. Any hair fibre can legally be marketed as wool or bear the common English name of the animal from which it was gathered camel's hair.

The principal hair fibre used to produce textile fabrics is sheep's wool. In wild sheep, the wool is a short, soft underlayer protected by longer, coarser hair. In domesticated sheep bred for their fleece, the wool is much longer.

Yarns made of wool are classified as either woolen or worsted. Wool fibres less than 5 cm (less than 2 in) in length are made into fuzzy, soft woolen yarns. Longer fibres are used for the smoother and firmer worsted yarns. Naturally crimped wool fibres produce air-trapping yarns that are used for insulating materials. Other animals used as sources of hair fibres for textiles include camels, llamas, alpacas, guanacos, vicuñas, rabbits, reindeer, Angora goats, and Kashmîr (or cashmere) goats.

Fur fibres from animals such as mink and beavers are sometimes blended with other hairs to spin luxury yarns but are most often found as fur pelts. Horsehair and cow's hair are used for felts and are sometimes spun as yarn, particularly for upholstery and other applications for which durability is important. Even human hair has been spun into yarn and used for textiles.

Vegetable Fibres

Vegetable fibres are predominantly cellulose, which, unlike the protein of animal fibres, resists alkalies. Vegetable fibres resist most organic acids but are destroyed by strong mineral acids. Improper use of most bleaches can also weaken or destroy these fibres.

There are four major types of vegetable fibres: *seed fibres,* which are the soft hairs that surround the seeds of certain plants; *bast fibres,* the tough fibres that grow between the bark and stem of many dicotyledonous plants; *vascular fibres,* the tough fibres found in the leaves and stems of monocotyledons; and *grass-stem fibres.* Other fibre types, of limited utility, include strips of leaf skins, such as raffia; the fibre of fruit cases, such as coir; and palm fibres.

Only two seed fibres, cotton and kapok, have commercial importance. Cotton fibre, which grows in the seed pod of cotton plants, is the only one that is useful for the manufacture of textiles. Different species of cotton plants produce fibres of different lengths.

Long-staple fibres are spun into fine, strong yarns, which are then woven into better-quality fabrics. Short-staple fibres produce coarser yarns for durable fabrics. Cotton yarns can be dyed and printed easily, so that they are useful for producing woven fabrics with a multitude of colours and designs. Kapok cannot be spun but is used as upholstery stuffing. Because it is hollow, kapok is buoyant. It was once used in flotation devices such as life preservers, but it has largely been replaced by other materials.

A wide variety of bast fibres are used in applications ranging from fine woven textiles to cordage. Linen cloth is made from flax. Coarser clothes and rope are produced from hemp, jute, ramie, and sunn.

Vascular fibres are used almost exclusively for making cordage. They include agave (sisal), henequen, manila hemp, and yucca. The vascular fibres of pineapple have been used in the production of textiles. Entire stems of some grasses and straws, such as esparto, are woven as fibres for hats and matting.

The papermaking industry also uses vegetable fibres extensively. Cotton and flax form the basis for fine rag papers. Grasses, hemp, jute, and manila are often used in wrapping papers and other coarse papers. Newsprint and kraft papers are produced from wood fibre after appropriate chemical treatment. Wood fibre and bagasse (the fibre of sugarcane) are made into building board by a process analogous to papermaking.

Mineral Fibres

Glass, which is made from silica sand, is the only inorganic (mineral) fibre widely used in commercial applications. There are two main forms of glass fibres: continuous and staple. *Continuous* glass fibre, which is made by drawing molten glass into threads, is used in textile materials. The use of air, steam, or gas to disrupt the flow of the molten glass stream produces *staple* fibres. These fibres can be fabricated into mats or into bulk-molding and sheet-molding compounds with the use of resins, or organic binders. Quartz mineral is high-silica, high-purity glass that is good for long-term use at temperatures as high as 1400° C (2552° F).

Since the early 1960s, ceramic fibres such as aluminum oxide, (also called alumina [$Al_2 0_3$]), silicon carbide (SiC), and boron carbide (B_4C) have been developed mainly for use in heat-resistant composite materials. Many components of helicopters, military aircraft, civil aircraft, missiles, and spacecraft, including satellites and space shuttles, are made from these high-strength, lightweight composites.

Fibres of asbestos, formerly used for insulation and fireproofing, were found to be carcinogenic and are no longer used. Thin metal wires are used for the production of gauze. Aluminum fibres coated with plastics possess a bright glitter and are used in decorative yarns.

Synthetic Fibres

Synthetic fibres derived from natural cellulose were first developed at the end of the 19th century and became known as rayons. In a typical rayon-making process, natural cellulose made from wood pulp is treated with chemicals to form a thick liquid. This liquid is then extruded as filaments into a weak acid bath that converts the filaments back into pure cellulose.

Rayons are not, therefore, completely synthetic but are actually regenerated fibres. Acetates and triacetates, which are true synthetic fibres, were developed shortly after rayon. They are derived from cellulose acetate in a process similar to that used for making rayon.

Most synthetic fibres are now derived from organic polymers, materials consisting of large organic molecules. Most of them are thermoplastic—that is, they are softened by heat.

The first commercially successful organic synthetic fibre, nylon (polyamide), dates from 1938. Since then many other fibres, including acrylic (polyacrylonitrile), aramid (aromatic polyamide), olefins (polyethylene and polypropylene), polyester, and spandex (polyurethane), have been developed. In a typical fibre-spinning process, a molten polymer or polymer solution is extruded through tiny holes in a spinneret into an environment that causes the filaments to solidify.

The fibre's properties depend on the base polymer, the spinning process, and the post-spinning treatment of the fibre, which can include drawing, annealing, applying a finish, and coating. Fibre properties such as weight, abrasion resistance, heat resistance, chemical resistance, moisture resistance, strength, stiffness, elasticity, and ease of dyeing and colouring can be optimized by such treatments.

Carbon and graphite fibres are high-strength materials that are used as reinforcing agents in composites. Carbon fibres are produced by using heat to chemically change rayon or acrylic fibres. Carbonization occurs at temperatures of 1000° C to 2500° C (1832° to 4532° F) in an inert atmosphere. Carbon fibres are converted to graphite at temperatures above 2500° C. Carbon and graphite fibres can also be made from pitch, a residual petroleum product.

Products that use carbon fibres include heat-shielding materials, aircraft fuselages and wings, spacecraft structures, and sports equipment. High-strength fibres such as aramid and polyethylene are also used in armor applications such as bullet-resistant garments, car doors, and crew seats for military helicopters and aircraft.

JUTE

Jute, common name for two species of woody herbs, and for the fibre of these herbs. They are cultivated in tropical countries throughout the world. They are annuals with sparsely branching stems, often growing as tall as 4 m (14 ft). The small yellow flowers, which grow singly or in pairs, give rise to capsular fruits. The fibres of the inner bark, called bast fibres or phloem fibres, are glossy and tenacious but are brittle and easily injured by moisture.

Most cultivated jute is grown in alluvial soils of the river valleys of India. The herb is planted, cultivated, and within four to five months of planting, harvested by hand. At harvest, roots and foliage are removed from the plants, and the stems, tied in bunches, are soaked in water (retted) for two to three weeks.

At the end of the retting process, the fibres are easily separable from most of the remaining stem tissue. While still in water, the stems are pounded with wooden mallets. They are then rinsed, wrung thoroughly to remove any remaining nonfibrous material, and hung up to dry. The dried fibres are yellowish white, soft, and lustrous. Jute is used in the manufacture of low-grade twine, burlap, and cheap varieties of paper.

RAMIE

Ramie, name of a natural fibre and the plant from whose bark it is derived. The perennial shrub of the nettle family is native to East Asia. Lustrous, durable, soft, stronger than cotton, and resistant to chemicals, mildew, and shrinking, the fibre is also readily dyed, but hard to spin. Twine and thread are made from the fibre, and the cloth (often mixed with other fibres) is used in upholstery, tapestries, and other materials.

BAOBAB

Baobab, common name for a tropical African tree. The baobab tree grows only to the height of a large maple tree, but extensive lateral growth makes it one of the largest trees. The trunk of the baobab sometimes attains a diameter of 9 m

(30 ft), and the branches, frequently as thick as the trunks of other large trees, form a hemispherical mass of foliage often 45 m (150 ft) in diameter. The fruit, called monkey bread, is about the size of a citron; the pulp, which has a pleasing acid taste, is used in the preparation of cooling drinks. The bark of the tree yields a strong cordage fibre. The baobab, native to Africa, is now cultivated in many tropical countries throughout the world.

MALLOW

Mallow, common name for a family comprising about 80 genera and 1500 species of herbs, shrubs, and some trees, and for its representative genus. Well-known members of the family are the hollyhock, the marshmallow, hibiscus, and okra. Cotton, and the potherb roselle are also members of the mallow family. The family belongs to a mostly woody order found throughout the temperate and tropical parts of the world. Five families and about 3500 species constitute the order, the members of which characteristically have fibrous stems and mucilaginous juice. The floral whorls (calyx and corolla) are present in groups of five, and the segments (sepals and petals) are free from one another. The sepals are typically valvate (meeting edge to edge) in bud, and the numerous stamens (male flower parts) are often fused at the base or along their entire length into a staminal tube.

The linden family, with about 450 species, is a member of the order and produces important timbers and jute. The baobab family is a tropical member of the order, with about 200 species. This family contains balsa, from which is obtained the world's lightest timber; kapok, used in upholstery and life jackets; and durian, which produces an edible fruit also named durian. The cacao family, with about 1000 species, contains the source of kola nuts. Chocolate, cocoa, and cocoa butter are obtained from cacao, another member of this family. The elaecarpus family contains about 400 species of tropical and subtropical trees and shrubs.

Scientific Classification: Mallows make up the family Malvaceae of the order Malvales. The representative genus of the family is *Malva*. The hollyhock is classified as *Alcea rosea*, and the marshmallow as *Althaea officinalis*. Hibiscus are classified in the genus *Hibiscus*. Okra is classified as *Abelmoschus esculentus*. Cottons are classified in the genus *Gossypium*. The potherb roselle is classified as *Hibiscus sabdariffa*. Balsa, classified as *Ochroma lagopus*, kapok, classified as *Ceiba pentandra*, and durian, classified as *Durio zibethinus*, belong to the family Bombacaceae.

HOLLYHOCK

Hollyhock, common name for any of a genus of biennial or perennial herbs. The most commonly known species, native to China, is cultivated in gardens of Europe and the United States. Hollyhocks are tall and erect, usually growing 2 to 3 m (5 to 9 ft) in height. The single stems and the undersides of the heart-shaped, wrinkled leaves are hairy. Most have single blossoms in late summer, but newer garden varieties are double-flowered. Common colours of the flowers are white, yellow, salmon, rose, red, violet, and purple.

MARSHMALLOW (PLANT)

Marshmallow (plant), common name for a tall, leafy, perennial plant, native to eastern Europe. It has toothed, heart-shaped, or three-lobed leaves and clusters of showy, pinkish flowers about 2.5 cm (about 1 in) across. It reaches a height of up to 1.2 m (4 ft). In the United States the marshmallow grows wild in marshy areas as far west as Michigan and Arkansas. The roots of the marshmallow were once used to make a creamy confection, a pufflike imitation of which is popular in the United States today.

HIBISCUS

Hibiscus, genus of plants, commonly called rose mallows, of the mallow family. The genus is native to warm, temperate regions of the northern hemisphere. The hibiscus flower is characterized by a five-pointed calyx that is surrounded by a set of coloured bracts growing just beneath it, giving the appearance of a double calyx. The large, showy flowers have five petals, a column of fused stamens with kidney-shaped anthers, and several pistils. The fruit is a many-seeded, five-celled pod. Rose of Sharon, or shrubby althea, is a tall Asian shrub with smooth leaves. Cultivated varieties have open, bell-shaped flowers in colours ranging from white to yellow, rose, red, and purple.

The Chinese hibiscus, or China rose, is a shrub or tree that grows as tall as 9 m (30 ft) and produces huge, showy flowers. Many species, such as mahoe, Cuban bast, and a species with yellow and purple-red flowers, have economic uses.

All three are used for fibre, and the third is a source of wood for cabinetmaking. Several species grow in the wild state in North America. The rose mallow is a tall perennial herb with ovate leaves and white flowers with rose-coloured centres. It grows along salt marshes of the eastern United States.

Scientific classification: The genus *Hibiscus* belongs to the family Malvaceae. Rose of Sharon, or shrubby althea, is classified as *Hibiscus syriacus,* the Chinese hibiscus, or China rose, as *Hibiscus rosa-sinensis,* and mahoe as *Hibiscus tiliaceus.* Cuban bast is classified as *Hibiscus elatus,* the economically useful plant with yellow and purple-red flowers as *Hibiscus macrophyllus,* and the rose mallow as *Hibiscus moscheutos.*

OKRA

Okra, also gumbo, an annual herb of the mallow family. The okra, which is native to Africa, is extensively cultivated in the southern United States and the West Indies for its long, many-seeded pod, which, when still young and green, is used to thicken soups and stews and as a cooked vegetable. The okra bears large, yellow flowers, similar to those of the closely related hibiscus, and is occasionally planted in flower gardens.

COTTON

Cotton, natural vegetable fibre of great economic importance as a raw material for cloth. Its widespread use is largely due to the ease with which its fibres are spun into yarns. Cotton's strength, absorbency, and capacity to be washed and dyed also make it adaptable to a considerable variety of textile products.

Cotton Plants

Cotton is produced by small trees and shrubs of a genus belonging to the mallow family, which also includes hibiscus, okra, and the familiar swamp mallow.

The immature flower bud, called a square, blossoms and develops into an oval boll that splits open at maturity, revealing a mass of long white seed hairs, called lint, that cover a large number of brown or black seeds. When fully mature and dry, each of these hairs is a thin flattened tubular cell with a pronounced spiral twist and is attached to a seed. The length of the individual fibres ranges from 1.3 to 6 cm (0.5 to 2.5 in). Shorter fibres that grow from the seeds are called linters.

A few species are grown commercially; these range from a small tree of Asia, to the common American Upland cotton, a low, multibranched shrub that is grown as an annual. Another species includes the long-fibre Egyptian and Sea Island cottons botanically derived from the Egyptian species brought to the United States about 1900.

Sea Island cotton thrives in the unique climate of the Sea Islands, located off the southeastern coast of the United States, and on the islands of the West Indies such as Barbados.

As with Egyptian cotton, the fibre is white and lustrous but its fibre length is longer than that of any other type of cotton, which permits the spinning of extremely fine yarns. Pima, originally called American-Egyptian cotton, is a hybrid type. It is the only variety of long-fibre cotton now grown in commercially significant quantities in the United States, where it is cultivated under irrigation in the Southwest.

It is almost impossible to determine the original habitats of the various species of cotton. Scientists have determined fibre and boll fragments from the Tehuacán Valley of Mexico to be about 7000 years old.

The plant has certainly been grown and used in India for at least 5000 years and probably for much longer. Cotton was used also by the ancient Chinese, Egyptians, and North and South Americans. It was one of the earliest crops grown by European settlers, having been planted at the Jamestown colony in 1607.

Cultivation

Successful cultivation of cotton requires a long growing season, plenty of sunshine and water during the period of growth, and dry weather for harvest. In general, these conditions are met within tropical and warm subtropical latitudes in the northern and southern hemispheres. The U.S. Cotton Belt stretches from northern Florida to North Carolina and westward to California.

In the United States, production of the crop for a given year starts soon after harvesting the preceding fall, when many cotton farmers chop or shred the stalks with machines. The residue is plowed under and the land usually left rough until spring tillage. Planting time varies from the beginning of February in southern Texas to the beginning of June in the northern sections of the Cotton Belt.

A number of methods, chemical and mechanical, have been used to control weeds and grass, including intensive spraying of herbicide before and after planting. The cultivator, rotary hoe, and flame cultivator are also used to destroy weeds.

Approximately 95 percent of the cotton in the United States is now harvested mechanically with spindle-type pickers or strippers. Pickers are used extensively in irrigated lands. The picker has vertical drums equipped with wire spindles that engage and pull the cotton from open bolls. Strippers are used primarily in western Texas and western Oklahoma. They are "once-over" machines that pull the bolls from the plant.

Cotton Insects and Diseases

In addition to the flowers, the underside of each leaf of the cotton plant contains a small cuplike structure holding nectar.

These deposits and the succulent stem make the plant attractive to a variety of insect pests. Chief among these is the boll weevil. The use of early maturing strains of cotton plus the application of several chemicals and control methods have greatly reduced losses from boll-weevil infestation.

The bollworm, the pink larva of a small moth, is believed to have been a native of India but is now parasitic on cotton all over the world. The larvae burrow into the bolls and eat the seeds. In the United States the pink bollworm is largely confined to Texas and the western sections of the Cotton Belt. Quarantine, fumigation of seed, and destruction of trash removed from the cotton in ginning are control measures. The bollworm-tobacco budworm also is one of the most damaging cotton pests in terms of losses and control costs. Armyworm, thrips, lygus, and red spider are among other significant pests.

Among the serious diseases to which the cotton plant is subject is the wilt caused by a fungus which enters the roots from the soil and manufactures a poison. No treatment is known, but wilt-resistant strains of cotton have been developed. Another fungus disease is boll rot or anthracnose, caused by sac fungus. The best control is using seed from fungus-free fields.

Processing

When cotton arrives at the cotton gin, it is sucked into the building through pipes placed in the trailers or trucks. In many plants it first enters driers that reduce the moisture content for easier processing. The cotton travels next to equipment that removes burrs, sticks, dirt, leaf trash, and other foreign matter. It then moves to the gin stand, where lint is separated from the seeds. After separation from the seeds, the lint is packed tightly into bales. For the processing of cotton fibre to make yarn, cloth, and cordage.

Marketing

In determining the value of cotton, workers class samples from each bale according to staple, grade, and character. Staple refers to fibre length. Short staple accounts for about 25 percent of the domestic crop and is used in many coarser textiles. Medium staple accounts for about 70 percent of U.S. cotton, and long staple and extra-long staple for about 5 percent.

Grade refers to colour, brightness, and amount of foreign matter. Standards for grading U.S. cotton are established by the U.S. Department of Agriculture and revised from time to time. The highest of the grades are Good Middling and Strict Middling. Six colour groupings indicate the degree of whiteness from white to gray. Character refers to the diameter, strength, body, maturity (that is, ratio of mature to immature fibres), uniformity, and smoothness of the fibres.

Cottonseed

Once a waste-disposal problem for gins, cottonseed is now a valuable by-product. The seed goes to oil mills, where it is delinted of its linters in an operation similar to ginning. The bare seed is then cracked and the kernel removed. The meal that remains after the oil has been extracted is high in protein. Linters are used for padding in furniture and automobiles, for absorbent cotton swabs, and for manufacture of many cellulose products such as rayon, plastics, lacquers, and smokeless powder for munitions.

The hulls, or husks, are used as feed for cattle. Kernels, or meats, provide cottonseed oil. The cake and meal are used for feed and flour. Foots, the sediment left by cottonseed oil refining, provides fatty acids for industrial products.

Production

Cotton ranks just behind corn, soybeans, wheat, and hay among the leading cash crops of United States agriculture and is among the nation's principal agricultural exports. The leading cotton-producing states are Texas, California, Georgia, Mississippi, Arkansas, Louisiana, North Carolina, and Arizona.

Surplus stocks of cotton on hand in the United States fluctuated widely during the 1970s. The world economic recession of 1973-74 ushered in a period during which both production and consumption of cotton dropped. Production, however, fell faster than consumption, and by the mid-1970s the U.S. surplus had been reduced to the lowest level in 50 years in order to compensate.

Toward the end of the decade, rising prices caused by the shortages had stimulated increased production, but at the same time these higher prices made domestic cotton more vulnerable to competition from artificial fibres and imported cotton goods. World demand for cotton continued to be erratic, and some groups lobbied for increased price-supports, but an upward trend began in the 1980s.

Cotton is still a principal raw material for the world's textile industry, but its dominant position has been seriously eroded by synthetic fibres. In the United States, cotton accounts today for about 35 percent of the materials processed in textile mills, as against 80 percent before World War II. Net per capita consumption of cotton fibres in the United States, after declining by more than one-third between 1950 and 1970, increased during the 1980s and by the early 1990s was about 12 kg (about 27 lb) per year.

World production of cotton in the early 1990s stood at 18.9 million metric tons annually. In the 1930s, the United States produced more than half the world's cotton; by the early 1990s it was turning out about a sixth. The other leading producers included China, India, Pakistan, Brazil, and Turkey.

TEXTILES

Textiles, generic term originally applied to woven fabrics, but now also applied to natural and synthetic filaments, yarns, and threads as well as to the woven, knitted, felted, tufted, braided, bonded, knotted, and embroidered fabrics made from them; and to nonwoven fabrics produced by mechanically or chemically bonding fibres.

Textile Fibres

The term *textile fibres* refers to fibres that can be spun into yarn or made into fabric by such operations as weaving, knitting, braiding, and felting. Weaving, one of the first crafts, was practiced as early as the New Stone Age, as shown by fragments of flax fibres found in the remains of lake dwellings in Switzerland. In ancient Egypt, the earliest textiles were woven from flax; in India, Peru, and Cambodia, from cotton; in the southern European area, from wool; and in China, from silk.

Linen

Made from flax, linen was first used by the ancient Egyptians. Because the earliest linen cloth was usually white, it became a symbol of purity for the Egyptians, and was used not only for clothing and household articles but also in religious practices. The Egyptians also produced textiles made of cotton imported from India. The term *linens,* now popularly used to designate such household items as cotton sheets, napkins, and towels, probably originated from the Egyptian word *linum.*

Wool

The Bible refers to the superior quality of wool sold in the ancient city of Damascus. The ancient peoples of the Caucasian peninsula wore woolen robes called *shal,* from which the word *shawl* is derived. Sheep were raised for fibre, as well as for meat and leather, throughout the Mediterranean area. Sicily and southern Italy provided wool for clothing in Rome until the time of the Roman Empire, when fabrics of silk, imported from China, became fashionable. The finest wool came from merino sheep, raised in Spain by the Basque people, whose reputation as the most able sheepherders in the world continues to the present day.

Subsequently, the Belgians became skillful in producing fine-quality wool textiles and taught their art to the Saxons in Britain, who also became noted for their fine woolen fabrics.

Cotton

Although cotton is the most common textile fibre now in use, it was the last natural fibre to attain commercial importance. In the 5th century BC the Greek historian Herodotus reported that among the valuable products in India was the wild plant that bears fleece as its fruit. In the following century cotton was introduced from India into Greece by Alexander the Great. Although the early Greeks and Romans used cotton for awnings and sails as well as for clothing, it was not adopted for widespread use in Europe until centuries later.

In the New World, the Mexicans used cotton for weaving in the pre-Columbian period. Cotton textiles were found in the West Indies and in South America by explorers in the 15th and 16th centuries. Cotton was cultivated by the early American colonists, and after the introduction of the cotton gin, invented in 1793 by the American inventor Eli Whitney, cotton became the most important staple fibre in the world for quantity, economy, and utility.

Silk

According to Chinese legend, the weaving of silk originated in the 27th century BC during the reign of Emperor Huang Ti, whose wife supposedly developed the technique of reeling the thread of the silkworm for use in weaving. Although for many centuries raw silk and silk fabrics were exported to the Mediterranean countries, the source of the fibre remained unknown to Europeans until the 6th century AD, when travellers returning from China smuggled eggs of the silkworm into the Western world. From this stock, silkworm culture was introduced into Greece and Italy. By the 12th century silk was used for the weaving of precious fibres throughout Europe.

In the western hemisphere, attempts to cultivate the silkworm began in 1620 when King James I of England urged the colonists to produce silk instead of tobacco. Some success was achieved by the Georgian colonists, but subsequent efforts in Connecticut and New Jersey failed because of the lack of efficient, low-cost labour required to raise the mulberry trees, upon which the silkworms feed, and to care for silkworms.

In the mid-20th century only Japan and China were important silk-producing countries. At the beginning of World War II, Japan supplied 90 percent of the world production of raw silk. When the Western world was cut off from this source during the war, nylon fibres, which had been developed in the 1930s, were used as a substitute.

Synthetic Fibres

The beauty and value of silk stimulated many early scientists to attempt to develop fibre resembling the thread of the silkworm. In 1664 the English scientist Robert Hooke suggested the possibility of synthesizing a glutinous substance similar to the fluid secreted by the silkworm when it spins its cocoon. Not until 200 years later, however, was the commercial production of manufactured fibres, originally named artificial silk, launched by the French scientist Count Hilaire de Chardonnet.

His process, which followed the principle suggested by earlier chemists, consisted of forcing a viscous fluid through small thimblelike nozzles called spinnerets and hardening the fluid into thread by coagulation in a chemical bath. This process continues to be the basic method that is used for the production of synthetic textile fibres.

In 1924 the term *artificial silk* was replaced by the more definitive name rayon, which in 1937 was officially recognized in the U.S. by the Federal Trade Commission as the generic term for the new fibre. Subsequently, two major processes used in rayon production led to the classification of rayons into two distinct categories, viscose rayon and acetate rayon.

Nylon was introduced in the 1930s. Stronger than silk, this fibre is used extensively in the production of clothing, hosiery, parachute fabric, and rope. After 1940 many other synthetic fibres achieved importance in the textile industry, including the polyesters, sometimes called dacrons, polyvinyls, polyethylenes, acrylics, and olefins. A silklike nylon known as Qiana was introduced in 1968. Fabrics made of Qiana resist wrinkles, retain creases and pleats, and have good colour clarity and stability when dyed.

The use of synthetic fibres brought many changes in the textile economy, because production methods and the physical characteristics of these fibres could be adjusted to suit specific requirements. Highly industrialized nations that previously had been forced to import cotton and wool as raw materials for textiles were able to manufacture their own fibres from such readily available resources as coal, petroleum, and wood pulp. The development of synthetic fibres led to the production of new types of durable and easily cared-for fabrics.

Textile Production

Production and distribution of textiles are relatively

complicated. Depending on the type of fabric, the raw material, which consists of both farm and chemical products, may be prepared as an independent operation or as a preliminary stage in the manufacture of the fabric. Thus, the number of separate processes involved in production varies with each textile product.

The initial stage of textile manufacturing involves the production of the raw material either by farmers who raise cotton, sheep, silkworms, or flax or by chemists who produce fibre from various basic substances by chemical processes. The fibre is spun into yarn, which is then processed into fabric in a weaving or knitting mill. After dyeing and finishing, the woven material is ready for delivery either directly to a manufacturer of textile products or to a retailer, who sells it to individuals for use in the making of clothes and such household articles as draperies, upholstery, and curtains.

Fibre Processing

The cotton fibre, the fleece from the sheep, and the flax must be processed to be made ready for the spinning plant. Raw cotton is put through the cotton gin, which removes seeds and other impurities, before the fibre is shipped in bales to the spinning mill. Various mechanical and chemical operations convert flax into spinnable linen fibre; wool must be sorted, graded, and scoured before it is ready for mill processing into yarn.

Silk is unwound from cocoons after the silk gum is softened in warm water to permit ready separation without rupturing the fine fibres. The continuous filaments are gathered and twisted to form multifilament yarns, in a process known as throwing. Broken filaments and waste are converted to staple (short fibres) for manufacture into spun silk yarns, in a manner similar to that used for spinning cotton, wool, or linen fibres.

Synthetic fibres are supplied in either filament or staple form. The continuous filament fibre is processed into yarn in the same manner as silk. Synthetic staple fibre, which consists of short lengths of fibre, is processed as are raw cotton and wool before spinning.

Spinning

Only twisting is required to process filament fibre into yarn, but staple fibres must be carded to combine the fibres into a continuous ropelike form, combed to straighten the long fibres, and drawn out into continuous strands, which are then twisted to the desired degree.

In general, the amount of twist given the yarns determines various characteristics. Light twisting yields soft-surfaced fabrics, whereas hard-twisted yarns produce hard-surfaced fabrics, which provide resistance to abrasion and are less inclined to retain dirt and wrinkles. Fabrics made from hard-twisted yarns, however, are subject to greater shrinkage. Hard-twisted yarns are used in producing hosiery and crepes.

Weaving

Two sets of yarns, called the warp and the woof (more commonly filling, or weft) are used in weaving, which is carried out on a mechanism known as a loom. Warp yarns run along the length of the loom; filling yarns run across it. The warp is wound on huge reels, called beams or creels, that are placed at the feet of the loom, and the warp yarns are threaded through the loom to form a series of parallel threads.

The filling is fed from the side of the loom by bobbins, which are changed either automatically or manually when the yarn runs out. The loom shuttle carries the filling yarns across the loom, interlacing them at right angles with the warp yarns.

Different patterns and textures are achieved by varying the number of warp yarns and by altering the sequence in which they are raised or lowered. A temporary protective coating known as sizing protects the warp yarns against damage during the weaving operation.

Knitting Machines

Knitting, which originated with the knotting of fishnets and snares by ancient peoples, is the craft of forming a fabric by the interlocking of yarn in a series of connected loops by means of hand or mechanized needles. The craft of knitting was introduced into continental Europe by the Arabs in the

5th century, and flourished in England and Scotland in the 14th and 15th centuries. The Scots have claimed both its invention and its introduction into France.

All knitting was done by hand early 1580s, when the English clergyman William Lee invented a machine that could knit stockings. Queen Elizabeth I of England refused Lee a patent for his machine, considering the new invention a threat to many of the hand knitters in the country.

The machine, however, was used in other countries, and paved the way for improvements. The first addition came in early 1750s, when a British cotton spinner, Jedediah Strutt, invented an attachment to the stocking frame that could produce ribbed fabric. In the early 19th century the British engineer Marc Isambard Brunel invented a circular knitting frame, to which he gave the name *tricoteur*.

The knitting of heavier yarns became possible when another British inventor, Matthew Townsend, introduced the latch needle, a needle having a latch-closed hook at one end, which he patented. An improvement in power machines that became known as Cotton's system. The improved machine was capable of shaping the heels and toes of hosiery, and it laid the foundation for the modern full-fashioned machines. Automatic knitting machines were first introduced.

Dyeing and Printing

Textiles may be dyed in a number of ways: The fabrics can be dyed after weaving or knitting is completed (piece-dyed), the loose fibres can be dyed in a vat (stock-dyed), or the yarn or filament can be dyed before weaving or knitting is begun (yarn-dyed). Synthetic yarns can also be precoloured by incorporating colour pigments in the spinning solution before the filaments are extruded through the spinneret (solution- or dope-dyed).

The principal method of printing designs on textiles is intaglio roller printing. In this process, the design is etched on copper rolls, a separate roll for each colour in the design, the depressions are filled with printing paste, and the fabric then passes through the rolls. Another method of printing fabrics is relief roller printing. In this process, the design is raised away from the surface of the roll, and the raised portions are covered with ink.

This is also called surface, peg, block, or kiss printing. Screen printing is accomplished with a design stenciled on a flat or roller screen. The screen is placed over the fabric and colour is applied by squeegeeing it through the openings in the stencil. Hand-screen printing is being replaced by automatic machines.

Other Finishing Processes

In addition to colouring and printing, other finishes applied to the fabric to improve its appearance and service include treatment to promote crease resistance in such textiles as cotton, linen, and spun rayons, which do not have the elasticity of silk and wool.

The latest developments in crease-resistant finishes are the so-called durable press, or permanent press, finishes. In addition to wrinkle resistance, these finishes impart permanent creases where desired, as in slacks. Resistance to shrinking, staining, and soiling also may be provided by various chemical treatments. Other finishing processes protect against slipping of threads or damage by mildew, moths, or flame.

Types of Textiles

Many woven fabrics are produced by variations in the weaving pattern.

Plain, or Taffeta, Weaves

The basic weaving pattern, in which each thread of the warp is interlaced with filling thread, or woof, is called the plain, or taffeta, weave. The word *taffeta* probably originated from the Persian *taftah,* meaning "twist." Familiar names for fabrics in the plain weave are batiste, broadcloth, calico, cambric, crepe, challis, cheesecloth, chintz, muslin, organdy, percale, seersucker, voile, and tweed. Variations of the plain weave are the basket and the ribbed weave.

Monk's cloth, oxford shirting, and plaids are examples of

the basket weave; poplins, bengalines, and piques are ribbed weaves.

Twill-Weave Fabrics

The twill weave is characterized by marked diagonal lines produced by the interlacing of two warp threads with one filling thread in alternate rows. This wale, or cord, effect may be observed in such twills as herringbone, serge, worsted cheviot, jersey, foulard, surah, covert cloth, gabardine, ticking, jean, and drill. The twill weave provides the cloth with superior strength, desirable for work clothes and suits.

Satin Weave

Although satins are heavier in texture than twills, the principal characteristic of the satin weave is its smoothness, which is achieved at the cost of strength. The smooth surface of the satin weave is produced by passing the warp yarns over a number of filling yarns, keeping the interlacing to a minimum. The reflection of light by the exposed yarns gives the satin weave its sheen. In a filling satin, the filling yarns are passed over a succession of warp yarns. Because the filling yarns are weaker than the warp, satin weaves are subject to more abrasion but are popular, nevertheless, for their beauty. The best-known satin weaves are the crepe satin, peau de soie, sateen, and damasks. The word *satin* is derived from the name of the Chinese seaport Chüanchow, formerly called Zaytun, from which this type of fabric was first exported in the Middle Ages.

Dobby and Jacquard Weaves

These two weaves are used to produce patterned fabrics. Small, repetitive motifs, such as the bird's eye, a small diamond with a dot at the centre, used in shirting and dress fabrics are dobby weaves. Intricate patterns are produced on the Jacquard loom, named for its French inventor, Joseph Marie Jacquard. Jacquard weaves are used extensively for upholstery and drapery materials, such as brocades, brocatelles, tapestries, and matelassés.

Pile Weaves

Some pile weaves, including velvets, plushes, corduroys, and Turkish toweling, are produced by a combination of the plain weave and the use of wires to draw from the cloth additional warp or filling yarn, forming loops that create the pile. Turkish toweling has uncut loops, in contrast to velvets in which the loops are cut. Pile fabrics may be produced also by weaving two pile fabrics face to face and then cutting them apart. This process is more economical than the cutting of loops, required in the production of velvets. Woven carpets and rugs are pile fabrics.

Choice of Fibres

The names of the weaves indicate a method of interlacing threads rather than fibre content. Any fibre or combination of fibres may be used for any type of weave. Some weaves initially were associated only with one particular fibre, as in the case of taffeta and satin, which were made of silk; serge, a twill weave formerly restricted to wool; and denim, a twill originally made only of cotton. Present-day production includes nylon taffetas, cotton satins, silk serge, and denims of blended fibre yarns.

The introduction of synthetic fibres has led to research to determine the most desirable fibre content for specific applications. Required characteristics are achieved by use of various combinations and blends of fibres, methods of weaving, and dyeing and finishing processes.

Nonwoven Textiles

The textile structure of a nonwoven fabric is produced by bonding or interlocking the fibres. This is accomplished by mechanical, chemical, thermal, or solvent methods, or by a combination of these methods.

The principal bonding methods are resin bonding and thermoplastic fibre bonding. In resin bonding, the resin is sprayed or applied as a foam directly onto the web of fibres as it emerges from the web-forming equipment. The web is then dried, heat cured, and, in some instances, pressed. In thermoplastic bonding, a thermoplastic (heat-setting) fibre, with a lower melting point than a base fibre, is blended with the base fibre in the form of a web. The web is pressed between heated rollers, bonding the plastic fibres to the base fibres.

The chief mechanical method of producing nonwoven fabrics is with a needle-punch machine, which was designed primarily to produce blankets. The machine uses small hooked needles to interlace and interlock the fibres.

Uses of Textiles

In addition to clothing and home furnishings, textiles are used for such industrial products as filters for air conditioners, life rafts, conveyor belts, tents, automobile tires, swimming pools, safety helmets, and mine ventilators. In many applications, textiles with protective plastic coatings provide greater suppleness, lighter weight, and better performance than metals. Although all types of fibre are used for such products, many industrial products use a combination of synthetic fibres on a backing of cotton. The synthetic fibres provide the fabric with mildew-proof, quick-drying properties, and the less expensive cotton backing provides bulk and stability. For the artistic use of textiles

Regulations

Some countries have enacted legislation to compel the identification of fibre content, irrespective of the fabric quality. The Federal Trade Commission (FTC) requires the identification of the fibre content of all fabrics. In woolens and worsteds, the percentage of wool fibre must be identified, and the label must state whether it is virgin, reprocessed, or reused wool. The term *virgin wool* is applied to wool that has never before been processed; *reprocessed wool,* to fibre recovered from the processing of virgin wool; and *reused wool,* to fibre recovered from used wool products such as carpets and clothing. Another requirement is that the terms *mohair* and *cashmere* be restricted to fibres obtained respectively from the hair of the Angora goat and of the Kashmîr goat. The term *linen* may be applied only to flax fibre.

Other regulations of the FTC govern textile finishes, that is, shrink-proofing, flameproofing, and weighting, which consists of adding metallic salts to delicate fabrics, such as silks, to provide more body. In textiles labeled shrink-proof, nonshrinkable, or preshrunk, the percentage of maximum shrinkage, as determined by government-sponsored tests, must be designated on the label. The Flammable Fabrics Act established safety standards with respect to the flammability of fabrics used for wearing apparel. The act was broadened to include fabrics used in interior furnishings. Only very sheer or loosely woven pile fabrics were found to exhibit rapid and intense burning. Administration of the act was transferred to the newly created Consumer Product Safety Commission.

CACAO

Cacao, common name for a tree, the seed of that tree, and for certain other related trees in a family that also contains the kola. The cacao tree is a perennial that yields several harvests annually. First cultivated in South America, it was introduced into Europe during the 16th century. Today it is grown chiefly in western Africa.

The average cacao tree attains a height of about 6 m (about 20 ft) and has shiny leaves, as long as 30 cm (12 in), and small pink flowers on the trunk and older branches. Only about 30 of the 6000 annual blossoms eventually bear seeds. Commonly called cocoa beans, the seeds are surrounded by a yellow or reddish-brown pod about 28 cm (about 11 in) long. Cocoa beans are either purple or off-white and resemble almonds. The high proportion of fat in the bean kernels (cocoa butter) is used in medications, cosmetics, and soaps. The pulverized residue, which is called cocoa, is used in beverages and as a flavouring. Chocolate is also derived from cocoa beans.

BALSA

Balsa, common name for a tropical American tree. The tree may grow to a height of 18 to 21 m (60 to 70 ft). Balsa wood, also called corkwood, weighs about 97 to 130 kg/cu m (about 6 to 8 lb/cu ft) and is lighter and stronger than cork. In colour it resembles white pine or basswood. Balsa has long been used, especially in South America, for raft and boat building, and the term *balsa* is applied to a type of raft made of two parallel cylindrical logs connected by a platform or grating. The wood is also used for life-preserver floats, surfboards, and model airplanes. It is used in the interiors of aircraft to reduce vibration and as a sound insulator. Balsa is used as a lining material in refrigerators and ship holds because of its heat-insulating qualities.

PINE (TREE)

Pine (tree), common name for a medium-size family of trees, mostly evergreen, of widespread distribution in the temperate areas of the northern hemisphere, and for its representative genus. The family, which contains about 210 species placed in 10 genera, has enormous economic importance as a source of timber and pulpwood, among other products. Members of the family characteristically have helically arranged, needlelike leaves. In several genera pine, cedar, and larch—the leaves are borne in clusters that are actually short branches, or spurs, on which the leaves are arranged in tight helices.

The members of the pine family have separate female and male cones; the former produce the seeds, and the latter, the pollen. Male and female cones are produced on the same plant; the seed-bearing cones are woody when mature; the seeds are winged. The family is distinguished from other conifers on the basis of its seed cones. Each of the flattened scales on which the seeds are borne is underlaid by a distinct, sterile bract (reduced leaf) that is usually shorter than the scale. The seed cones are drooping in all members of the family except the fir and a small genus confined to South China and Southeast Asia. All members of the family have evergreen leaves except the golden larch and the larch.

The pine genus itself is the largest in the family, with about 110 species, about 35 of which are in North America. Pines grow in a wide range of habitats, from sea level to altitudes of 4,000 m (13,000 ft) and are distinguished from other members of the family by the leaves, which are in bundles. Each bundle contains a specific number of leaves, depending on the species, with a sheath of short, scalelike leaves at the base.

Pines are divided into two groups, based on the scale leaves and other characteristics. The soft pines have leaves in bundles of five, and the scale leaves fall away from mature leaf bundles. Their wood is soft and has a coarse grain. Well-known soft pines are the eastern white pine, of northeastern North America; piñon pine, of the Southwest, the seeds of which are edible; bristlecone pine, the Rocky Mountain species; and the Great Basin bristlecone, which can live more than 4,000 years and is one of the oldest known living things on the planet. Through analysis of bristlecone rings, scientists can tell what the climate was more than 10,000 years ago. The hard pines have leaves in clusters of two or three, and the scale leaves persist in mature clusters.

The wood is usually hard, with a close grain. Well-known species include lodgepole pine, extending from Alaska to Baja California; longleaf pine, of the southeastern coastal plain; and ponderosa pine, of the American West. Both pine groups are economically important for their timber, pulp, tar, and turpentine and for their use as ornamentals. Members of a pine family thought to be extinct for 50 million years were discovered in a rain forest near Sydney, Australia, in 1994. Other members of the pine family include Douglas fir, hemlock, and spruce.

CEDAR (TREE)

Cedar (tree), common name for three or four species of large trees native to mountainous areas of North Africa and Asia. Cedar trees belong to the pine family, the members of which have needlelike leaves and, like all conifers, bear their seeds on scales clustered into cones. They differ from other members of the family in their evergreen four-angled leaves borne on short side-branches. The genus produces fragrant, durable, red-coloured wood used in construction and cabinetry. Although no true cedars are native to North America, they are planted as ornamentals in milder areas, and various horticultural varieties, based on growth form and leaf colour, exist.

The best-known cedar is the cedar of Lebanon, mentioned often in the Old Testament; the First Temple of Solomon was built of this wood. It is native to Asia Minor, and today only a few original groves remain, although they contain some trees of great age. Trees may reach 30 m (100 ft) in height and produce spreading branches that split off from the main trunk, unlike most conifers, which have a single dominant trunk. The dark to bright green leaves are about 2.5 cm (about 1 in) long, and the upright cones are about 10 cm (about 4 in) long. The Cyprus cedar, usually considered only a variety of the cedar of Lebanon, occurs on the island of Cyprus in the Mediterranean.

The Atlas cedar is closely related to the cedar of Lebanon and occurs in the Atlas Mountains of North Africa. The remaining cedar, deodar, occurs in the Himalayas and is an important timber tree in India. Unlike the other species, which have horizontal branches and cones flat at the apex, the deodar has pendulous branches and rounded cones.

The name cedar is also applied to other conifer trees with fragrant wood. The well-known white cedar grows in swamps of the eastern United States and reaches a height of 24 m (80 ft). An arborvitae is also called cedar; western cedar and eastern white cedar are both important timber trees in the United States. Eastern red cedar, widespread in the eastern United States, is a juniper. A flowering tropical American mahogany is known as Spanish or West Indian cedar.

LARCH

Larch, common name for a small genus of trees, restricted to the colder parts of the northern hemisphere. Larches belong to the pine family and are unusual among the conifers in that they are deciduous: their soft, needlelike leaves, borne in dense clusters, drop in the fall, and new leaves do not appear until the following spring. Of the ten species of larch in the world, three occur in North America.

The American larch, also called tamarack or hackmatack,

occurs from Newfoundland and Labrador to Alaska. The strong durable wood is used in rough construction and as poles, posts, and railway ties.

Western larch occurs in the northwestern United States and southeastern Canada. Its close-grained, durable wood is used in flooring. The subalpine larch, occurs in the same areas as the western larch but usually at higher altitudes. The European larch is an important timber tree in Europe, where it has been planted extensively as a crop. It is grown in North America as an ornamental.

BOWSTRING HEMP

Bowstring Hemp, common name for any of a genus of plants and for the hemplike fibre produced by the plants. Formerly used for bowstrings, this fibre is long, silky, elastic, resistant to rotting in water, and about equal in strength to hemp. The individual strands of fibre are obtained from the elongated leaves of the plant. Cordage and coarse, strong cloth are made from it.

Ceylon bowstring hemp is a stemless perennial that grows wild in the jungles and increases by runners. It is also cultivated for fibre. The thick and fleshy leaves are sword- or lance-shaped, hollowed, and banded crosswise with white. The leaves of the African species are banded lengthwise with yellow. Several species are cultivated in the United States under the name of snakeplant.

LILY

Lily, common name for a family comprising more than 250 genera and about 4000 species of mostly herbaceous flowering plants, many with showy flowers. It contains many horticulturally important plants, including tulips, lilies, daffodils, hyacinths, day lilies, and amaryllis. Another important genus, the onion genus, contains about 700 species, usually with bulbs or corms underground and long, slender leaves starting at the ground (basal leaves).

Several species are cultivated as food crops: onions and shallots, garlic, chives, and leeks. In the asparagus genus, the leaves are reduced to tiny scales, and the needlelike "leaves" are actually highly modified branches. Tender young shoot tips of asparagus are eaten as a delicacy. Asparagus fern is another species grown as a houseplant for its attractive foliage and for its pretty red berries. The aloe genus also belongs to the lily family and contains about 250 species native to Arabia; Africa, especially South Africa; and Madagascar.

The hardy plants are often potted outdoors, and the juice from the leaves has medicinal uses.The order that lilies belong to is distinguished by having all perianth parts (sepals and petals) relatively undifferentiated and petaloid, a three-chambered gynoecium with nectaries generally present between the chambers (sepal nectaries), and larger seeds with well-developed storage tissue (endosperm) and embryos.Stems are usually fleshy in all types; they rise from underground storage organs and bear characteristically narrow leaves with parallel veins. The order occurs throughout the world, but most of its members flourish only in subtropical and temperate areas.

Many members of the lily order show adaptations to arid climates. During unfavourable periods, food and water are stored in bulbs or other forms of enlarged underground stem, such as corms, rhizomes, and tubers. Aboveground structures such as stems and leaves may also act as storage organs; they often have thickened bark or epidermal layers to prevent water loss. Many plants in the group have developed asexual means of reproducing, including the production of bulblets on parent bulbs or on inflorescences (flower clusters) and the production of seeds by parthenogenesis.

The pickerel weed family has about 35 species of freshwater plants found throughout the tropics. The water hyacinth floats freely on the water's surface because of its swollen, hollow petioles (leafstalks); due to its rapid growth and lack of natural predators, it has become a troublesome weed in some waterways.

In the iris family, about 1800 species are placed in about 92 genera. The family's horticulturally important plants include crocuses, gladiolus, and irises.

The agave family contains about 18 genera and 410 species; many are succulent plants of the tropics and subtropics, especially common in arid areas. The typically long, stiff leaves are usually basal (arising from the base of the stem) and may yield useful fibres. Sisal hemp is native to Mexico. Other fibres known as hemp are also obtained; true hemp comes from an unrelated plant. The Joshua tree of the American Southwest and the century plant are also members of this family.

The catbrier family contains mostly tropical to temperate herbs and woody climbing or trailing plants. About 225 species are placed in 10 genera. Sarsaparilla is obtained from the roots of some species of the family. Familiar species include carrion flower and the greenbrier or horse brier.

The yam family is a medium-size tropical and subtropical group with 8 genera and about 630 species. Most are weak-stemmed vines with large, underground food-storage organs—tubers or rhizomes. Yams are edible tubers of several cultivated species of the family's representative genus. Sweet potatoes are called yams in the southern United States but are unrelated to true yams.

PARTHENOGENESIS

Parthenogenesis, growth of an organism from an unfertilized gamete, or sex cell. It is common in the animal kingdom up through the class Insecta, but it occurs much more rarely thereafter. The mechanisms involved in the process are not yet well understood. A few kinds of amphibians, reptiles, and birds can reproduce parthenogenetically, but mammal embryos derived experimentally in this manner have thus far died within a period of days. Parthenogenesis also occurs, less commonly, among the lower plants. Among plants, the biological reproduction of fruit without fertilization is called parthenocarpy. Such fruit is seedless.

REPRODUCTION

Reproduction, process whereby all living organisms produce offspring. Reproduction is one of the essential functions of plants, animals, and single celled organisms, as necessary for the preservation of the species as eating is for the preservation of the individual.

In almost all animal organisms, reproduction occurs during or after the period of maximum growth. In plants, which continue to grow throughout their lifetime, the relationship between growth and reproduction is more complex. Individual plants have growth limitations imposed by inherited characteristics and environmental conditions; if the plant grows excessively, any of a number of reproductive processes may be stimulated. Environmental conditions also play some part in the reproduction of higher animals, but hormonal elements are more important.

Asexual Reproduction

Most single-celled organisms reproduce by a process known as fission, in which the parent organism splits into two or more so-called daughter organisms, thereby losing its original identity. Cell division, which results in the multiplication of cells constituting the tissues, organs, and systems of a multicellular organism, is not considered true reproduction; it is almost identical, however, with the binary fission of single-celled organisms.

In certain multicellular animals, such as the cnidarians, sponges, and tunicates, cell division often results in the production of buds that arise from the body of the parent and then later separate to develop into a new organism identical with the parent; this process, known as gemmation, is analogous to the process of vegetative reproduction or propagation in plants. Reproductive processes such as those cited above, in which only one parent gives rise to the offspring, are scientifically classified as asexual reproduction. The offspring produced are identical with the parent.

Sexual Reproduction

A number of single-celled organisms multiply by conjugation. In this process, which is analogous to fertilization, two similar unicellular organisms fuse, exchange nuclear materials, and then break apart. Each organism then reproduces by fission; occasionally, after conjugation, the participating organisms do not reproduce, the process in these instances seeming merely to revitalize the organisms. Conjugation is the most primitive method of sexual reproduction by which organisms having genetic characteristics derived from two parents are produced.

Most multicellular animals and plants undergo a more complex form of sexual reproduction in which especially differentiated male and female reproductive cells (gametes) unite to form a single cell, known as a zygote, which later undergoes successive divisions to form a new organism. The terms *fecundation* and *fertilization* are applied to the union of the male and female cells. In this form of sexual reproduction, half the genes, the carriers of inheritable characteristics, in the zygote come from one parent and half from the other parent.

Many lower multicellular organisms and all higher plants undergo an alternation of generations. In this process, a sexually produced generation alternates with an asexually produced generation. In some organisms that reproduce sexually, a process known as parthenogenesis occurs in which the female sex cell develops without fertilization.In higher animals, individuals of a single species are either male or female, according to whether they produce male reproductive cells or female reproductive cells.

The typical male reproductive cell, which is known as a sperm, spermatozoon, or spermatozoan, is a motile cell with a head containing the nucleus and a whiplike tail with which it swims. The typical female reproductive cell, which is known as an egg or ovum, is a rounded cell many times larger than the sperm and containing large amounts of cytoplasm surrounding the nucleus. Plant reproductive cells are roughly similar to animal cells, the male cell being known as the sperm or microgamete and the female cell as the ovum or macrogamete.

Hermaphroditism

In some relatively simple animals such as the earthworms

and leeches, organs producing sperm and ova occur in the same individual. Although such animals produce both male and female gametes, the production of sperm and ova usually occurs at different times, so that these animals generally do not fertilize themselves but rather other individuals of the same species. Certain hermaphroditic animals, such as the planarian flatworms, habitually undergo self-fertilization. Among plants, one individual may bear reproductive organs of only one sex, separate reproductive organs of both sexes, or reproductive organs containing both male and female elements. Individuals among higher animals bear reproductive organs of only one sex.

Cross-Fertilization

This requires the bringing together of sperms and ova that are produced at a distance from each other. In plants, wind and insects carry the sperm to the stationary egg, or, in a liquid medium, the sperm swims to the egg. In lower animals, deposition of sperm and eggs in water is common. This method is haphazard, as only a few of the many sperm discharged reach the eggs. In higher animals, various adaptations have evolved by means of which the spermatozoa, contained in a liquid known as semen, are deposited in the lower segment of the female reproductive tract.

Insemination

In vertebrates this internal deposition of semen occurs in the process of copulation, also known as coitus or sexual intercourse. During copulation animals are locked in close embrace, and the male inserts the male genital organ, the penis, into the female genital orifice, the vagina, discharging the semen therein. This process is known as insemination. Both animal and human spermatozoa can be kept alive outside the body for long periods by freezing; artificially introduced into the female reproductive tract, such spermatozoa produce pregnancy. The method, called artificial insemination, has been used in human reproduction to produce offspring where either the male or the female is sterile and in animals for breeding purposes.

Mating

The union of male and female, necessary for internal fertilization, is encouraged in nature. Most lower animals have definite seasons, governed by endocrine secretions. In most female mammals, estrus, or receptivity to mating, is operative only for short periods during the year. Animals such as the cow have several such periods of estrus during the year, the dog one or two. The human female normally has a 28-day reproductive, or menstrual, cycle, with ovulation usually occurring about 14 days before the onset of the menstruation, but sexual interest in humans is more culturally determined than tied to the reproductive cycle. In most animals, copulation is preceded by a period of courtship; the courtship ritual is stereotyped to a large extent. In humans, courtship and mating practices have been strongly modified by social and religious codes of behaviour set by society.

Gestation

After fertilization of the egg, the resulting zygote undergoes cell division and differentiation to form the embryo. In most higher plants, the embryo is enclosed in a layer of nutritive material surrounded by a hard outer covering, forming the seed. In most lower animals the embryo, surrounded by the nutritive material of the former ovum, is enveloped by a leathery or calcareous shell and is extruded from the body of the female. Animals, such as birds, that lay their eggs before the young are completely developed are termed oviparous.

Ovoviviparous animals are those that produce eggs in shells but that hatch the eggs within the body of the mother. The placental mammals never produce shelled eggs; the embryo is implanted in the uterus and is nourished by the mother until almost completely developed. Animals that give birth to live young without forming eggs are termed viviparous. The period during which viviparous animals carry their young internally is known as the period of gestation.In humans the period of years during which reproduction can occur begins with the onset of puberty, and the reproductive capacity of the female ends at what is known as menopause, or when menstruation ceases.

FIR

Fir, common name for any of a genus of trees. The trees, known as true firs, generally have a straight trunk with somewhat pyramidal growth. The branches grow in whorls from the trunk. The cones, which are erect at maturity, are composed of thin, close scales. Each scale bears two winged seeds. The flat leaves are scattered, with the midribs showing clearly on the whitish undersides.

About 25 species of true firs are widely scattered throughout the northern hemisphere. The silver fir of Europe sometimes reaches a height of 46 m (150 ft), with large boughs curved upward at their outer extremities. The leaves are dark green above, with two white lines beneath. When seen from below, the tree appears to have a silvery colour. It is abundant in the mountains of southern and central Europe. It is also found in Asia, in the Caucasus Mountains.

Ten species of fir are native to North America, growing chiefly in the region west of the Rocky Mountains. They achieve maximum growth in the Sierra Nevada and Cascade mountain ranges. The balsam fir is found from Virginia to the island of Newfoundland and northwestward to the Yukon and Labrador. It grows from 12 to 18 m (40 to 60 ft) high, and its leaves are highly fragrant and resinous. The balsam fir, probably the best known of the true firs, is used for pulpwood and yields the oleoresin known as Canada balsam.

The noble fir, found in California, Washington, and Oregon, grows to a height of 30 to 60 m (100 to 200 ft), with a trunk as large as 2.4 m (8 ft) in diameter. The alpine fir is smaller than the noble fir, growing commonly from 24 to 30 m (80 to 100 ft) high. It is found from New Mexico to Alaska in the Rocky Mountains. The lowland or grand fir, growing from Montana to the Pacific Coast, at times reaches a height of 91 m (300 ft). True firs do not have the resin ducts that typify true pines or spruce, although these trees all resemble one another in softness of wood.

OAK

Oak, common name for a large genus of hardwood trees that are widespread in the North Temperate Zone. The oak genus contains about 450 species. Oaks are distinguished from the other ten or so genera in the beech family, to which the oak genus belongs, by various technical characteristics of their minute, clustered flowers, but they are easily recognized by their distinctive fruit, the acorn. The related tan oak, one species of which occurs in the coastal ranges of California and Oregon, also produces an acorn. The tan oak differs from the oak genus in its upright rather than hanging male flower clusters.

About 60 species of oak occur in the United States and Canada, with about 150 additional species in Mexico. They grow in a variety of habitats, from seacoasts to high mountain slopes and from wet lowlands to high, dry mesas. Flowering occurs in the spring, before the new leaves appear, and large quantities of pollen are shed into the wind. The trees may be deciduous (losing their leaves in the fall) or evergreen. Most eastern United States species are deciduous—the live oak of the southeastern coastal plain being a notable exception—whereas the western United States has both many evergreen and many deciduous species.

Oaks produce durable, tough wood and are important lumber trees. The wood is used in cabinetry and barrel making and as flooring and veneers. Corks are made from the thick, spongy bark of the cork oak, which occurs in the Mediterranean region. Several species yield tannins, which are used in the leather-tanning industry, and others yield dyes from their bark. Oaks are of some horticultural importance, but because most are slow growing, they are more often planted in public parks and gardens than in private lawns. Scarlet oak, willow oak, and pin oak, however, are moderate to fast-growing species that are well suited to both purposes.

BEECH

Beech, common name for a family of woody flowering plants that often dominate temperate forests, and for its representative genus. The beech family contains some 7 genera and nearly 800 species. Many of its members—including oaks, chestnuts, and beeches—are important sources of timber, food, and other useful materials.

The flowers in the beech groups are usually individually inconspicuous, with bractlike floral tubes (perianths); female and male flowers are borne separately in dense clusters called spikes or, if pendulous, catkins. The male catkins are often conspicuous in the spring, when they shed their pollen, as in oaks. A unique feature of the family is the cupule, a cuplike, often scale-covered structure that surrounds the single-seeded nut. The cap of an acorn is a good example of a cupule.

They also occur in the Andes of southern South America. Members of the family are conspicuous or dominant in the hardwood forests of both the northern and southern hemispheres.

The beech genus itself is a group of about ten species of deciduous trees native to the North Temperate Zone. The pale, smooth bark and elongated winter buds are characteristic features. The American beech is the only species native to the United States, where it occurs extensively east of the Mississippi River. The European beech was introduced into North America in Colonial times and is often found in parks. The copper beech, with late-appearing, copper-coloured leaves, and the weeping beech, with hanging branches, are cultivated varieties of the European beech. The fruits of beech, called beechnuts or beechmast, contain nearly 50 percent oil and are used as pig feed in Europe. The wood is extensively used in furniture and flooring. Old-fashioned clothespins are also made of beech.

Beeches are placed in an order with three other families. The southern beech family contains a single genus confined to the southern hemisphere. Its some 35 species include both deciduous and evergreen trees. Southern beeches are exploited for timber and indirectly as food: Fungi that grow on some are eaten, and the wood of others, partially rotted, is used as cattle feed. The other families of the order are the birch family and a one-genus family of shrubs and trees restricted to Queensland and northeastern Australia.

BIRCH

Birch, common name for a family of woody trees or shrubs that produce separate, abundant, tiny male and female flowers in dense clusters. The family is widely distributed in temperate and arctic regions of the northern hemisphere, reaching the southern hemisphere only in South America. The family contains 6 genera and about 150 species.

Birch trees of the family's representative genus produce close-grained wood of uniform texture that is used in furniture, flooring, plywood, and veneers. Birch beer, once popular, is derived from the sap. The bark of paper birch was used by Native Americans to build canoes. Oil of wintergreen, once derived from the bark of sweet birch, is now manufactured synthetically. Several species are useful ornamentals the European white birch, which has many horticultural varieties. One genus is the source of hazelnuts and filberts, which have been used as food since ancient times.

The family also contains alder, hornbeam, ironwood or hop hornbeam, among others. Most are shrubs or short-lived trees that are too small when mature to provide useful lumber. Red alder of the Pacific Northwest is an important exception, providing wood for inexpensive furniture.

Members of the birch family exhibit several adaptations to fertilization by wind pollination, which is common throughout the group. Separate clusters of male and female flowers are produced on the same plant, developing in the fall and maturing in the early spring. Sepals and petals are very small or entirely absent, exposing the pollen-bearing stamens and pollen-collecting pistils to the wind. Enormous quantities of small, easily wind-dispersed pollen grains are shed in the spring by male flowers. The female flowers, however, are not fully mature when the pollen is shed; the styles and pollen-receiving stigmas have formed, but the ovules, which must be fertilized to mature into seeds, have not formed. The pollen remains lodged in the tissue of the styles for several weeks while the ovules mature. Fertilization and seed production follow this process.

Chapter 7

Rubber Yielding Plants

MULBERRY

Mulberry, common name for a family of mostly woody flowering dicot plants, widespread in the tropics, with some extensions into temperate areas, and for its representative genus. The family contains about 48 genera and 1200 species and has small, clustered, unisexual flowers, typical of the nettle order, to which it belongs. Members of the mulberry family are distinguished from the other members of the order by the presence of milky sap containing latex.

The female flowers are often borne on the inside of a fleshy structure called a receptacle, which expands greatly as the fruit matures. Two well-known examples are the fig and the breadfruit. The fruits of these plants actually are derived from many flowers borne on a common receptacle and are termed compound fruits.

The mulberry genus contains about seven species of trees native to the temperate and subtropical northern hemisphere. Two species are native to North America: red mulberry, widespread in the eastern United States; and Texas mulberry, a small tree or shrub that occurs scattered across the southwestern United States and northern Mexico. White mulberry has been cultivated for centuries in China, and its leaves are the main food of the silkworm. Both the tree and the worm were introduced into the United States; the attempt to form a silk industry failed, but the white mulberry has become naturalized in the eastern and southern United States. Another important member of the family is osage orange.

NETTLE

Nettle, common name for a flowering plant family, and for its representative genus. The family comprises over 1000 species placed in 45 genera. Their stems and leaves are often armed with hollow hairs filled with a stinging liquid. The brittle, gland-tipped hairs are easily broken, and the liquid, if injected into the skin, produces a burning sensation that may be of temporary or long duration. The sting of the stinging nettle lasts only a few minutes, whereas that of an Australian species produces such a severe reaction that death has been reported in a few cases. Nettles are of little economic importance. Ramie fibre, or China grass, obtained from a nettle species of Southeast Asia, is finer than hemp and stronger than cotton, but it is difficult to extract.

The family belongs to an order, mainly tropical in distribution although with many temperate members as well, that has traditionally included about 2400 species placed in six families, although recent information places 6000 species divided into three families in the order. Other important families in the order are the mulberry family, with about 3000 species, and the elm family, with about 2000 species. The elm and mulberry families are mostly woody, whereas the nettle family is mostly herbaceous. The flowers, usually unisexual (either male or female), are small and lack petals. They are often wind-pollinated, and each female flower produces a single seed.

HEMP

Hemp, common name for an Asian annual herb, and also for its strong, pliable fibres. This species is often called true hemp or Indian hemp. It is cultivated in Eurasia, the United States, and Chile. A hemp plant may be as small as 91 cm (36 in) or as high as 5 m (15 ft), depending upon the climate and soil type. The male plants bear flowers in axillary racemes and die soon after pollination. Female plants bear flowers in short, crowded spikes and die soon after the seed matures. Plants of both sexes are used for fibre.

Hemp stems are hollow and have a fibrous inner bark. The fibres from this bark are used to make a great variety of textile products, including coarse fabrics, ropes, sailcloth, and packing cloth. Soft fibres, used for making clothing fabrics in Asia, are obtained from hemp harvested at the time of pollination; strong, coarse fibres are obtained from mature plants. The fibres are removed and processed by methods similar to those used in processing flax. Partially decomposed, the stalks are dried, broken, and shaken to separate the woody stalks from the fibres.

The seed of hemp is commonly used as birdseed. Hempseed also yields an oil, called oil of hemp, used in the manufacture of soap and oil paints. A resin, called charas, produced by female flower heads and seeds of hemp, is used in narcotic smoking mixtures in India. Flowers and leaves of hemp are used to produce the narcotics bhang, hashish, and marijuana.

Unrelated plants that are commonly called hemp include henequen, sisal, bowstring hemp, and Manila hemp. Sunn hemp is obtained from a leguminous herb native to India.

ELM

Elm, common name for trees and shrubs of a family widespread throughout the North Temperate Zone. The tall, deciduous trees of the representative genus have straight-veined elliptic leaves. The purple or yellowish flowers bloom in clusters and appear before the leaves unfold.

The most common and most popular of the North American elms is the American elm, a tree valued for its ornamental shade qualities, which often grows to 37 m (120 ft). Five other species from which numerous horticultural varieties have been developed, are native to the United States. The Chinese elm is a small half-evergreen tree, frequently planted in the South and in California. The red (or slippery) elm is a common species of medium height. The rock (or cork) elm, valued for its corky, winged twigs, is hardy in the New England area and northern portions of the United States. The wahoo (or winged) elm, is a small tree found primarily in Florida, Louisiana, and Arkansas.

Another important species of elm is the English elm, which grows up to 30 m (100 ft) high; occasional specimens are much taller. Found throughout western Asia, Europe, and northern Africa, it has been introduced into the United States and planted along the streets of many cities. The wood is compact, durable, and water resistant and is used for the manufacture of numerous items. The outer bark is used medicinally; dyes are also made from it. Also in the family, the hackberry genus contains about 80 species of trees and shrubs, some of which produce edible fruits.

In recent years the elm population in the United States has been markedly decreased by Dutch elm disease. The disease was introduced into the United States accidentally from the Netherlands. Although Dutch elm disease can not be eliminated, effective control programmes can slow the spread of the disease and greatly reduce the loss of trees. Several disease-resistant varieties of elm have also been developed.

Elm trees are also frequently destroyed by insects that feed on their foliage. Examples of these insects include the gypsy moth, the tussock moth, and the bagworm. The elm-leaf beetle is perhaps the most destructive to the foliage of the elm. It is a small yellowish-brown beetle, which begins to feed while the leaves are still young, eating large, round holes into them. The adult elm-leaf beetle deposits clusters of eggs on the undersides of the leaves and dies soon thereafter. The larvae feed voraciously on the leaves. Phloem necrosis, another serious disease, is caused by a virus carried by an insect, the leafhopper.

Japanese zelkova, an elm species resistant to Dutch elm disease, has replaced the American elm as an ornamental tree in many areas of the United States. The name elm is also applied in Australia to a tall shrub of the nightshade family.

CANNABIS

Cannabis, genus containing a coarse, tall, hairy annual herb that provides fibre from its stems, oil from its seeds, and drugs from its leaves and flowers. The only species of Cannabis, also called hemp or India hemp, is a native of Central Asia but is widely cultivated and found as a weed throughout North

America. The plant grows up to 1.8 m (6 ft) tall, with coarsely-toothed, palmately divided leaves and inconspicuous clusters of flowers. Depending on the product desired, the methods and areas of production vary.

Hemp is grown mainly in temperate regions. Seeds yield a drying oil used in the manufacture of varnish, paints, and soap. The seeds are also used as bird feed. The fibres have a variety of uses in textiles and in rope. The drugs bhang, hashish, and marijuana contain as their principal component narcotic resins found mostly in the glandular hairs of the plants. These resins are most abundant under hot, tropical conditions. In the United States, cannabis may be grown only under government permit.

ROPE

Rope, a flexible line made of fibres or wires twisted or braided together for tensile strength. Ropes may be made of natural fibres, such as cotton, hemp, jute, flax, manila, or sisal; of synthetic filaments, such as nylon, polyester, or glass fibres; or of metallic wire.

Rope making as a craft dates back to prehistory. At first fibres were twisted by hand, but by 3500 BC the Egyptians were using special tools to fashion ropes from papyrus fibres and leather strips. Hemp, used in Asia as early as 2800 BC, was adopted in Europe around 200 BC and remained the standard material for ropes until the 19th century, when it was replaced by Manila hemp, an unrelated plant from the Philippines. The introduction of synthetic fibres in the 1950s in turn replaced Manila hemp as the prime rope material.

Fibres for rope making must first be *carded* (combed), then spun by a process similar to that used for wool or cotton yarn. The spun fibres are twisted into strands by a process known as forming. Several strands are then twisted together by rope-laying machines. Although machines that automate the combing, forming, and rope-laying processes were developed in the mid-19th century, rope is still made in many places by an earlier method known as the *rope walk.* In this method, a device equipped with hooks, known as a traveller, moves slowly on rails and twists the fibres into strands; a second traveller twists the strands into rope.

MARIJUANA

Marijuana, common name for a drug made from the dried leaves and flowering tops of the Indian hemp plant *Cannabis sativa*. People smoke, chew, or eat marijuana for its hallucinogenic and intoxicating effects. It is known by a number of slang names, including "pot," "grass," "reefer," "weed," and "Mary Jane."

The flowering tops of the *Cannabis* plant secrete a sticky resin that contains the active ingredient of marijuana, known as delta-9-tetrahydrocannabinol (THC). The plant has both male and female forms, and the sticky flowers of the female plant are the most potent. Hashish is a similar drug prepared from the same plant. It differs from marijuana in that it is comprised of only the resin from the plant, whereas marijuana is made up of flowering tops and leaves.

Known in India, Central Asia, and China as early as 3000 BC, marijuana has long been used as both a medicine and an intoxicant. It gained widespread use in the United States in the 1960s and 1970s, becoming the second most popular drug after alcohol. In subsequent decades its use continued to increase, particularly among American teens. According to a survey prepared in 1998 by the United States Drug Enforcement Agency, marijuana use among teenagers increased almost 300 percent from 1992 to 1998.

Most countries consider marijuana an illegal substance, but individual countries vary on how they prosecute the use and possession of marijuana. Some countries only impose small fines, while others impose harsher punishment, including imprisonment.

Effects

Many users describe two phases of marijuana intoxication: initial stimulation, which includes giddiness and euphoria, followed by sedation and pleasant tranquility. Mood changes are often accompanied by altered perceptions of time and space.

Thinking processes become disrupted by fragmentary ideas and memories. Many users report increased appetite, heightened sensory awareness, and general feelings of pleasure.

Negative effects of marijuana use can include confusion, acute panic reactions, anxiety attacks, fear, a sense of helplessness, and loss of self-control. Chronic marijuana users may develop amotivational syndrome characterized by passivity, decreased motivation, and preoccupation with taking drugs. Like alcohol intoxication, marijuana intoxication impairs judgment, comprehension, memory, speech, problem-solving ability, reaction time, and driving skills.

The effects of long-term marijuana use on the intellect have not been established, and there is no evidence that marijuana causes brain damage. Smoking marijuana can damage the lungs, however, and long-term use may increase the risk of lung cancer. Although marijuana is not physically addicting and no physical withdrawal symptoms occur when use is discontinued, psychological dependence develops in some 10 to 20 percent of long-term regular users.

Medical Uses

Some people find that marijuana combats the unpleasant symptoms associated with medical conditions. But the potential medical uses of marijuana are hard to assess, as there have been few clinical trials. Pure THC has been shown to improve appetite and prevent the severe weight loss associated with acquired immunodeficiency syndrome (AIDS), and it also reduces the nausea caused by cancer chemotherapy and radiation treatments. A synthetic version of THC sold under the brand name Marinol is available in capsule form as a prescription medicine in the United States for these uses.

Compared to smoked marijuana, however, this drug is slower to provide symptom relief due to the time required for the drug to be absorbed into the bloodstream. Marijuana is also reported to have beneficial effects in treating pain and muscle spasms in patients with multiple sclerosis (MS). Many people who suffer from MS and other chronic diseases report that marijuana provides symptom relief when all other medications fail.

In the United States, the potential medical benefits of marijuana have sparked a debate about the legalization of marijuana for medical purposes. Federal laws prohibit the use, possession, growth, or distribution of marijuana for any purpose. Marijuana is classified in the United States as a Schedule I substance, defined as having a high potential for abuse, no accepted medical use, and no accepted safety for use in medically supervised treatment.

However, since 1996 voters in 11 states—Alaska, Arizona, California, Colourado, Hawaii, Maine, Montana, Nevada, Oregon, Vermont, and Washington—have approved so-called medical marijuana laws. Except in Arizona, these laws allow patients with certain diseases, such as cancer and AIDS, to grow and use marijuana with a physician's approval for medical purposes, mainly to alleviate extreme pain, nausea, lack of appetite, and other chronic symptoms when other drugs are ineffective. Under most of these laws, qualifying patients must carry special identification cards.

The Court ruled that marijuana distributors cannot offer a medical-necessity defence to avoid a federal conviction for marijuana manufacture, distribution, and possession. In 2005 the Court ruled in *Gonzales* v. *Raich* that the federal government can prosecute violators of federal drug laws even in states that have medical marijuana laws. Although the decision did not overturn those state laws, it did override any provisions exempting patients in possession of medical marijuana from raids, arrest, and prosecution by federal authorities.

In the United Kingdom large-scale clinical trials of cannabis-based medicines for pain and multiple sclerosis (MS) were initiated in 2000. In 2001 the federal government of Canada approved the use of marijuana for medical purposes. In April 2005 a cannabis-derived drug developed by a U.K.-based pharmaceutical company was approved for use by prescription in Canada for relief of neuropathic pain from MS.

BANANA

Banana, common name for any of a genus of tropical, treelike herbs and also for their fruit. Species of the genus are native to Southeast Asia but are now grown extensively in all tropical countries for their fruit, fibre, or foliage. The banana is a large, herbaceous plant with a perennial root, or rhizome, from which the plant is perpetuated by sprouts or suckers. In the tropics the stems are annual—that is, they die after perfecting the fruit, and new stems are developed from buds in the rootstock.

These stems, or buds, are the common means of propagating and making new plantations, and the growth is so rapid that the fruit is usually ripe within ten months after the offsets are planted. When fully grown the stem attains a height of 3 to 12 m (10 to 40 ft) and is surmounted by a crown of large oval leaves up to 3 m (10 ft) long, with a strong fleshy footstalk and midrib.

The flowers spring in great spikes from the centre of the crown of leaves and are arranged in whorl-like clusters along the spike; the female flowers occupy the base of the spike, and the male the apex. The fruits vary in length from about 10 to 30 cm (about 4 to 12 in). The average weight of a bunch is about 11 kg (about 25 lb), but individual bunches often exceed 18 kg (40 lb). A stalk bears only once, dies down, and is replaced by sprouts, two or three of which are allowed to bear fruit.

The fruit of the plantain, or cooking banana, is larger, coarser, and less sweet than the kinds that are generally eaten raw. The edible part of the banana contains, on the average, 75 percent water, 21 percent carbohydrate, and about 1 percent each of fat, protein, fibre, and ash. Other parts of the plant abound in fibre, which can be used in the manufacture of paper and cordage. One species is the source of Manila hemp.

POLYMER

Polymer, substance consisting of large molecules that are made of many small, repeating units called monomers, or mers. The number of repeating units in one large molecule is called the degree of polymerization. Materials with a very high degree of polymerization are called high polymers. Polymers consisting of only one kind of repeating unit are called homopolymers. Copolymers are formed from several different repeating units.

Most of the organic substances found in living matter, such as protein, wood, chitin, rubber, and resins, are polymers. Many synthetic materials, such as plastics, fibres (; Rayon), adhesives, glass, and porcelain, are also to a large extent polymeric substances.

Structure of Polymers

Polymers can be subdivided into three, or possibly four, structural groups. The molecules in *linear polymers* consist of long chains of monomers joined by bonds that are rigid to a certain degree—the monomers cannot rotate freely with respect to each other. Typical examples are polyethylene, polyvinyl alcohol, and polyvinyl chloride (PVC).

Branched polymers have side chains that are attached to the chain molecule itself. Branching can be caused by impurities or by the presence of monomers that have several reactive groups. Chain polymers composed of monomers with side groups that are part of the monomers, such as polystyrene or polypropylene, are not considered branched polymers.

In *cross-linked polymers,* two or more chains are joined together by side chains. With a small degree of cross-linking, a loose network is obtained that is essentially two dimensional. High degrees of cross-linking result in a tight three-dimensional structure. Cross-linking is usually caused by chemical reactions. An example of a two-dimensional cross-linked structure is vulcanized rubber, in which cross-links are formed by sulfur atoms. Thermosetting plastics are examples of highly cross-linked polymers; their structure is so rigid that when heated they decompose or burn rather than melt.

Synthesis

Two general methods exist for forming large molecules from small monomers: *addition polymerization* and *condensation polymerization.* In the chemical process called addition polymerization, monomers join together without the loss of atoms from the molecules. Some examples of addition polymers are polyethylene, polypropylene, polystyrene, polyvinyl acetate, and polytetrafluoroethylene (Teflon).

In condensation polymerization, monomers join together with the simultaneous elimination of atoms or groups of atoms. Typical condensation polymers are polyamides, polyesters, and certain polyurethanes.

In 1983 a new method of addition polymerization called *group transfer polymerization* was announced. An activating group within the molecule initiating the process transfers to the end of the growing polymer chain as individual monomers insert themselves in the group. The method has been used for acrylic plastics; it should prove applicable to other plastics as well.

FIG

Fig, common name for plants of a genus of the mulberry family, and for the fruits of these plants. The common commercial fig, native to southwest Asia, is widely cultivated in tropical and subtropical countries. It is a low, deciduous tree, about 5 to 8 m (about 15 to 25 ft) tall, having deeply lobed, alternate leaves that are rough above and smooth beneath; branches are covered with downy, greenish bark.

The small flowers of the fig plant are borne on the inner surface of a fleshy, hollow organ called a receptacle, and the fruit is the result of further growth of the receptacle. Many commercial fig varieties produce no fertile pollen, and as fruit development cannot proceed without fertilization, pollen of the wild fig is used for these varieties. Fruits of other varieties develop without fertilization. To ensure pollination in fig orchards, flower branches of the wild fig are suspended in the vicinity of cultivated fig trees, a process known as caprification. Propagation is usually accomplished by cuttings.

Commercial production of cultivated figs is widespread throughout the Mediterranean region. Most of the fruit is dried before marketing. In the United States, the major centres are California and Texas. The more popular Californian varieties are packed fresh or dried. Most Texas figs are canned.

Another species of fig, the sycamore fig, is a taller tree that also bears edible fruit. The figs are pear-shaped, sweet, and slightly aromatic but inferior to the common fig. This tree is the true sycamore, mentioned several times in the Old Testament, and is a favourite shade tree in the Middle East. The pipal, or sacred fig, is another tall member of the genus, growing in Southeast Asia. It is venerated by Buddhists and Brahmins, to whom it is known as the bo tree.

The common rubber plant, which is familiar in United States homes and conservatories, is a species of fig. In Southeast Asia, its native home, the plant's overall growth is much greater than under temperate conditions, and in this form it is known as the India rubber tree, a source of Assam rubber.

The banyan tree, or Indian fig, produces edible fruits. Two figs native to the subtropical United States develop from seeds germinated on the trunks of trees. Aerial roots are extended down the sides of the trunks, eventually establishing contact with the ground.

BO TREE

Bo Tree, common name for a fig tree of India, also known as bodhi tree, pipal, or peepul. Buddha is said to have received his Enlightenment (*bodhi*) while sitting under a bo tree at the site of the present-day town of Buddh Gaya, India, and the bo tree is therefore sacred to the followers of Buddhism. In the ruins of Anuradhapura, Sri Lanka, is a sacred bo tree that, according to tradition, was planted in the 3rd century BC and grown from a branch of the tree at Buddh Gaya. Each year thousands of pilgrims pay homage to the tree. Bo trees grow to a great age and to a height of about 30 m (about 100 ft).

BANYAN

Banyan, common name for a large Indian tree, remarkable for numerous aerial roots that, growing down from the branches, take root in the soil and form prop roots or secondary trunks. In this manner the tree spreads over a large area. As the tree ages, the original trunk decays, and the tree breaks up into several sections, the props becoming separate trunks for the various sections.

The banyan is a species of fig, with ovate, heart-shaped, entire leaves about 15 cm (about 6 in) long. The fruit is scarlet, not larger than a cherry, and grows in pairs from the axils of the leaves. The seeds seldom germinate in the ground, but, deposited by birds in the crowns of palm trees, germinate there and send down roots that embrace and eventually kill the palms.

A famous banyan in the Botanical Gardens in Kolkata is more than a century old. The main trunk is more than 12 m (more than 40 ft) in circumference; it has 230 prop roots 1.8 to 3 m (6 to 10 ft) around, and more than 3000 smaller trunks.

PLASTICS

Plastics, materials made up of large, organic (carbon-containing) molecules that can be formed into a variety of products. The molecules that compose plastics are long carbon chains that give plastics many of their useful properties. In general, materials that are made up of long, chainlike molecules are called polymers.

The word *plastic* is derived from the words *plasticus* and *plastikos* (Greek "to mold," or "fit for molding"). Plastics can be made hard as stone, strong as steel, transparent as glass, light as wood, and elastic as rubber. Plastics are also lightweight, waterproof, chemical resistant, and produced in almost any colour. More than 50 families of plastics have been produced, and new types are currently under development.

Like metals, plastics come in a variety of grades. For instance, nylons are plastics that are separated by different properties, costs, and the manufacturing processes used to produce them. Also like metals, some plastics can be alloyed, or blended, to combine the advantages possessed by several different plastics. Some types of impact-resistant (shatterproof) plastics and heat-resistant plastics are made by blending different plastics together.

Plastics are moldable, synthetic (chemically-fabricated) materials derived mostly from fossil fuels, such as oil, coal, or natural gas. The raw forms of other materials, such as glass, metals, and clay, are also moldable. The key difference between these materials and plastics is that plastics consist of long molecules that give plastics many of their unique properties, while glass, metals, and clay consist of short molecules.

Uses of Plastics

Plastics are indispensable to our modern way of life. Many people sleep on pillows and mattresses filled with a type of plastic—either cellular polyurethane or polyester. At night, people sleep under blankets and bedspreads made of acrylic plastics, and in the morning, they step out of bed onto polyester and nylon carpets.

The cars we drive, the computers we use, the utensils we cook with, the recreational equipment we play with, and the houses and buildings we live and work in all include important plastic components. The average car contains almost 136 kg (almost 300 lb) of plastics—nearly 12 percent of the vehicle's overall weight. Telephones, textiles, compact discs, paints, plumbing fixtures, boats, and furniture are other domestic products made of plastics. In 1979 the volume of plastics produced in the United States surpassed the volume of domestically produced steel.

Plastics are used extensively by many key industries, including the automobile, aerospace, construction, packaging, and electrical industries. The aerospace industry uses plastics to make strategic military parts for missiles, rockets, and aircraft. Plastics are also used in specialized fields, such as the health industry, to make medical instruments, dental fillings, optical lenses, and biocompatible joints.

General Properties of Plastics

Plastics possess a wide variety of useful properties and are relatively inexpensive to produce. They are lighter than many materials of comparable strength, and unlike metals and wood, plastics do not rust or rot. Most plastics can be produced in any colour. They can also be manufactured as clear as glass, translucent (transmitting small amounts of light), or opaque (impenetrable to light).

Plastics have a lower density than that of metals, so plastics are lighter. Most plastics vary in density from 0.9 to 2.2 g/cm^3 (0.45 to 1.5 oz/cu in), compared to steel's density of 7.85 g/cm^3 (5.29 oz/cu in). Plastic can also be reinforced with glass and other fibres to form incredibly strong materials.

Nylon reinforced with glass can have a tensile strength (resistance of a material to being elongated or pulled apart) of up to 165 Mega Pascal (24,000 psi).

Plastics have some disadvantages. When burned, some plastics produce poisonous fumes. Although certain plastics are specifically designed to withstand temperatures as high as 288° C (550° F), in general plastics are not used when high heat resistance is needed. Because of their molecular stability, plastics do not easily break down into simpler components. As a result, disposal of plastics creates a solid waste problem.

Chemistry of Plastics

Plastics consist of very long molecules each composed of carbon atoms linked into chains. One type of plastic, known as polyethylene, is composed of extremely long molecules that each contain over 200,000 carbon atoms. These long, chainlike molecules give plastics unique properties and distinguish plastics from materials, such as metals, that have short, crystalline molecular structures.

Although some plastics are made from plant oils, the majority are made from fossil fuels. Fossil fuels contain hydrocarbons (compounds containing hydrogen and carbon), which provide the building blocks for long polymer molecules. These small building blocks, called monomers, link together to form long carbon chains called polymers. The process of forming these long molecules from hydrocarbons is known as polymerization. The molecules typically form viscous, sticky substances known as resins, which are used to make plastic products.

Ethylene, is a gaseous hydrocarbon. When it is subjected to heat, pressure, and certain catalysts (substances used to enable faster chemical reactions), the ethylene molecules join together into long, repeating carbon chains. These joined molecules form a plastic resin known as polyethylene.

Joining identical monomers to make carbon chains is called addition polymerization, because the process is similar to stringing many identical beads on a string. Plastics made by addition polymerization include polyethylene, polypropylene, polyvinyl chloride, and polystyrene. Joining two or more different monomers of varying lengths is known as condensation polymerization, because water or other by-products are eliminated as the polymer forms. Condensation polymers include nylon (polyamide), polyester, and polyurethane.

The properties of a plastic are determined by the length of the plastic's molecules and the specific monomer present. Elastomers are plastics composed of long, tightly twisted molecules. These coiled molecules allow the plastic to stretch and recoil like a spring. Rubber bands and flexible silicone caulking are examples of elastomers.

The carbon backbone of polymer molecules often bonds with smaller side chains consisting of other elements, including chlorine, fluorine, nitrogen, and silicon. These side chains give plastics some distinguishing characteristics. When chlorine atoms substitute for hydrogen atoms along the carbon chain, the result is polyvinyl chloride, one of the most versatile and widely used plastics in the world. The addition of chlorine makes this plastic harder and more heat resistant.

Different plastics have advantages and disadvantages associated with the unique chemistry of each plastic. Longer polymer molecules become more entangled (like spaghetti noodles), which gives plastics containing these longer polymers high tensile strength and high impact resistance. However, plastics made from longer molecules are more difficult to mold.

Thermoplastics and Thermosetting Plastics

All plastics, whether made by addition or condensation polymerization, can be divided into two groups: thermoplastics and thermosetting plastics. These terms refer to the different ways these types of plastics respond to heat. Thermoplastics can be repeatedly softened by heating and hardened by cooling. Thermosetting plastics, on the other hand, harden permanently after being heated once.

The reason for the difference in response to heat between thermoplastics and thermosetting plastics lies in the chemical structures of the plastics. Thermoplastic molecules, which are linear or slightly branched, do not chemically bond with each other when heated. Instead, thermoplastic chains are held together by weak van der Waal forces (weak attractions between the molecules) that cause the long molecular chains to clump together like piles of entangled spaghetti. Thermoplastics can be heated and cooled, and consequently softened and hardened, repeatedly, like candle wax. For this reason, thermoplastics can be remolded and reused almost indefinitely.

Thermosetting plastics consist of chain molecules that chemically bond, or cross-link, with each other when heated. When thermosetting plastics cross-link, the molecules create a permanent, three-dimensional network that can be considered one giant molecule. Once cured, thermosetting plastics cannot be remelted, in the same way that cured concrete cannot be reset. Consequently, thermosetting plastics are often used to make heat-resistant products, because these plastics can be heated to temperatures of 260° C (500° F) without melting.

The different molecular structures of thermoplastics and thermosetting plastics allow manufacturers to customise the properties of commercial plastics for specific applications. Because thermoplastic materials consist of individual molecules, properties of thermoplastics are largely influenced by molecular weight. For instance, increasing the molecular weight of a thermoplastic material increases its tensile strength, impact strength, and fatigue strength (ability of a material to withstand constant stress). Conversely, because thermosetting plastics consist of a single molecular network, molecular weight does not significantly influence the properties of these plastics. Instead, many properties of thermosetting plastics are determined by adding different types and amounts of fillers and reinforcements, such as glass fibres

MANUFACTURING PLASTIC PRODUCTS

The process of forming plastic resins into plastic products is the basis of the plastics industry. Many different processes are used to make plastic products, and in each process, the plastic resin must be softened or sufficiently liquefied to be shaped.

Forming Thermoplastics

Although some processes are used to manufacture both thermoplastics and thermosetting plastics, certain processes are specific to forming thermoplastics.

Injection Molding

Injection molding uses a piston or screw to force plastic resin through a heated tube into a mold, where the plastic cools and hardens to the shape of the mold. The mold is then opened and the plastic cast removed. Thermoplastic items made by injection molding include toys, combs, car grills, and various containers.

Extrusion

Extrusion is a continuous process, as opposed to all other plastic production processes, which start over at the beginning of the process after each new part is removed from the mold. In the extrusion process, plastic pellets are first heated in a long barrel. In a manner similar to that of a pasta-making or sausage-stuffing machine, a rotating screw then forces the heated plastic through a die (device used for forming material) opening of the desired shape.

As the continuous plastic form emerges from the die opening, it is cooled and solidified, and the continuous plastic form is then cut to the desired length. Plastic products made by extrusion include garden hoses, drinking straws, pipes, and ropes. Melted thermoplastic forced through extremely fine die holes can be cooled and woven into fabrics for clothes, curtains, and carpets.

Blow Molding

Blow molding is used to form bottles and other containers from soft, hollow thermoplastic tubes. First a mold is fitted around the outside of the softened thermoplastic tube, and then the tube is heated. Next, air is blown into the softened tube (similar to inflating a balloon), which forces the outside of the softened tube to conform to the inside walls of the mold. Once the plastic cools, the mold is opened and the newly molded container is removed. Blow molding is used to make many plastic containers, including soft-drink bottles, jars, detergent bottles, and storage drums.

Blow Film Extrusion

Blow film extrusion is the process used to make plastic garbage bags and continuous sheets. This process works by extruding a hollow, sealed-end thermoplastic tube through a die opening. As the flattened plastic tube emerges from the die opening, air is blown inside the hollow tube to stretch and thin the tube (like a balloon being inflated) to the desired size and wall thickness.

The plastic is then air-cooled and pulled away on take-up rollers to a heat-sealing operation. The heat-sealer cuts and seals one end of the thinned, flattened thermoplastic tube, creating various bag lengths for products such as plastic grocery and garbage bags. For sheeting (flat film), the thinned plastic tube is slit along one side and opened to form a continuous sheet.

Calendering

The calendering process forms continuous plastic sheets that are used to make flooring, wall siding, tape, and other products. These plastic sheets are made by forcing hot thermoplastic resin between heated rollers called calenders. A series of secondary calenders further thins the plastic sheets. Paper, cloth, and other plastics may be pressed between layers of calendered plastic to make items such as credit cards, playing cards, and wallpaper.

Thermoforming

Thermoforming is a term used to describe several techniques for making products from plastic sheets. Products made from thermoformed sheets include trays, signs, briefcase shells, refrigerator door liners, and packages. In a vacuum-forming process, hot thermoplastic sheets are draped over a mold. Air is removed from between the mold and the hot plastic, which creates a vacuum that draws the plastic into the cavities of the mold.

When the plastic cools, the molded product is removed. In the pressure-forming process, compressed air is used to drive a hot plastic sheet into the cavities and depressions of a concave, or female, mold. Vent holes in the bottom of the mold allow trapped air to escape.

Forming Thermosetting Plastics

Thermosetting plastics are manufactured by several methods that use heat or pressure to induce polymer molecules to bond, or cross-link, into typically hard and durable products.

Compression Molding

Compression molding forms plastics through a technique that is similar to the way a waffle iron forms waffles from batter. First, thermosetting resin is placed into a steel mold. The application of heat and pressure, which accelerate cross-linking of the resin, softens the material and squeezes it into all parts of the mold to form the desired shape. Once the material has cooled and hardened, the newly formed object is removed from the mold. This process creates hard, heat-resistant plastic products, including dinnerware, telephones, television set frames, and electrical parts.

Laminating

The laminating process binds layers of materials, such as textiles and paper, together in a plastic matrix. This process is similar to the process of joining sheets of wood to make plywood. Resin-impregnated layers of textiles or paper are stacked on hot plates, then squeezed and fused together by heat and pressure, which causes the polymer molecules to cross-link.

The best-known laminate trade name is Formica, which is a product consisting of resin-impregnated layers of paper with decorative patterns such as wood grain, marble, and coloured designs. Formica is often used as a surface finish for furniture, and kitchen and bathroom countertops. Thermosetting resins known as melamine and phenolic resins form the plastic matrix for Formica and other laminates.

Electric circuit boards are also laminated from resin-impregnated paper, fabric, and glass fibres.

Reaction Injection Molding (RIM)

Strong, sizable, and durable plastic products such as automobile body panels, skis, and business machine housings are formed by reaction injection molding. In this process, liquid thermosetting resin is combined with a curing agent (a chemical that causes the polymer molecules to cross-link) and injected into a mold. Most products made by reaction injection molding are made from polyurethane.

Forming Both Types of Plastics

Certain plastic fabrication processes can be used to form either thermoplastics or thermosetting plastics.

Casting

The casting process is similar to that of molding plaster or cement. Fluid thermosetting or thermoplastic resin is poured into a mold, and additives cause the resin to solidify. Photographic film is made by pouring a fluid solution of resin onto a highly polished metal belt. A thin plastic film remains as the solution evapourates. The casting process is also used to make furniture parts, tabletops, sinks, and acrylic window sheets.

Expansion Processes

Thermosetting and thermoplastic resins can be expanded by injecting gases (often nitrogen or methyl chloride) into the plastic melt. As the resin cools, tiny bubbles of gas are trapped inside, forming a cellular plastic structure. This process is used to make foam products such as cushions, pillows, sponges, egg cartons, and polystyrene cups.

Foam plastics can be classified according to their bubble, or cell, structure. Sponges and carpet pads are examples of open-celled foam plastics, in which the bubbles are interconnected. Flotation devices are examples of closed-celled foam plastics, in which the bubbles are sealed like tiny balloons. Foam plastics can also be classified by density (ratio of plastic to cells), by the type of plastic resin used, and by flexibility (rigid or flexible foam). Rigid, closed-celled polyurethane plastics make excellent insulation for refrigerators and freezers.

IMPORTANT TYPES OF PLASTICS

A wide variety of both thermoplastics and thermosetting plastics are manufactured. These plastics have a spectrum of properties that are derived from their chemical compositions. As a result, manufactured plastics can be used in applications ranging from contact lenses to jet body components.

Thermoplastics

Thermoplastic materials are in high demand because they can be repeatedly softened and remolded. The most commonly manufactured thermoplastics are presented in this section in order of decreasing volume of production.

Polyethylene

Polyethylene (PE) resins are milky white, translucent substances derived from ethylene (CH_29CH_2). Polyethylene, with the chemical formula $[8CH_28CH_28]_n$ (where *n* denotes that the chemical formula inside the brackets repeats itself to form the plastic molecule) is made in low- and high-density forms. Low-density polyethylene (LDPE) has a density ranging from 0.91 to 0.93 g/cm3 (0.60 to 0.61 oz/cu in). The molecules of LDPE have a carbon backbone with side groups of four to six carbon atoms attached randomly along the main backbone. LDPE is the most widely used of all plastics, because it is inexpensive, flexible, extremely tough, and chemical-resistant. LDPE is molded into bottles, garment bags, frozen food packages, and plastic toys.

High-density polyethylene (HDPE) has a density that ranges from 0.94 to 0.97 g/cm3 (0.62 to 0.64 oz/cu in). Its molecules have an extremely long carbon backbone with no side groups. As a result, these molecules align into more compact arrangements, accounting for the higher density of

HDPE. HDPE is stiffer, stronger, and less translucent than low-density polyethylene. HDPE is formed into grocery bags, car fuel tanks, packaging, and piping.

Polyvinyl Chloride

Polyvinyl chloride (PVC) is prepared from the organic compound vinyl chloride (CH_29CHCl). PVC is the most widely used of the amorphous plastics. PVC is lightweight, durable, and waterproof. Chlorine atoms bonded to the carbon backbone of its molecules give PVC its hard and flame-resistant properties.

In its rigid form, PVC is weather-resistant and is extruded into pipe, house siding, and gutters. Rigid PVC is also blow molded into clear bottles and is used to form other consumer products, including compact discs and computer casings.

PVC can be softened with certain chemicals. This softened form of PVC is used to make shrink-wrap, food packaging, rainwear, shoe soles, shampoo containers, floor tile, gloves, upholstery, and other products. Most softened PVC plastic products are manufactured by extrusion, injection molding, or casting.

Polypropylene

Polypropylene is polymerized from the organic compound propylene ($CH_38CH9CH_2$) and has a methyl group ($8CH_3$) branching off of every other carbon along the molecular backbone. Because the most common form of polypropylene has the methyl groups all on one side of the carbon backbone, polypropylene molecules tend to be highly aligned and compact, giving this thermoplastic the properties of durability and chemical resistance. Many polypropylene products, such as rope, fibre, luggage, carpet, and packaging film, are formed by injection molding.

Polystyrene

Polystyrene, produced from styrene ($C_6H_5CH9CH_2$), has phenyl groups (six-member carbon ring) attached in random locations along the carbon backbone of the molecule. The random attachment of benzene prevents the molecules from becoming highly aligned. As a result, polystyrene is an amorphous, transparent, and somewhat brittle plastic. Polystyrene is widely used because of its rigidity and superior insulation properties. Polystyrene can undergo all thermoplastic processes to form products such as toys, utensils, display boxes, model aircraft kits, and ballpoint pen barrels. Polystyrene is also expanded into foam plastics such as packaging materials, egg cartons, flotation devices, and styrofoam.

Polyethylene Terephthalate

Polyethylene terephthalate (PET) is formed from the reaction of terephthalic acid ($HOOC8C_6H_48COOH$) and ethylene glycol ($HOCH_28CH_2OH$), which produces the PET monomer $[8OOC8C_6H_48COO8CH_2CH_28]_n$. PET molecules are highly aligned, creating a strong and abrasion-resistant material that is used to produce films and polyester fibres. PET is injection molded into windshield wiper arms, sunroof frames, gears, pulleys, and food trays. This plastic is used to make the trademarked textiles Dacron, Fibre V, Fortrel, and Kodel. Tough, transparent PET films (marketed under the brand name Mylar) are magnetically coated to make both audio and video recording tape.

Acrylonitrile Butadiene Styrene

Acrylonitrile butadiene styrene (ABS) is made by copolymerizing (combining two or more monomers) the monomers acrylonitrile (CH_2CHCN) and styrene ($C_6H_5CH9CH_2$). Acrylonitrile and styrene are dissolved in polybutadiene rubber $[8CH9CH8CH9CH8]_n$, which allows these monomers to form chains by attaching to the rubber molecules.

The advantage of ABS is that this material combines the strength and rigidity of the acrylonitrile and styrene polymers with the toughness of the polybutadiene rubber. Although the cost of producing ABS is roughly twice the cost of producing polystyrene, ABS is considered superior for its hardness, gloss, toughness, and electrical insulation properties. ABS plastic is injection molded to make telephones, helmets, washing machine agitators, and pipe joints. This plastic is thermoformed to make luggage, golf carts, toys, and car grills. ABS is also extruded to make piping, to which pipe joints are easily solvent-cemented.

Polymethyl Methacrylate

Polymethyl methacrylate (PMMA), more commonly known by the generic name acrylic, is polymerized from the hydrocarbon compound methyl methacrylate ($C_4O_2H_8$). PMMA is a hard material and is extremely clear because of the amorphous arrangement of its molecules. As a result, this thermoplastic is used to make optical lenses, watch crystals, aircraft windshields, skylights, and outdoor signs. These PMMA products are marketed under familiar trade names, including Plexiglas, Lucite, and Acrylite. Because PMMA can be cast to resemble marble, it is also used to make sinks, countertops, and other fixtures.

Polyamide

Polyamides (PA), known by the trade name Nylon, consist of highly ordered molecules, which give polyamides high tensile strength. Some polyamides are made by reacting dicarboxylic acid with diamines (carbon molecules with the ion $-NH_2$ on each end), as in nylon-6,6 and nylon-6,10. (The two numbers in each type of nylon represent the number of carbon atoms in the diamine and the dicarboxylic acid, respectively.) Other types of nylon are synthesized by the condensation of amino acids.

Polyamides have mechanical properties such as high abrasion resistance, low coefficients of friction (meaning they are slippery), and tensile strengths comparable to the softer of the aluminum alloys. Therefore, nylons are commonly used for mechanical applications, such as gears, bearings, and bushings. Nylons are also extruded into millions of tons of synthetic fibres every year.

The most commonly used nylon fibres, nylon-6,6 and nylon-6 (single number because this nylon forms by the self-condensation of an amino acid) are made into textiles, ropes, fishing lines, brushes, and other items.

Thermosetting Materials

Because thermosetting plastics cure, or cross-link, after being heated, these plastics can be made into durable and heat-resistant materials. The most commonly manufactured thermosetting plastics are presented below in order of decreasing volume of production.

Polyurethane

Polyurethane is a polymer consisting of the repeating unit $[8R8OOCNH8R'8]_n$, where R may represent a different *alkyl group* than R'. Alkyl groups are chemical groups obtained by removing a hydrogen atom from an *alkane*—a hydrocarbon containing all carbon-carbon single bonds. Most types of polyurethane resin cross-link and become thermosetting plastics. However, some polyurethane resins have a linear molecular arrangement that does not cross-link, resulting in thermoplastics.

Thermosetting polyurethane molecules cross-link into a single giant molecule. Thermosetting polyurethane is widely used in various forms, including soft and hard foams. Soft, open-celled polyurethane foams are used to make seat cushions, mattresses, and packaging. Hard polyurethane foams are used as insulation in refrigerators, freezers, and homes.

Thermoplastic polyurethane molecules have linear, highly crystalline molecular structures that form an abrasion-resistant material. Thermoplastic polyurethanes are molded into shoe soles, car fenders, door panels, and other products.

Phenolics

Phenolic (phenol-formaldehyde) resins, first commercially available in 1910, were some of the first polymers made. Today phenolics are some of the most widely produced thermosetting plastics. They are produced by reacting phenol (C_6H_5OH) with formaldehyde (HCOH). Phenolic plastics are hard, strong, inexpensive to produce, and they possess excellent electrical resistance.

Phenolic resins cure (cross-link) when heat and pressure are applied during the molding process. Phenolic resin-impregnated paper or cloth can be laminated into numerous products, such as electrical circuit boards. Phenolic resins are also compression molded into electrical switches, pan and iron handles, radio and television casings, and toaster knobs and bases.

Melamine-Formaldehyde and Urea-Formaldehyde

Urea-formaldehyde (UF) and melamine-formaldehyde (MF) resins are composed of molecules that cross-link into clear, hard plastics. Properties of UF and MF resins are similar to the properties of phenolic resins. As their names imply, these resins are formed by condensation reactions between urea (H_2NCONH_2) or melamine ($C_3H_6N_6$) and formaldehyde (CH_2O).

Melamine-formaldehyde resins are easily molded in compression and special injection molding machines. MF plastics are more heat-resistant, scratch-proof, and stain-resistant than urea-formaldehyde plastics are. MF resins are used to manufacture dishware, electrical components, laminated furniture veneers, and to bond wood layers into plywood.

Urea-formaldehyde resins form products such as appliance knobs, knife handles, and plates. UF resins are used to give drip-dry properties to wash-and-wear clothes as well as to bond wood chips and wood sheets into chip board and plywood.

Unsaturated Polyesters

Unsaturated polyesters (UP) belong to the polyester group of plastics. Polyesters are composed of long carbon chains containing $[8OOC8C_6H_48COO8CH_28CH_2]_n$. Unsaturated polyesters (an *unsaturated* compound contains multiple bonds) cross-link when the long molecules are joined (copolymerized) by the aromatic organic compound styrene.

Unsaturated polyester resins are often premixed with glass fibres for additional strength. Two types of premixed resins are bulk molding compounds (BMC) and sheet molding compounds (SMC). Both types of compounds are doughlike in consistency and may contain short fibre reinforcements and other additives. Sheet molding compounds are preformed into large sheets or rolls that can be molded into products such as shower floors, small boat hulls, and roofing materials. Bulk molding compounds are also preformed to be compression molded into car body panels and other automobile components.

Epoxy

Epoxy (EP) resins are named for the epoxide groups (cycl-CH_2OCH; *cycl* or *cyclic* refers to the triangle formed by this group) that terminate the molecules. The oxygen along epoxy's carbon chain and the epoxide groups at the ends of the carbon chain give epoxy resins some useful properties. Epoxies are tough, extremely weather-resistant, and do not shrink as they cure (dry).

Epoxies cross-link when a catalyzing agent (hardener) is added, forming a three-dimensional molecular network. Because of their outstanding bonding strength, epoxy resins are used to make coatings, adhesives, and composite laminates. Epoxy has important applications in the aerospace industry. All composite aircraft are made of epoxy. Epoxy is used to make the wing skins for the F-18 and F-22 fighters, as well as the horizontal stabilizer for the F-16 fighter and the B-1 bomber. In addition, almost 20 percent of the Harrier jet's total weight is composed of reinforcements bound with an epoxy matrix. Because of epoxy's chemical resistance and excellent electrical insulation properties, electrical parts such as relays, coils, and transformers are insulated with epoxy.

Reinforced Plastics

Reinforced plastics, called composites, are plastics strengthened with fibres, strands, cloth, or other materials. Thermosetting epoxy and polyester resins are commonly used as the polymer matrix (binding material) in reinforced plastics. Due to a combination of strength and affordability, glass fibres, which are woven into the product, are the most common reinforcing material. Organic synthetic fibres such as aramid (an aromatic polyamide with the commercial name Kevlar) offer greater strength and stiffness than glass fibres, but these synthetic fibres are considerably more expensive.

The Boeing 777 aircraft makes extensive use of lightweight reinforced plastics. Other products made from reinforced plastics include boat hulls and automobile body panels, as well as recreation equipment, such as tennis rackets, golf clubs, and jet skis.

HISTORY OF PLASTICS

Humankind has been using natural plastics for thousands of years. The early Egyptians soaked burial wrappings in natural resins to help preserve their dead. People have been using animal horns and turtle shells (which contain natural resins) for centuries to make items such as spoons, combs, and buttons.

During the mid-19th century, shellac (resinous substance secreted by the lac insect) was gathered in southern Asia and transported to the United States to be molded into buttons, small cases, knobs, phonograph records, and hand-mirror frames. During that time period, gutta-percha (rubberlike sap taken from certain trees in Malaya) was used as the first insulating coating for electrical wires.

In order to find more efficient ways to produce plastics and rubbers, scientists began trying to produce these materials in the labouratory. American inventor Charles Goodyear vulcanized rubber by accidentally dropping a piece of sulfur-treated rubber onto a hot stove. Goodyear discovered that heating sulfur and rubber together improved the properties of natural rubber so that it would no longer become brittle when cold and soft when hot.

In 1862 British chemist Alexander Parkes synthesized a plastic known as pyroxylin, which was used as a coating film on photographic plates. American inventor John W. Hyatt began working on a substitute for ivory billiard balls. Hyatt added camphor to nitrated cellulose and formed a modified natural plastic called celluloid, which became the basis of the early plastics industry. Celluloid was used to make products such as umbrella handles, dental plates, toys, photographic film, and billiard balls.

These early plastics based on natural products shared numerous drawbacks. Many of the necessary natural materials were in short supply, and all proved difficult to mold. Finished products were inconsistent from batch to batch, and most products darkened and cracked with age. Celluloid proved to be a very flammable material.

Due to these shortcomings, scientists attempted to find more reliable plastic source materials. American chemist Leo Hendrik Baekeland made a breakthrough when he created the first commercially successful thermosetting synthetic resin, which was called Bakelite (known today as phenolic resin). Use of Bakelite quickly grew. It has been used to make products such as telephones and pot handles.

The chemistry of joining small molecules into macromolecules became the foundation of an emerging plastics industry. Between 1920 and 1932, the I.G. Farben Company of Germany synthesized polystyrene and polyvinyl chloride, as well as a synthetic rubber called Buna-S. Du Pont made a breakthrough when it introd7uced nylon—a material finer, stronger, and more elastic than silk. Acrylics were being produced by German, British, and U.S. companies.

That same year, the British company Imperial Chemical Industries developed polyethylene. In 1937 polyurethane was invented by the German company Friedrich Bayer & Co, but this plastic was not available to consumers until it was commercialized by U.S. companies in the 1950s. In 1939 the German company I.G. Farbenindustrie filed a patent for polyepoxide (epoxy), which was not sold commercially until a U.S. firm made epoxy resins available to the consumer market almost four years later.

After World War II, the pace of new polymer discoveries accelerated. A small English company developed polyethylene terephthalate (PET). Although Du Pont and Imperial Chemical

Industries produced PET fibres (marketed under the names Dacron and Terylene, respectively) during the postwar era, the use of PET as a material for making bottles, films, and coatings did not become widespread until the 1970s. In the postwar era, research by Bayer and by General Electric resulted in production of plastics such as polycarbonates, which are used to make small appliances, aircraft parts, and safety helmets.

In 1965 introduced a linear, heat-resistant thermoplastic known as polysulfone, which is used to make face shields for astronauts and hospital equipment that can be sterilized in an autoclave (a device that uses high pressure steam for sterilization).

Today, scientists can tailor the properties of plastics to numerous design specifications. Modern plastics are used to make products such as artificial joints, contact lenses, space suits, and other specialized materials. As plastics have become more versatile, use of plastics has grown as well. Annual global demand for plastics is projected to exceed 200 million metric tons (441 billion lb).

Plastics and the Environment

Every year in the United States, consumers throw millions of tons of plastic away—of the estimated 210 million metric tons (232 short tons) of municipal waste produced annually 10.7 percent are plastics. As municipal landfills reach capacity and additional landfill space diminishes across, alternative methods for reducing and disposing of wastes—including plastics—are being explored. Some of these options include reducing consumption of plastics, using biodegradable plastics, and incinerating or recycling plastic waste

Source Reduction

Source reduction is the practice of using less material to manufacture a product. The wall thickness of many plastic and metal containers has been reduced in recent years, and some European countries have proposed to eliminate packaging that cannot be easily recycled.

Biodegradable Plastics

Due to their molecular stability, plastics do not easily break down into simpler components. Plastics are therefore not considered biodegradable. However, researchers are working to develop biodegradable plastics that will disintegrate due to bacterial action or exposure to sunlight. Scientists are incorporating starch molecules into some plastic resins during the manufacturing process.

When these plastics are discarded, bacteria eat the starch molecules. This causes the polymer molecules to break apart, allowing the plastic to decompose. Researchers are also investigating ways to make plastics more biodegradable from exposure to sunlight. Prolonged exposure to ultraviolet radiation from the sun causes many plastics molecules to become brittle and slowly break apart. Researchers are working to create plastics that will degrade faster in sunlight, but not so fast that the plastic begins to degrade while still in use.

Incineration

Some wastes, such as paper, plastics, wood, and other flammable materials can be burned in incinerators. The resulting ash requires much less space for disposal than the original waste would. Because incineration of plastics can produce hazardous air emissions and other pollutants, this process is strictly regulated.

Recycling Plastics

All plastics can be recycled. Thermoplastics can be remelted and made into new products. Thermosetting plastics can be ground, commingled (mixed), and then used as filler in moldable thermoplastic materials. Highly filled and reinforced thermosetting plastics can be pulverized and used in new composite formulations.

Chemical recycling is a depolymerization process that uses heat and chemicals to break plastic molecules down into more basic components, which can then be reused. Another process, called pyrolysis, vapourizes and condenses both thermoplastics and thermosetting plastics into hydrocarbon liquids.

Collecting and sorting used plastics is an expensive and time-consuming process. While about 27 percent of aluminum products, 45 percent of paper products, and 23 percent of glass products are recycled in the United States, only about 5 percent of plastics are currently recovered and recycled. Once plastic products are thrown away, they must be collected and then separated by plastic type. Most modern automated plastic sorting systems are not capable of differentiating between many different types of plastics. However, some advances are being made in these sorting systems to separate plastics by colour, density, and chemical composition. X-ray sensors can distinguish PET from PVC by sensing the presence of chlorine atoms in the polyvinyl chloride material.

If plastic types are not segregated, the recycled plastic cannot achieve high remolding performance, which results in decreased market value of the recycled plastic. Other factors can adversely affect the quality of recycled plastics. These factors include the possible degradation of the plastic during its original life cycle and the possible addition of foreign materials to the scrap recycled plastic during the recycling process. For health reasons, recycled plastics are rarely made into food containers. Instead, most recycled plastics are typically made into items such as carpet fibres, motor oil bottles, trash carts, soap packages, and textile fibres.

Chapter 8

Beverage

DRINKING

Drinking, referring to the drinking of alcoholic beverages, has social, medical, and legal aspects. Alcoholic beverages are present in many cultures and have been used by humans for many centuries, under widely differing customs and mores.

CAFFEINE

Caffeine, an alkaloid ($C_8H_{10}O_2N_4 \cdot H_2O$) found in coffee, tea, cacao, and some other plants. It is also present in most cola beverages. Caffeine was discovered in coffee in 1820. In 1838 it was established that theine, discovered in tea in 1827, is identical to caffeine. The drug increases the blood pressure, stimulates the central nervous system, promotes urine formation, and stimulates the action of the heart and lungs. Caffeine is used in treating migraine because it constricts the dilated blood vessels and thereby reduces the pain. It also increases the potency of analgesics such as aspirin, and it can somewhat relieve asthma attacks by widening the bronchial airways. Caffeine is produced commercially chiefly as a byproduct in making caffeine-free coffee.Caffeine has been suggested as a possible cause of cancer and of birth defects. No studies, however, have yet confirmed any of these charges. Persons who stop drinking coffee do sometimes experience withdrawal headaches.

COFFEE

Coffee, common name for any of a genus of trees of the

madder family, and also for their seeds (beans) and for the beverage brewed from them. Of the 30 or more species of the genus, only three are important: Arabian, robusta, and Liberian. The shrub or small tree, 4.6 to 6 m (15 to 20 ft) high at maturity, bears shiny green, ovate leaves that persist for three to five years and white, fragrant flowers that bloom for only a few days.

During the six or seven months after appearance of the flower, the fruit develops, changing from light green to red and, ultimately, when fully ripe and ready for picking, to deep crimson. The mature fruit, which resembles a cherry, grows in clusters attached to the limb by very short stems, and it usually contains two seeds, or beans, surrounded by a sweet pulp.

Coffee grows well on the islands of Java and Sumatra and in Arabia, India, Africa, the West Indies, and South and Central America. The Americas, where Arabian coffee is grown, produce approximately two-thirds of the world's supply.

Production

The soil in which coffee is grown must be rich, moist, and absorbent enough to accept water readily, but sufficiently loose to allow rapid drainage of excess water. The best soil is composed of leaf mold, other organic matter, and disintegrated volcanic rock. Although coffee trees are damaged easily by frost, they are cultivated in cooler regions.

The growing temperatures range from 13° to 26° C (55° to 80° F). Altitudes of coffee plantations range from sea level to the tropical frost level, about 1,800 m (about 6,000 ft). Robusta coffee and Liberian coffee grow best at altitudes below 900 m (3,000 ft); Arabian coffee flourishes at the higher altitudes. The seeds are planted directly in the field or in specially prepared nurseries.

In the latter case, young selected plants are transplanted later to the fields. Commercial fertilizers are used extensively to promote the growth of stronger, healthier trees with heavier yields. Both the trees and the fruit are subject to insect infestation and microbial diseases, which may be controlled by spraying and proper agricultural management.

Harvesting

The coffee tree produces its first full crop when it is about five years old. Thereafter it produces consistently for 15 or 20 years. Some trees yield 0.9 to 1.3 kg (2 to 3 lb) of marketable beans annually, but 0.45 kg (1 lb) is considered an average annual yield.

Two methods of harvesting are used. One is based on selective picking; the other involves shaking the tree and stripping the fruit. Beans picked by the first technique are generally processed, if water is available, by the so-called wet method, in which the beans are softened in water, depulped mechanically, fermented in large tanks, washed again, and finally dried in the open or in heated, rotating cylinders.

The so-called dry method, used generally for beans harvested by the second technique, entails only drying the beans and removing the outer coverings. In either case the final product, called green coffee, is sorted by hand or machine to remove defective beans and extraneous material and is then graded according to size.

Commercial Crops

The major types of commercial coffee are the arabicas and the robustas. In the western hemisphere the arabicas are subdivided into Brazils and milds. Robustas are produced in the eastern hemisphere exclusively, together with substantial quantities of arabicas. The Brazils consist principally of Santos, Paraná, and Rio, named for the ports from which they are shipped.

Milds are identified by the names of countries or districts in which they are grown, such as Medellín, Armenia, and Manizales coffees from Colombia. Robustas and other arabicas are similarly identified. Green coffee is a major import of the United States; about two-thirds of the 1.2 million metric tons comes from Central and South America, with Brazil and Colombia the two largest suppliers.

Several varieties of green coffee usually are blended and roasted together to produce the tastes, aromas, and flavours popular with consumers. As a rule the beans are heated in rotating, horizontal drums that provide a tumbling action to prevent uneven heating or scorching. Temperatures for roasting range from about 193° C (about 380° F) for a light roast, through about 205° C (about 400° F) for a medium roast, to about 218° C (about 425° F) for a dark roast. The roasted beans are cooled rapidly. Roasted coffee may be packaged and shipped to retail stores, which custom grind it for the customers on purchase, or it may be ground in plate- or roller-type grinding mills before shipment.

Ground coffee loses its unique flavour within about a week unless it is specially packaged. Plastic-and-paper combinations are popular packaging media that afford protection to freshly roasted and ground coffee. Hermetically sealed vacuum, or pressure, cans keep coffee fresh for up to three years.

Characteristics

Coffee contains a complex mixture of chemical components of the bean, some of which are not affected by roasting. Other compounds, particularly those related to the aroma, are produced by partial destruction of the green bean during roasting. Chemicals extracted by hot water are classified as nonvolatile taste components and volatile aroma components. Important nonvolatiles are caffeine, trigonelline, chlorogenic acid, phenolic acids, amino acids, carbohydrates, and minerals. Important volatiles are organic acids, aldehydes, ketones, esters, amines, and mercaptans.

The principal physiological effects of coffee are due to caffeine, an alkaloid that acts as a mild stimulant. In recent years controversy arose over the possibly harmful effects of coffee beyond those recognized for people who should take few or no stimulants, and the dangers of caffeine for the fetuses of pregnant women. These debated studies were not substantiated, however.

Soluble Coffee

Soluble or instant coffee is an important production of the United States coffee industry. In its manufacture an extract is prepared by mixing coarsely ground and roasted coffee with hot water. The water is evapourated from the extract by various methods, including the use of spray driers or high-vacuum equipment. In freeze-dried coffee the coffee extract is frozen, and the water is removed by sublimation. The product is packed in vacuumized, sealed jars or in cans.

Decaffeinated Coffee

Caffeine can be removed from coffee by treating the green beans with chlorinated hydrocarbon solvents. The beans are roasted by ordinary procedures after removal of the solvents. Decaffeinated coffee is used by people hypersensitive to the caffeine present in regular coffee. In the 1980s nonchemical methods of decaffeination became more common.

Coffee Substitutes

The use of substitutes for coffee in the United States is limited. The most important substitute is chicory, although chicory is usually used as an extender. Under United States law, the addition of chicory or any other substance must be clearly stated on the brand label.

TEA

Tea, common name for a family of mostly woody flowering plants, and for one of its important genera. The family, which contains about 600 species placed in 28 genera, is distributed through tropical and subtropical areas, but most species occur in eastern Asia and South America.

Characteristics of the Order

The order to which the tea family belongs is primarily tropical in distribution, centreed in southeastern Asia, with few temperate members. Most members are evergreen trees with broad, simple, resin-containing leaves, although a few climbers and herbs occur. The flowers usually have four or five free, or unfused, sepals (outer flower whorls) and petals (inner floral whorls) and are radially symmetrical. The numerous stamens (male floral organs) are fused either into a ring, as in the tea genus, or into distinct bundles, as in Saint John's wort. When the stamens are united into a ring, the petals are often joined to the ring, as in tea genus. The ovary (female floral organ) is superior; that is, the sepals, petals, and stamens are produced from its base.

The most important source of timber in the order is a family that dominates the rain forests of Malaysia and is also a source of useful resins. This family contains more than 500 species. Members of the family produce a characteristic two-winged fruit, which is distributed by the wind; the wings are formed by persistent sepals.

The Beverage

The tea plant itself is a native of Southeast Asia. The tea brewed from the dried leaves of this plant has been drunk in China since perhaps the 28th century BC and certainly since the 10th century BC, from which time written records of its use survive. It was first brought to Europe by the Dutch in the early 17th century AD.

After the introduction of tea there in 1657, England became the only European country of tea drinkers rather than coffee drinkers. Tea was introduced into North America by early settlers but was heavily taxed by the British, eventually resulting in the well-known Boston Tea Party of 1773, and it has never competed successfully with coffee as the staple beverage. Tea is drunk by about half of the world's population; China, India, Indonesia, Sri Lanka, and Japan are the main producers.

Leaf buds and young leaves are used in making tea, the age of the leaves determining the taste and name of the particular commercial variety. Thus, orange pekoe is made from the youngest leaves, and souchong from the fourth leaves. After picking, the leaves either are dried immediately and completely to produce green teas—such as pan-fired, basket-fired, hyson, and gunpowder—or are partially dried and then allowed to ferment to produce various kinds of black teas, such as orange pekoe, pekoe, congou, and souchong. Oolong tea is partially fired and then steamed, thus being intermediate between green and black teas. After being sorted, all grades of tea are packed in foil-lined chests to prevent the absorption of unpleasant odors or the loss of aroma during shipment. In China, tea is sometimes allowed to absorb the scent from various flowers; jasmine is a particular favourite.

Tea is an aromatic stimulant, containing various polyphenols, essential oils, and caffeine. The concentration of caffeine in tea ranges from 2.5 to 4.5 percent, as contrasted to an average concentration of about 1.5 percent in coffee.

Pests

The tea plant is attacked by several injurious insects, the most important of which is the fagot worm. The tea borer, which is the larva of a cossid moth, attacks the stems and branches of the tea plant. Several species of scale insects attack the tea plant. Several mites also feed on it, including a red spider and the yellow tea mite, which destroys the buds.

CIDER

Cider, sweet or fermented juice of apples, used as a beverage and for making vinegar. Fermented, or hard, cider contains only 2 to 3 percent solids, instead of 12 to 15 percent as in the apple juice, and 2 to 8 percent alcohol. Cider brandy, or applejack, is derived by distillation from fermented cider. It contains 40 to 50 percent alcohol.

VINEGAR

Vinegar, sour-tasting condiment and preservative prepared by two successive microbial processes, the first being an alcoholic fermentation effected by yeasts and the second an oxidation of alcohol by *Acetobacter*, a genus of aerobic bacteria.

Regulations of the. Food and Drug Administration prescribe that the unmodified name *vinegar* apply only to the product derived from apples and that this product contain not less than 4 g of acetic acid in 100 ml of vinegar. Vinegar also contains small quantities of ash, sugars, phosphoric acid, alcohol, and glycerol. A quick method of manufacture is to pour fermented apple cider containing about 10 percent alcohol over wood shavings while air is blown through the mixture. The resulting liquid is then clarified and filtered. Malt vinegar is preferred in Britain, and wine vinegar in continental Europe. Other varieties of vinegar are produced from beetroot and alcoholic spirits; and it is sometimes flavoured with tarragon, dill, or other herbs.

DISTILLATION

Distillation, process of heating a liquid until its more volatile constituents pass into the vapour phase, and then cooling the vapour to recover such constituents in liquid form by condensation. The main purpose of distillation is to separate a mixture of several components by taking advantage of their different volatilities, or the separation of volatile materials from nonvolatile materials.

In evapouration and in drying, the purpose usually is to obtain the less volatile constituent; the more volatile constituent, in most cases water, is discarded. In distillation, on the other hand, the principal object of the operation is to obtain the more volatile constituent in pure form. The removal of water from glycerin by vapourizing the water is called evapouration, but the removal of water from alcohol by vapourizing the alcohol is called distillation, although similar apparatus is used in both cases.

If the difference in volatility (and hence in boiling point) between the two constituents is great, complete separation may be easily accomplished by a single distillation. Seawater which contains about 4 percent dissolved solids (principally common salt), may be readily purified by vapourizing the water, condensing the steam thus formed, and collecting the product, distilled water. This product is, for most purposes, equivalent to pure water, although actually it contains some impurities in the form of dissolved gases, the most important of which is carbon dioxide.

If the boiling points of the constituents of a mixture differ only slightly, complete separation cannot be achieved in a single distillation. An important example is the separation of water, which boils at 100° C (212° F), and alcohol, which boils at 78.5° C (173° F). If a mixture of these two liquids is boiled, the vapour that rises is richer in alcohol and poorer in water than the liquid from which it came, but it is not pure alcohol. In order to concentrate a 10 percent solution of alcohol (such as might be obtained by fermentation) to obtain a 50 percent solution (common for whiskey), the distillate must be redistilled once or twice, and if industrial (95 percent) alcohol is desired, many redistillations are needed.

Theory of Distillation

In the simplest mixture of two mutually soluble liquids, the volatility of each is undisturbed by the presence of the other. In such a case, the boiling point of a 50-50 mixture would be halfway between the boiling points of the pure substances, and the degree of separation produced by a single distillation would depend only on the vapour pressure, or the volatility, of the separate components at this temperature.

This simple relationship was first stated by the French chemist François Marie Raoult and is called Raoult's law. Raoult's law applies only to mixtures of liquids that are very similar in chemical structure, such as benzene and toluene. In most cases wide deviations occur from this law.

Thus, one component is only slightly soluble in the other, its volatility is abnormally increased. In the example above, the volatility of alcohol in dilute aqueous solution is several times as great as predicted by Raoult's law. In extremely concentrated alcohol solutions, the deviation is even more striking: The distillation of 99 percent alcohol produces vapour that has less than 99 percent alcohol. For this reason, alcohol cannot be concentrated by distillation beyond 97 percent, even by an infinite number of distillations.

Distillation Apparatus

Technically, the term *still* is applied only to the vessel in which liquids are boiled during distillation, but the term is sometimes applied to the entire apparatus, including the fractionating column, the condenser, and the receiver in which the distillate is collected. The term *still* is also extended to cover apparatus for destructive distillation, or cracking. Stills for labouratory work are usually made of glass, but industrial stills are generally made of iron or steel. In cases in which iron would contaminate the product, copper is often employed, and small stills for the distillation of whiskey are frequently made of glass and copper. (The term *retort* is also sometimes used for a still.)

Fractional Distillation

If a portion of the distillate is returned from the condenser and made to drip down through a long column onto a series of plates, and if the vapour as it rises on its way to the condenser is made to bubble through this liquid at each plate, the vapour and liquid will interact so that some of the water in the vapour condenses and some of the alcohol in the liquid vapourizes.

The interaction at each plate is thus equivalent to a redistillation, and by building a column with a sufficient number of plates, 95 percent alcohol can be obtained in a single operation. Moreover, by feeding the original 10 percent alcohol solution gradually at a point in the middle of the column, virtually all the alcohol may be stripped from the water as it descends to the lowest plate, so that no alcohol need be wasted.

This process, known as rectification, fractionation, or fractional distillation, is common in industrial usage, not only for simple mixtures of two components (such as alcohol and water in fermentation products, or oxygen and nitrogen in liquid air) but also for highly complex mixtures such as those found in coal tar and petroleum.

The fractionating column most often used is the so-called bubble tower, in which the plates are arranged horizontally a few centimeters apart and the ascending vapours are forced to rise through bubble caps in each plate and then bubble through the liquid.

The plates are baffled so that the liquid flows from left to right on one plate, then overflows onto the plate below, and there flows from right to left. If the interaction between liquid and vapour is incomplete, or if frothing and entrainment occur so that some of the liquid is carried up by the vapour to the plate above, five actual plates might be required to do the work of four theoretical plates, producing four redistillations. An inexpensive equivalent of a bubble tower is the so-called packed column, in which the liquid flows down over a packing of earthenware rings or bits of glass tubing.

The only disadvantage of fractional distillation is that a large fraction (as much as one-half) of the condensed distillate must be refluxed, or returned to the top of the tower and eventually boiled again, and more heat must therefore be supplied. On the other hand, the continuous operation made possible by fractionation allows great heating economies, because the outgoing distillate may be used to preheat the incoming feed.

When the mixture consists of many components, they are drawn off at different points along the tower. Industrial distillation towers for petroleum often have over 100 plates, with as many as ten different fractions being drawn off at suitable points. Towers with more than 500 plates have been used for the separation of isotopes by distillation.

Steam Distillation

If two insoluble liquids are heated, each is unaffected by the presence of the other (as long as they are agitated so that the lighter liquid does not form an impenetrable layer over the heavier), and vapourizes to an extent determined only by its own volatility. Such a mixture, therefore, always boils at a temperature lower than that of either constituent; and the percentage of each constituent in the vapour depends only on its vapour pressure at this temperature. This principle may be applied to substances that would be damaged by overheating if distilled in the usual fashion.

Vacuum Distillation

Another method of distilling substances at temperatures below their normal boiling points is to partially evacuate the still. Thus, aniline may be distilled at 100° C (212° F) by removing 93 percent of the air from the still. This method is as effective as steam distillation, but somewhat more expensive. The greater the degree of vacuum, the lower is the distillation temperature. If the distillation is carried on in a practically perfect vacuum, the process is called molecular distillation. This process is regularly used industrially for the purification of vitamins and certain other unstable products.

The substance is placed on a plate in an evacuated space and heated. The condenser is a cold plate, placed as close to the first as possible. Most of the material passes across the space between the two plates, and therefore very little is lost.

Centrifugal Molecular Distillation

If a tall column of mixed gases is sealed and placed upright, a partial separation of the gases takes place as a result of gravity. In a high-speed centrifuge or an instrument called a vortex, the forces separating the lighter and heavier components from each other are thousands of times greater than gravity, making the separation more efficient. Separation of gaseous uranium hexafluoride, UF_6, into molecules containing two different uranium isotopes, uranium-235 and uranium-238, may be effected by means of centrifugal molecular distillation.

Sublimation

If a solid substance is distilled, passing directly into the vapour phase and back into the solid state without a liquid being formed at any time, the process is called sublimation. Sublimation does not differ from distillation in any important respect, except that special care must be taken to prevent the solid from clogging the apparatus. Rectification of such materials is impossible. Iodine is purified by sublimation.

Destructive Distillation

If a substance is heated to a high temperature and decomposed into several valuable products, and these products are separated by fractionation in the same operation, the process is called destructive distillation. The important applications of this process are the destructive distillation of coal for coke, tar, gas, and ammonia, and the destructive distillation of wood for charcoal, acetic acid, acetone, and wood alcohol. The latter process has been largely displaced by synthetic processes for making the various by-products. The cracking of petroleum is similar to destructive distillation.

ALCOHOL

Alcohol term applied to members of a group of chemical compounds and, in popular usage, to the specific compound ethyl alcohol, or ethanol. The Arabic word denotes kohl, a fine powder of antimony used as an eye makeup. The word *alcohol* originally denoted any fine powder; the alchemists of medieval Europe later applied it to essences obtained by distillation, and this led to the current usage.

Alcohols are a class of organic compounds containing the hydroxyl group, OH, attached to a carbon atom. Alcohols have one, two, or three hydroxyl groups attached to their molecules and are thus classified as monohydric, dihydric, or trihydric, respectively. Methanol and ethanol are monohydric alcohols. Alcohols are further classified as primary, secondary, or tertiary, according to whether one, two, or three other carbon atoms are bound to the carbon atom to which the hydroxyl group is bound. Alcohols, although analogous to inorganic bases, are neither acid nor alkaline.

They are characterized by many common reactions, the most important of which is the reaction with acids to form substances called esters, which are analogous to inorganic salts. Alcohols are normal by-products of digestion and chemical processes within cells and are found in the tissues and fluids of animals and plants.

Wood Alcohol

Methyl alcohol, or methanol, CH_3OH, is the simplest of all the alcohols. It was formerly made by the destructive distillation of wood; however, almost all of the methanol produced today is synthetic, made from hydrogen and carbon monoxide. Methanol is used as a denaturant for grain alcohol as an antifreeze, as a solvent for gums and lacquers, and in the synthesis of many organic compounds, particularly formaldehyde. When taken internally, by either drinking the liquid or inhaling the vapours, methanol is extremely poisonous. Methanol melts at -97.8° C (-144.0° F), boils at 64.7° C (148.5° F), and has a specific gravity of 0.7915 at 20° C (68° F).

Grain Alcohol

Ethyl alcohol, or ethanol, C_2H_5OH, is a clear, colourless liquid, with a burning taste and characteristic, agreeable odor. Ethanol is the alcohol in such beverages as beer, wine, and brandy. Because of its low freezing point, it has been used as the fluid in thermometers for temperatures below -40° C (-40° F), the freezing point of mercury, and for other special low-temperature purpose, such as for antifreeze in automobile radiators. Ethanol is normally concentrated by distillation of dilute solutions.

Commercial ethanol contains 95 percent by volume of ethanol and 5 percent of water. Dehydrating agents remove the remaining water and produce absolute ethanol. Ethanol melts at -114.1° C (-173.4° F), boils at 78.5° C (173.3° F), and has a specific gravity of 0.789 at 20° C (68° F).

Ethanol has been made since ancient times by the fermentation of sugars. All beverage ethanol and more than half of industrial ethanol is still made by this process. Starch from potatoes, corn, or other cereals can be the raw material. The yeast enzyme, zymase, changes the simple sugars into ethanol and carbon dioxide. The fermentation reaction, represented by the simple equation

$$C_6H_{12}O_6'!\ 2C_2H_5OH + 2CO_2$$

is actually very complex because impure cultures of yeast produce varying amounts of other substances, including fusel oil, glycerin, and various organic acids. The fermented liquid, containing from 7 to 12 percent ethanol, is concentrated to 95 percent by a series of distillations.

In the production of beverages such as whiskey and brandy, some of the impurities, which supply the flavour, are of great value. Much ethanol not intended for drinking is now made synthetically, either from acetaldehyde made from acetylene, or from ethylene made from petroleum. A small amount is made from wood pulp.

Ethanol can be oxidized to form first acetaldehyde and then acetic acid. It can be dehydrated to form ether. Other products made from ethanol include butadiene, used in making synthetic rubber; ethyl choride, used as a local anesthetic; and many other organic chemicals.

Ethanol can also be mixed with gasoline to form the automobile fuel called gasohol. Ethanol is *miscible* (mixable) in all proportions with water and with most organic solvents. It is an excellent solvent for many substances and is used in making such products as perfumes, lacquer, celluloid, and explosives. Alcoholic solutions of nonvolatile substances are called tinctures; if the solute is volatile, the solution is called a spirit.

Most industrial ethanol is denatured to prevent its use as a beverage. Denaturing involves mixing ethanol with small amounts of poisonous or unpleasant substances to make the ethanol undrinkable. The removal of all these substances would involve a series of treatments more expensive than the federal excise tax on alcoholic beverages.

Higher Alcohols

Higher alcohols, those of greater molecular weight than ethyl alcohol, have many specific and general uses. Isopropyl alcohol is used extensively as a rubbing alcohol, butyl alcohol is a base for perfumes and fixatives, and others are important flavouring agents and perfumes. Polyhydric alcohols, those containing more than one OH group, are also important as the trihydric alcohol known as glycerol.

BEER

Beer, alcoholic beverage made from cereal grains, usually barley, but also corn, rice, wheat, and oats. Beer is made using a process called fermentation, in which microscopic fungi called yeast consume sugars in the grain, converting them to alcohol and carbon dioxide gas. This chemical process typically produces beer with an alcohol content of 2 to 6 percent. Over 70 styles of beer are available today. Each style derives its unique characteristics from its ingredients and subtle differences in its brewing process.

Throughout history, wherever cereal grains were grown, humans made a beerlike beverage from them: they used wheat in Mesopotamia, barley in Egypt, millet and sorghum in other parts of Africa, rice in Asia, and corn in the Americas. Today, beer making is a major industry worldwide. In 2002 in the United States, 1,800 brewers produced almost 175 million barrels of beer, and on average, each American consumed nearly 83 liters (22 gallons) of beer.

Beer Ingredients

Four basic ingredients are used to brew beer: grain, hops, yeast, and water. Grain contains the natural sugars required for fermentation. It also provides beer with flavour, colour, body, and texture. Hops are small, green, cone-shaped flowers from the hop plant, a vine related to the nettle plant. Over 50 varieties of hops are grown throughout the world, mostly in Europe, Australia, and North America. Hops provide beer with a spicy, bitter flavour and contribute natural substances that prevent bacteria from spoiling beer. Two species of yeast used to make beer, called brewer's yeast, are *Saccharomyces cerevisiae* and *Saccharomyces uvarum*. Each yeast species is used in a slightly different method of fermentation and produces a distinct type of beer.

Water constitutes as much as 95 percent of the ingredients used in the brewing process. The mineral content in water—in particular, the levels of salts such as calcium, sulfate, and chloride dissolved in the water—influences the quality and flavour of the beer it is used to produce. Modern brewers add minerals and other natural elements to water or eliminate them by boiling or filtration so that the water used in the brewing process always produces beer with the same flavours. This enables brewers to produce identical-tasting beer at different brewing locations throughout the world.

The Brewing Process

The first step in brewing, called malting, involves steeping the grain in water for several days until it begins to germinate, or sprout. During germination, enzymes within the grain convert the hard, starchy interior of the grain to a type of sugar called maltose. At this point, the grain is called malt. After several days, when the majority of the starch has been converted to sugar, the malt is heated and dried. This process, called kilning, stops the malt from germinating any further. A portion of the malt may be further roasted to varying depths of colour and flavour to create different styles of beer.

After kilning, the dried malt is processed in a mill, which cracks the husks (the outer coating of the grain). The cracked malt is transferred to a container called a mash tun, and hot water is added. The malt steeps in the liquid, usually for one to two hours. This process, called mashing, breaks down the complex sugars in the grain and releases them in the water, producing a sweet liquid called wort. The temperature and amount of time used to mash the malt affects the body and flavour of the finished beer.

In the next step, called brewing, the wort is transferred to a large brew kettle and boiled for up to two hours. Boiling effectively sterilizes the wort to kill any bacteria that may spoil the wort during fermentation. During this stage of the brewing process, hops are added to the wort to provide a spicy flavour and bitterness that balances the sweetness of the wort. The types of hops used and the length of time they are boiled are determined by the style of beer being made. To produce a beer with a stronger, more bitter flavour, hops are boiled for at least 30 minutes and often longer. This enables the bitter oils in the hops to fully infuse into the wort.

Other ingredients may also be used to influence the flavour of the finished beer. Brewers of pale and light-bodied beers often add other cereal grains, such as corn and rice, to achieve the desired lightness in their product. Many large American breweries add corn and rice that has first been cooked to a gel-like consistency. This gives the beer a lighter colour and body and a more mellow taste than beers produced from barley alone.

After brewing, the wort is cooled and then strained to

remove the hop leaves and other residue. The brewer transfers the wort to a container in which it can ferment. This vessel may be a deep, flat container with an open top or a tall cylindrical vat with a conical base. Yeast is then added or *pitched* into the wort to begin fermentation. *Saccharomyces cerevisiae* floats on top of the liquid as it ferments the grain sugars and prefers warm temperatures ranging from 16° to 22° C (60° to 72° F). *Saccharomyces uvarum* sinks to the bottom of the liquid and ferments best at cool temperatures ranging from 3° to 10° C (38° to 50° F). The first fermentation lasts from a few days to two weeks. When the yeast has consumed most of the fermentable sugar, the wort becomes beer.

The beer is transferred to an airtight container, called a conditioning tank, for a second fermentation or aging period, where the beer becomes naturally carbonated. Some brewers inject carbon dioxide gas into the beer when aging is complete to give it a bubbly, effervescent quality. Aging lasts for a few weeks to several months, depending on the type of beer being produced.

After aging, the beer may appear somewhat cloudy from yeast cells and other particles that remain suspended in the liquid. The most common method of removing these impurities is filtration, a process in which the finished beer is pumped, under pressure, through a sterile filtering system that traps nearly all of the suspended particles from the liquid, resulting in a clear liquid. Even after filtration, however, some yeast may remain in the beer.

To kill the remaining yeast, the beer is pasteurized, or heated to 82° C (180° F) after it has been sealed in cans or bottles. Draught beer, which is stored in metal kegs, usually is not pasteurized and must be kept refrigerated to prevent it from spoiling. Some brewers and beer drinkers believe that filtering and pasteurizing beer robs it of much of its original flavour and character.

Beer Characteristics

The two major categories of beer are ales and lagers, and the yeast used in fermentation determines the differences between the two. Ales are fermented with *Saccharomyces cerevisiae* at warm temperatures for short periods of time, typically a week. This yeast ferments in warmer temperatures to produce a fruity flavour that characterizes ale. Ales are aged, or conditioned, for one to three weeks. Ales should be served at room or cellar temperature—about 13° C (about 55° F).

Lagers are usually drier, crisper, and less fruity in taste than ales. Lagers are fermented with *Saccharomyces uvarum* at cooler temperatures for longer periods up to two weeks, which encourages the flavour components in lagers to combine and mellow. Lagers are aged for up to 12 weeks. Lagers are best served chilled.

All beer can be further described by three additional variables: colour, bitterness, and gravity. Colour is determined by the type and amount of malt used to make the beer. lightly roasted malt produces a light-coloured beer, while beer made only with barley that has been dark roasted is nearly black in colour.

Bitterness depends on the type and amount of grain and hops used in the beer's production. Beers made with wheat are generally less bitter than beers made with dark-roasted barley. The mineral content of the brewing water can also accentuate hop bitterness. Beer made with water that has a high level of dissolved minerals is more bitter than beer made with water low in minerals.

Gravity refers to the beer's density, or the amount of dissolved sugars in the wort. As more sugars dissolve in the brewing water during mashing, the density of the wort increases. The yeast consumes these sugars to produce alcohol during fermentation, so elevated sugar levels translate into a higher alcohol content in the finished beer.

Types of Beer

Porter and stout are dark ales that are nearly black in colour and have a hearty flavour and dense body. A London brewer created porter in 1722 as a more nourishing drink for porters and other heavy labourers. Arthur Guinness, an Irish brewer, developed a darker version of porter in the late 1700s, calling it extra stout porter. This designation was later shortened to stout. The barley used to produce these beers is roasted to a dark, rich colour. Both beers range in taste from sweet to dry (lacking any sweetness). Porter is lighter in body and higher in alcohol than stout, but stout tends to be more bitter.

Mild ale, originally produced in England, has a gentle, sweet taste that is meant to quench the thirst. It is usually tawny to dark in colour. Bitter ale is a popular style of British ale that ranges in colour from light to dark. It tastes dry and bitter because the hops are added early in the cooking process, enabling the bitter oils to impart a strong flavour. Pale ale is a clear beer with a dry, malty, nutty flavour.

It has a less pronounced hop flavour than bitter ale. Brown ale, in contrast, is deep amber or darker in colour and may have a strong, dry, nutty taste or be somewhat sweet and fruity, depending on how it is brewed. Barleywine has a bronze to mahogany colour and a heavy, fruity taste. Although it is an ale, it may have been named wine originally because of its high alcohol content, which, at around 10 percent, is closer to wine than beer.

Pilsner, the most popular of all the lagers, originated in the Bohemian town of Plzeò in 1842. It is a clear, golden lager with a dry but soft malty taste and flowery hop aroma. Dark lager, also known as Munich *dunkel*, was first produced in Munich, Germany. It is a dark brown brew with a spicy, malty taste with flavours of chocolate and licorice. Vienna-style *Märzen*, or *Oktoberfest*, is a lager that ranges in colour from amber-red to bronze or copper and has a soft malty taste and smell.

Bock beer is a full-bodied, smooth lager with a somewhat sweet taste. It is usually dark in colour and may have an alcohol content as high as 8 percent. *Doppel* bock is a variation of bock beer that is very dark and strong. Bock and doppel bock beer are usually brewed in the winter and consumed in the spring. Light beer and ice beer are typically lagers. Light beer contains fewer calories and usually less alcohol—about 2 percent—than regular beer. It is produced by using a lower grain-to-water ratio during the brewing process.

Ice beer, which has a higher alcohol content, is made by

cooling a beer to below freezing and then filtering out the ice crystals that form. California common beer, marketed under the brand name Steam Beer, is produced in very shallow fermentation vessels using lager yeast but fermented at warmer, ale, temperatures.

Wheat beer is brewed by mixing wheat with barley—usually in equal parts. The result is a light-coloured and somewhat cloudy beer with a refreshing, tart flavour. Wheat beer typically contains less alcohol than other types of beer. German-style *hefeweizen* is an unfiltered wheat beer. Additional yeast is added to the bottle before it is capped to enhance its flavour and cloudy appearance. *Lambic* beer, brewed primarily in Belgium, is a type of wheat beer fermented using only wild airborne yeast.

Rye beer, as its name suggests, is made with rye, but it may also be combined with oats. Estonia and Finland make a traditional rye beer called *sahti* that is seasoned with juniper as well as hops. Rye beer is native to Eastern, Central, and Baltic Europe but more recently has been produced by breweries in the Pacific Northwest of the United States.

Sake, a Japanese beer made from fermented rice, is clear in colour and tastes and looks more like wine than beer. It contains approximately 15 percent alcohol. Sake is typically served warm to enhance its flavours.

Some beers are brewed with additional ingredients to enhance their flavours. Fruit beer is flavoured with raspberries and cherries or other fruit. Herbs and spices, such as chili peppers, are added to some beers. Smoked beer is made using malt dried on mesh screens over an open fire. Black beer is a very dark lager containing flavours of tangy, dry, toffee combined with bitter chocolate.

WINE

Wine, alcoholic beverage made from the juice of grapes. During fermentation, microscopic single-celled organisms called yeasts digest sugars found in fruit juice, producing alcohol and carbon dioxide gas in the process. Although grapes are the most common fruit used to make wine, wine is also made from the fermented juice of pears, apples, berries, and even flowers such as dandelions. Wine naturally contains about 85 to 89 percent water, 10 to 14 percent alcohol, less than 1 percent fruit acids, and hundreds of aroma and flavour components in very small amounts. Wine character—its taste and smell—is derived from many factors including the grapes it is made from, where they were grown, and the production techniques applied by the wine maker, or *enologist.*

The practice of making wine is as old as our most ancient civilizations, and wine has played a central role in human culture for more than 8,000 years. In contrast to most foods and beverages that spoil quickly or that can spread disease, wine does not spoil if stored properly.

The alcohol in wine, called ethanol, is present in sufficient concentrations to kill disease-causing microorganisms, and throughout history, wine was often safer to drink than water or milk. This property was so significant that before the connection between microorganisms, poor sanitation, and disease was understood, ancient civilizations regarded wine as a gift from the gods because it protected against disease.

Wine Grapes and Vineyards

The main grapevine cultivated for wine production is the European wine grape, *Vitis vinifera.* Native to areas along the Black, Caspian, and Mediterranean seas, today there are more than 5,000 varieties of *Vitis vinifera* grown in the world. Because this grape plant prefers warm, dry summers and mild winters, successful cultivation is limited to temperate climates in both the northern and southern hemispheres. The most popular red varieties in the United States are zinfandel, cabernet sauvignon, grenache, merlot, and pinot noir. The most popular white grapes are colombard, chardonnay, chenin blanc, and sauvignon blanc.

Natural factors make wine from a particular region unique. Known in the wine industry as *terroir*, these factors include local climate (temperature, rainfall, and sunlight), location of grapevines (altitude and slope), and soil (structure, composition, and water drainage). In general, a grapevine produces the best fruit when the moderate climate provides much sunshine and cool nights without frost, and the soil is well drained. Grapevines grow best in sandy, chalky, or rocky soils. Wine grapes are grown in vineyards, where individual vines are grown or *trained* on a system of stakes and wires, called a *trellis,* to optimize sun exposure. The first harvest of grapes can be made in the third year after planting, and a full crop suitable for commercial use can be expected after five years. Grapevines may produce fruit for 20 to over 100 years. The grapevine growth cycle begins in early spring when new shoots appear on the buds of the grapevine.

These shoots develop flowers that blossom and then produce clusters of tiny green grapes. The grapes begin to ripen in midsummer and are ready to be harvested beginning in midfall, depending on the location, grape variety, weather, and the type of wine to be produced. By the end of fall, the vines lose their leaves and become dormant until the following spring.

A wine's character is strongly affected by wine growing, or *viticultural* practices such as training, trellising, harvesting, and pruning. Training and trellising enable the viticulturalist to control the sun exposure to ensure the grapes ripen evenly. Grapes harvested when they are not ripe may be low in sugar and may not ferment properly. Overly ripe grapes have very high sugar content and produce wine high in alcohol.

Once the vines are dormant, the viticulturalist prunes the vines to remove the dead wood. Pruning enables the grower to control the size and shape of the vines, as well as the number of buds that will develop the next year. Too many buds on a vine may stress nutrient availability, reducing the quality of the future harvest.

Grapevines have many natural enemies: insects, molds, bacteria, viruses, and animals such as deer and birds that eat the young shoots or the sweet grapes. Certain soilborne pests, such as the root louse *Phylloxera,* destroy the roots of European grapevines. Vines native to North and South America have a natural resistance to this insect, but they often produce grapes with an undesirable flavour.

To counter this problem, American vineyards use grapevines grown from two different parts: the roots from resistant American vines and the part above the ground from European vines. The process of combining parts of two different plants is known as grafting and works much like healing a broken bone.

There are 8 million hectares (20 million acres) of vineyards in the world producing 62 million tons of grapes each year. About 29 billion liters (8 billion gallons) of wine are made from those grapes. The biggest wine producers worldwide are France (19 percent), Italy (17 percent), and Spain (13 percent). The United States is the fourth largest producer in the world, producing about 9 percent of the world's wine. California produces 90 percent of all the wine in the United States, with enologists in New York, Washington, Oregon, and at least 41 other states making the remainder of U.S. wine.

Made of Wine

Wine is the product of the fermentation by yeast of grape juice or grape *must,* grape juice that still contains the fruit's skins and seeds. Once the grape sugar has been completely consumed, fermentation is complete, and wine has been produced. The science that deals with wine making is known as enology.

While the basic production elements of wine are simple, manipulation of the grapes, juice or must, and wine to produce the desired combination of flavours and aromas is very difficult, and many recognize this process as an art form. Wine makers try to optimize production of specific aromas and flavours—described with terms like cherry, chocolate, vanilla—and minimize the formation of negative flavours and aromas—described as wet dog, plastic, and rotten egg. It is also important that the wine acids and alcohol are balanced. If the wine is too acidic, the wine may taste sour. If the ethanol level is too high, the wine will have a strong taste of alcohol.

The single most important factor that contributes to a wine's character is the grapes that are used. Grapes influence the wine's flavour, alcohol content, acidity, and even its colour. White wine, which is actually straw to golden-yellow in colour, is produced from white grapes, and red wine is produced from red grapes. Red and white wine production is basically the same except for one primary difference: the presence of the grape skins during fermentation. White grapes are crushed and the juice separated from the skins prior to fermentation. Red wine is fermented with the grape skins. Red pigments called anthocyanins and other compounds in the grape skins are extracted during the fermentation process to impart the characteristic red colour of the wine as well as other features. A blush or rosé wine is light pink in colour and is produced from red grapes not fermented with the skins. A little pigment is released when the red grapes are crushed, but not to the same extent as during fermentation.

In modern wine production, the grapes are harvested from the vineyards and taken to a winery where they are passed through a machine called a destemmer-crusher that separates the fruit from the stems and cracks the berries open to release the juice. To make white wine, the must is transferred to a press where pressure is applied to separate the juice from the skins. The amount of pressure used influences what flavour compounds are extracted from the skins. After pressing, the white juice without the skins is transported to a fermentation tank. In red wine production, the must from the crusher is transferred directly to a tank for fermentation.

The containers used for fermentation are mostly stainless steel or wood. The type of container used and the temperature of fermentation influence the characters of the wine. Many of the aroma components of wine are volatile—that is, they leave the wine by evapouration. This evapouration occurs faster at higher temperatures, so to retain fruity characters in the wine the temperature of fermentation must be controlled, usually by direct cooling of the fermentation tanks. Stainless steel is much easier to cool than wood and is preferred for temperature-crucial fermentation.

The wine maker may allow fermentation to proceed relying only on the yeast naturally present on the grape skins and in the winery equipment, or the wine maker may add extra yeast in a process known as *inoculation.* Two yeast species are used in fermentation, *Saccharomyces cerevisiae* or *Saccharomyces*

bayanus. Yeast is responsible for the presence of positive but also negative aroma characters in wine. When yeast is under stress it produces a compound called hydrogen sulfide, which smells like rotten eggs. To avoid this undesirable quality, a wine maker may add nutrients to the fermentation tank. The duration of fermentation also influences wine character.

Other naturally occurring microorganisms may grow in the must or juice, affecting the flavours and aromas of the finished wine. Lactic acid bacteria use the acids in wine as a source of energy, reducing the wine's acidity. These bacteria also produce other aromas and are responsible for the buttery smells that can be found in wine. Sometimes the wine maker restricts the growth of lactic acid bacteria, especially if the wine is already low in acidity or if the buttery character would clash with other aromas of the wine. *Acetobacter,* another type of bacteria, can spoil the wine by converting ethanol to acetic acid to make vinegar.

When fermentation is complete, red wine is separated from the stems and grape skins by passing it through a press. Both red and white wines appear cloudy after fermentation, and the wine maker must wait for the yeast and other solids to settle to the bottom of the fermentation tank, forming a sediment called the *lees.* The clear wine is *racked* or drawn off the lees and stored in a clean cask. In a process called *fining,* the wine maker may further clarify the wine by adding ingredients that attract unwanted particles, such as proteins that can cause cloudiness. These added ingredients settle to the bottom and can be easily collected and removed.

After fermentation, the wine maker has to decide how the wine will be aged. Aging of wine significantly affects the flavours and aromas present, and several different techniques are used. Wine aged in oak barrels picks up some flavour and aroma characters from the oak wood, a very desirable quality in some wines. A wine may be aged under conditions encouraging the loss of some of the fruity, volatile compounds, producing a wine rich in other characters, such as spicy or toasted flavours.

Air exposure during aging can cause the phenolic wine

compounds, extracted from grape skins and seeds, to combine with each other, producing large chemical compounds called *tannins*. Over time the tannins become so large that they form reddish-brown sediment in the bottle. This reduces wine bitterness and astringency. The length of time a wine is aged before it is bottled determines the extent to which these reactions occur. Once the wine has been aged, it is ready to be put into bottles, where it may continue to slowly age for many years.

Classification of Wine

Wines are categorized using a number of different methods. Sometimes they are grouped into different categories by grape variety, region of origin, by colour, by the name of the wine maker or viticulturalist, or by production technique. Three basic groups of wines are most easily distinguishable for the consumer: table wines, sparkling wines, and fortified wines.

Table wines, also known as still or natural wines, are produced in many different styles and make up the majority of wines on the market. Traditionally consumed as part of a meal, table wines contain between 10 and 14 percent alcohol and are further classified by their colour, sugar content, and the variety and origin of the grapes that were used. Depending on the grape variety and wine-making technique, wines can be white, red, or pink in colour. Most table wines are fermented until they are *dry*—that is, all the grape sugar has been turned to alcohol by the yeast. Slightly sweet or *off-dry* wines are made by stopping the fermentation before all the sugar is gone or by adding grape juice back to the wine afterwards.

In wine-producing regions outside of Europe, particularly California and Australia, table wines are often classified by the grape variety they are made from. At least 75 percent of the grapes used to produce the wine must be of the named grape variety. Chardonnay is wine made from at least 75 percent chardonnay grapes. Wines classified this way are sometimes called varietals, and include wines such as riesling, cabernet sauvignon, and merlot.

The traditional European classification system puts more

emphasis on the region—or *appellation*—where the wine is from. The French system of *Appellation d'Origine Contrôlée* labels wines based on their geographical pedigree. The most renowned wine-producing regions in France, and possibly the world, are Burgundy, in central France, and Bordeaux, a region on the southwestern coast of the country. Bordeaux maintains a famous geographical classification system for some of its viticultural areas, dating back to the year 1855. Bordeaux ranks its best wineries, called *châteaux*, and their vineyards—*crus*, into five classes called *grand crus*.

The highest class, called *premier grand crus*, is still held by only five wineries: Château Margaux, Château Latour, Château Mouton-Rothschild and Château Lafite-Rothschild in Pauillac, plus Château Haut-Brion in Graves. Wines from these vineyards in France are considered to be among the highest-quality wines in the world. Altogether, France produces about 200 million cases (containing 12 bottles each) of table wine each year.

The French *Appellation d'Origine Contrôlée* system has been adopted by most other wine-producing countries. In addition to the primary grape variety used to make the wine, American wineries use a tag on their wine bottle labels called Appellation of Origin to indicate where the grapes were grown.

An appellation can be a country, state, county, or geographically defined American Viticultural Area (AVA). At least 85 percent of the grapes used to produce the wine must be from the viticultural area stated on the label. The United States currently recognizes about 150 AVAs, distinguishable by geographical features. The largest growing region in the United States, California, has at least 85 AVAs, including the Napa and Sonoma valleys. About 223 million cases of table wine are produced in the United States each year.

Sparkling wine is made from table wine that has undergone a second fermentation. The wine maker adds a measured amount of sugar and fresh yeast to the dry wine. This can happen in a closed tank, or directly in the bottle, which is the way the most famous sparkling wine, French champagne, is produced. The yeast ferments the added sugar, but this time the carbon dioxide gas remains in the sealed

bottle, creating carbonation. When the sparkling wine is poured into a glass, the gas bubbles to the surface.

Under the *Appellation d'Origine Contrôlée* system, only sparkling wines produced in the Champagne region of northeastern France can officially use the name *champagne*. Sparkling wines produced in all other regions of the world, even those produced using the traditional champagne method, are simply referred to as sparkling wines. About 11 million cases of sparkling wine are produced in the United States each year.

Fortified wines contain additional alcohol and are usually consumed in small amounts as *aperitifs* before meals or *dessert wines* after a meal. Popular examples are port and sherry. In port wine making, which originated in Portugal, the grapes are crushed and the fermentation started but then stopped by the addition of more alcohol, which kills the yeast. The resulting wine is sweet and has an alcohol content that is 5 to 10 percent higher than table wine.

Originally from Spain, sherry is made by adding alcohol to a young dry wine in an oak barrel intentionally filled only halfway. Special yeasts called *flor yeast* grow on the surface of the wine and create the distinct nutty flavour characteristic of sherry. About 8 million cases of fortified wines are produced in the United States each year.

Brandy is made from wine but is classified as distilled liquor, not as wine. Brandy is distilled from wine to concentrate the alcohol in the wine. To make a distillate, wine is heated in an enclosed copper pot until it boils and the alcohol evapourates. The alcoholic vapour passes through a coiled pipe where it is cooled down until it forms a liquid again, or condenses. After distillation the brandy is aged. Bottled brandy typically contains 40 percent alcohol and has been aged in oak barrels for several years.

Storing and Serving Wine

If stored properly, wines can be aged for many years without spoiling or losing quality. The most important factor in wine spoilage is air exposure. Oxygen from the air permits

microorganisms to grow on the surface of the wine, producing negative flavours and aromas, such as those that smell like vinegar or nail polish. Oxygen can also trigger chemical reactions that lead to flavour losses and colour changes. To avoid these changes, wine should be stored in a way that limits or eliminates oxygen exposure. Very little oxygen exposure occurs in completely full wine barrels. While the wine is aging in a barrel, wine makers take great care to limit the air space in the barrel by regularly adding wine to the barrels to fill vacant space formed as the wine evapourates. This process is called *topping off*.

Wines last best if bottled with little or no air space in the bottle. The traditional closure for a wine bottle is a stopper made from the bark of the cork oak tree, which when properly used prevents air from entering the wine. Optimally, wine bottles should be stored horizontally, enabling contact between the wine in the bottle and the cork.

This prevents the cork from drying out and letting oxygen to seep into the bottle. Bottled wines can be stored for decades in a cellar at low temperature, approximately 16° C (60° F). As wine ages in the bottle, precipitates may still form and appear as crystals or sediment. These sediments are not harmful, and their appearance does not mean that the wine has been stored improperly or is otherwise spoiled. The salts of the fruit acids in wine, especially tartaric acid, form a precipitate that looks like fine crystals and is sometimes mistaken for glass by consumers. These so-called wine diamonds are harmless and readily sink to the bottom of the wine.

White wines are usually served chilled because at warmer temperatures they quickly lose their volatile characters and become flat and tasteless. Blush wines are also served chilled like white wines. Normal refrigerator temperatures of 4° to 10° C (40° to 50° F) are sufficient for chilling white and blush wines. Red wines, which usually contain more flavour and aroma components than white wines, are served at room temperature to release the aroma characters, and the wine smells and tastes better than it would if it were chilled.

Traditionally, different types of wines are served in glasses of different shapes to enhance their individual characteristics. Robust red wines may be served in a glass with a generous, wide bowl and a narrower mouth. The bowl enables the wine to be easily swirled in the glass without spilling to encourage evapouration of some of the volatile compounds. The smaller mouth of the glass concentrates the ensuing aroma—sometimes referred to as the *bouquet*—so that the nose can readily appreciate the wine's aroma. Sparkling wines are often served in tall, narrow glasses that clearly display the beautiful bubbles as they rise to the surface. Wine can be enjoyed in any glass, however, and ultimately, personal preference should determine the type of glass used.

The flavours of different wines are very distinctive and some are considered to taste better with certain kinds of foods. A wine with a very delicate flavour goes best with lightly flavoured foods rather than with strong flavours that overpower the wine, making it appear tasteless. Likewise, if the wine is too strong in flavour for the food, the food tastes bland. Great chefs are considered masters of pairing wine with food so each enhances the flavour and aroma of the other.

GRAPE

Grape, common name of an edible fruit in the buckthorn family, and of the vines that produce the fruit. The European grape has been used as food since prehistoric times. Grape seeds have been found in remains of lake dwellings of the Bronze Age in Switzerland and Italy and in tombs of ancient Egypt. Botanists believe that the Caspian Sea region was the original home of the European grape.

Distribution of seeds by birds, wind, and water carried the plant westward to the Asian shores of the Mediterranean. Grape culture, practiced in Palestine during biblical times, was introduced in the Mediterranean region by seagoing Phoenicians. The ancient Greeks cultivated grapes, and use of the fruit was later adopted by Rome and its tributary territories.

The European grape is now commercially cultivated in

warmer regions all over the world, particularly in western Europe, the Balkans, California, Australia, South Africa, and parts of South America. It was introduced to eastern North America during colonial times, but in those days grape cultivation failed due to the attacks of diseases and pests. Successful grape varieties of the eastern United States, such as Concord and Delaware, are strains developed from hybrids between the European grape and several native species, particularly the northern fox grape, the summer grape, the riverbank grape, and the muscadine grape. Eastern U.S. grapes are characterized by a juicy layer between the skin and pulp of the fruit, which permits easy removal of the skin. Grape varieties, whether European or eastern U.S., are classified according to their ultimate use.

Grapes used to make table wine must have relatively high acidity and moderate sugar content; those used for dessert wines and other sweet wines must have high sugar content and moderate acidity. Table grapes must be low in both acidity and sugar content and must conform to definite standards of size, colour, and shape. Grapes used to make juices and jellies must have a pronounced flavour combined with high acidity and moderate sugar content. Raisin grapes are preferably seedless, with high sugar content and low acidity. European varieties are considered superior to eastern U.S. varieties for use as table wines, table grapes, dessert wines, and raisins; eastern U.S. grapes are preferred for juices and jellies.

Grapevines are stems that climb on walls and fences by means of specialized supporting organs, called tendrils. Palmately veined leaves arise alternately along the stem. In most varieties, tendrils arise opposite two of every three successive leaves. Flowers, usually greenish, are borne in clusters and have staminate and pistillate flowers sometimes occurring on separate plants. Fruit is borne on 2-year-old canes, which are removed after harvesting the grapes.

Grapevines planted in commercial vineyards are usually started in spring from year-old rooted or grafted cuttings. Roots are trimmed to 7.6 to 10 cm (3 to 4 in) for convenience, and vines are planted 2.4 to 3 m (8 to 10 ft) apart. All the shoots except the strongest one on the vine are later pruned; the remaining shoot is cut back to two or three buds.

This process is repeated in the spring of the following two years. The resulting plant develops a strong main stem, resembling a small tree trunk, before it is allowed to bear fruit. Such strong stems are able to stand erect without support. During the expansion of the main stem, the vine is loosely tied to an upright support 1.8 m (6 ft) tall or higher. After the fruit-producing stage is reached, the vines are carefully pruned to reduce the number of buds. Shoots that develop from the remaining buds are more prolific and bear grapes of high quality.

BRANDY

Brandy, alcoholic beverage produced by the distillation of grape wine and matured by aging in wooden casks. When freshly distilled, the brandy is clear and colourless and will remain so if kept in glass containers. Placed in wooden casks, the spirits dissolve a colouring matter from the wood and acquire a light brownish tint, which dealers often deepen by adding burnt sugar.

The distinctive aroma of brandy is due to the presence of traces of higher alcohols and volatile oils. The very high alcoholic content of the raw spirits is reduced somewhat by aging and is adjusted usually to 40 to 45 percent by dilution with water when the brandy is bottled for sale.

Perhaps the most famous brandy is cognac, named after a town in the wine-producing department of Charente, France. The amber-hued cognac is made by distilling white wine, which is then aged in an oak cask.

Other notable brandies are kirsch, produced in the Alsace area of France, in Switzerland, and in the Black Forest region of Germany, by distilling the fermented juice of the black morello cherry; and šljivovica, a dry, colourless plum brandy made in the Balkans.

In the United States, liquors made from fruits other than grapes are also called brandies, but are more correctly termed cordials or liqueurs.

ADULTERATION

Adulteration, act of making any commodity impure by admixture of other or baser ingredients. This admixture may corrupt the nature of the original to the extent of destroying its identity, or it may merely lower the value or effectiveness of the finished product.

Adulteration of foods and beverages has been performed with the same aim—increasing profits for the manufacturer or merchant—since early times, when laws in ancient Greece and Rome addressed the colouring and flavouring of wine. England has had laws against adulteration of beer, bread, and other commodities since the 13th century, culminating in the Adulteration of Food or Drink Act of 1872 with its stiff penalties—six months at hard labour for a second offense. The law was modernized with the 1955 Food and Drug Act.

In the U.S. numerous state and federal bills were introduced in the 1890s, finally resulting in the Pure Food and Drugs Act of 1906. This act was ineffective because of its light penalties, and in 1938 it was superseded by the Federal Food, Drug, and Cosmetic Act, which outlaws foods and drugs dangerous to health that are sold in interstate commerce.

The 1938 law has been amended to cover food colourings and additives and supplemented by similar state legislation aimed at foods and drugs that do not come within the scope of interstate commerce.

Adulteration not only functions to defraud consumers but it can also pose a health threat. In the case of illegal drugs sold on the street, adulteration is generally in the form of inert or harmless compounds, but deadly poisons, such as sodium cyanide, have sometimes been sold as heroin.

Adulteration is not the only source of poor-quality or dangerous foods and drugs: The ingredients of junk foods need not be adulterated to ensure a virtual absence of nutritional value; potentially hazardous medicines will have more adverse effects if unadulterated. The consumer movement of recent times has focused not only on adulteration, but also on the nature of various unadulterated ingredients.

PASTEURIZATION

Pasteurization, process of heating a liquid, particularly milk, to a temperature between 55° and 70° C (131° and 158° F), to destroy harmful bacteria without materially changing the composition, flavour, or nutritive value of the liquid.

The process is named after the French chemist Louis Pasteur, who devised it in 1865 to inhibit fermentation of wine and milk. Milk is pasteurized by heating at a temperature of 63° C (145° F) for 30 minutes, rapidly cooling it, and then storing it at a temperature below 10° C (50° F). Beer and wine are pasteurized by being heated at about 60° C (140° F) for about 20 minutes; a newer method involves heating at 70° C (158° F) for about 30 seconds and filling the container under sterile conditions.

MILK

Milk, highly nutritious, versatile food. People enjoy drinking milk in its natural form and also use it to make a wide range of food products, including cream, butter, yogurt, cheese, and ice cream.

Female mammals produce milk to feed their newly born young. Milk is produced in the mother's mammary glands, which are found in the breasts of humans or the udders of cows, sheep, or goats. Each species of mammal produces milk with a unique composition designed to meet the specific needs of its infants. For instance, the milk of animals that need to develop a thick layer of insulating fat, such as seals, has a high fat content. The milk of animals that grow rapidly, such as cows, which double their birth weight in 50 days, is rich in protein and minerals.

Humans drink the milk produced from a variety of domesticated mammals, including cows, goats, sheep, camels, reindeer, buffaloes, and llama. By far the vast majority of milk used for commercial production and consumption is from cows. This article focuses on the nutritional value and production of cow milk. For information on the branch of agriculture concerned with the raising of cows (or other domesticated mammals) for the purpose of collecting their milk.

Nutritional Value of Milk

Most milk is composed of 80 to 90 percent water. The remaining 10 percent consists of an abundance of the major nutrients needed by the body for good health, including fats, carbohydrates, proteins, minerals, and vitamins.

Cow milk typically contains about 3.5 to 5 percent fat, which is dispersed throughout the milk in globules. In addition to providing milk's characteristic taste and texture, fat supplies vitamins A, D, E, and K, as well as certain fatty acids that the body cannot produce on its own.

Lactose, a kind of sugar found only in milk, gives milk its sweet taste. Making up about 5 percent of milk's content, lactose is a carbohydrate that is broken down by the body to supply energy. Infants digest lactose easily, but many adults, especially those of Asian and African ancestry, have lost some of their ability to digest this sugar. When these adults drink milk, they often suffer gastric distress and diarrhea.

The most important protein in milk is casein, accounting for 80 percent of milk protein. Casein is a complete protein, meaning that it contains all of the essential amino acids, which the body cannot manufacture on its own. Casein molecules and globules of fat deflect light rays passing through milk, giving milk its opalescent appearance. Other proteins present in milk include albumin and globulin.

Milk contains many minerals, the most abundant of which are calcium and phosphorus, as well as smaller amounts of potassium, sodium, sulfur, aluminum, copper, iodine, manganese, and zinc. Milk is perhaps the best dietary source of calcium—one liter (about 1 qt) of milk supplies as much calcium as 21 eggs, 12 kg (26 lb) of lean beef, or 2.2 kg (5 lb) of whole wheat bread.

Milk is an excellent source of vitaminsA and B_2. All other vitamins are present also, but in lower doses. Vitamin D is typically added to commercially sold milk. Vitamin A, which is found in the globules of fat, is removed when fat is skimmed away to make low-fat or skim milk. Generally, vitamin A is replaced during the production of commercially sold low-fat milk.

Human Breast Milk

Human milk provides distinct advantages over formula or cow milk for human infants. Not only is breast milk's nutritional composition uniquely designed for the needs of human babies, but it also contains antibodies from the mother's immune system that help the infant fight off infections and diseases.

During the first few days after giving birth, a mother releases colostrum, a yellowish liquid that contains less fat and lactose and more protein and antibodies than regular breast milk. After about three or four days, colostrum is replaced by a bluish-white milk that is higher in fats and carbohydrates, reflecting the energy needs of a growing baby.

Whole Milk, Low-fat Milk, and Skim Milk

Since the fat in raw milk is lighter in weight than the rest of the milk, it will naturally rise to form a layer of cream if allowed to stand. Spinning the milk in a large machine, called a centrifuge, accelerates the formation of a cream layer, or the separation of fat, from raw milk. Varying amounts of fat are removed from the raw milk, resulting in different kinds of fresh milk. If the fat content is lowered to 3.25 percent, the milk is sold as *whole milk*. *Low-fat milk* typically has 1 percent or 2 percent fat. *Skim milk*, or *nonfat milk*, is the liquid that remains after removing all the cream; it contains about half a percent milk fat. About half of the milk produced in the United States is consumed as one of these types of fresh milk; the rest is processed into other products such as cream, butter, cheese, yogurt, and ice cream.

Once the fat level has been reduced to the desired level, most fresh milk is homogenized to prevent the further separation of a cream layer. Homogenization is accomplished by forcing hot milk under high pressure through small nozzles. The fat globules become so small that they remain evenly dispersed throughout the milk.

In order to insure its safety for human use, almost all milk undergoes pasteurization, in which milk is heated to a high temperature for a specified length of time to destroy pathogenic bacteria. Pasteurized milk can be stored in a refrigerator for a week or longer.

Ultrapasteurized milk, common in Europe and Canada, is heated to an even higher temperature and can be stored at room temperature for several weeks. Condensed, evapourated, and powdered milk are produced by evapourating some or all of the water in milk. Sweetened condensed milk is sweetened with the addition of sugar. These products have very long shelf lives.

Cream, Butter, and Ice Cream

In order for a product to be labeled as cream, it must contain 18 percent milk fat or more. Light whipping cream must contain at least 30 percent fat, and 36 percent fat is the minimum fat content for heavy whipping cream. Half-and-half, an equal mixture of both milk and cream, must have at least 10.5 percent fat. The various grades of cream are valued for their smooth, thick texture.

They are often used in cooking instead of milk, because they are less likely to form a skin when heated and can be whipped into a stiff foam. When chilled cream is churned gently, the fat globules gather together to form butter, leaving buttermilk as the by-product. Butter contains at least 82.5 percent fat. In the past, before the advent of widespread refrigeration, salt was added to butter to retard bacterial spoilage; now salt is added mainly for flavour.

Ice cream, a popular frozen dessert, is made of milk, cream, sugar, and flavouring. The mixture is slowly beaten while chilled until it is partially frozen, then packed into containers, and chilled until firm. Variants of ice cream include ice milk, which contains less fat; sherbet, which has even less fat; and French ice cream, which is enriched with egg yolks.

Yogurt, Cheese, and Other Fermented Milk Products

Fermented milk products, including yogurt and cheese, are formed when bacteria break down lactose to produce lactic acid, which sours the milk. Yogurt is usually made from milk that has been fortified by the addition of nonfat powdered milk to improve its texture and taste. The fortified milk is pasteurized at a very high temperature and homogenized. A culture containing the bacteria *Streptococcus thermophilus* and *Lactobacillus bulgaricus*, and sometimes *Lactobacillus acidophilus*, is then added. The two most popular types of yogurt sold are Swiss-style, with added fruit mixed throughout, and sundae-style, with fruit on the top or bottom.

Cultured buttermilk and sour cream, like yogurt, are produced by the breakdown of lactose by bacteria. Cultured buttermilk used to be made from buttermilk, but is now more commonly made from skim milk. Sour cream is made from cream. Both have a tangy, sour taste imparted by lactic acid.Cheese making is a complex process, with each of the more than 400 varieties of cheeses differing in the details of the process.

However, most cheese making follows the same basic steps. Bacteria are introduced into milk that consume lactose and produce lactic acid. Cheeses are allowed to ferment longer than yogurt, buttermilk, and sour cream, which gives the bacteria time to also digest some of the fat and protein present. The waste products produced by bacteria from digesting fats and proteins provide cheeses with their distinctive and stronger flavours.

Acidification of milk or the addition of the enzyme rennin precipitates moist lumps of protein called curds. The curds contain all of the milk's protein and most of the fat, minerals, and vitamins. The residual thin liquid is known as whey. The curds are salted (for taste) and pressed into shape, which eliminates more of the whey. The pressed curd is then cured under controlled temperature and humidity for varying lengths of time to produce cheese.

ICE CREAM

Ice Cream, popular frozen food made of milk, cream, sugar, and flavouring. Ice cream probably originated in China around 2000 BC. It was first made in Italy in the 17th century and appeared in the United States in the early 18th century. The U.S. ice-cream manufacturing industry began in 1851.

Early production methods consisted of placing the ingredients in a metal container, surrounded by a freezing mixture of ice and coarse salt, and mixing them until smooth. In modern plants the basic ingredients, plus gelatin, used as a stabilizer to give the product a smooth consistency, are poured into a tank, where they are mixed and pasteurized.

The mixture is then homogenized to break up particles of butterfat, cooled, piped to a freezing tank, and beaten until smooth; at this stage nuts or fruits are sometimes added. The ice cream emerges from the freezing tank partially frozen and is packed into containers that are stored in a refrigerated room until hard.

BOOTLEGGING

Bootlegging, in popular usage, term applied to the practice of illegally transporting or selling intoxicating liquors. Such liquor is known as "bootleg," and the seller of it as a "bootlegger." Bootlegging may also refer to the smuggling or illegal selling of other goods such as pornographic and narcotics. The term probably came into use during the American Civil War, when an illegal liquor traffic was carried on among federal troops by peddlers who hid bottled whiskey in their cowhide bootlegs. Bootlegging was widespread throughout the U.S.

During Prohibition, when the manufacture and sale of alcoholic beverages was illegal.Several forms of ice cream are made. French ice cream is ice cream enriched with egg yolks; parfait and mousse are ice-cream preparations that have not been beaten during the freezing process; biscuit tortoni is a rich ice cream sprinkled with powdered almonds or macaroons; and spumoni is a mousselike ice cream to which fruits and nuts have been added.

Soft ice cream, made of the same ingredients as ordinary ice cream, is sold as it comes from the freezer before hardening. Ice milk, made from milk with four percent butterfat, is also sold before hardening. Frozen custard—soft ice cream with eggs added—is cooked to a custard before freezing.

PROHIBITION

Prohibition, legal ban on the manufacture and sale of

intoxicating drink; by extension, the term also denotes those periods in history when such bans have been in force, as well as the political and social movements advocating them. Such movements (also called temperance movements) have occurred whenever significant numbers of people have believed that the consumption of alcoholic beverages presented a serious threat to the integrity of their most vital institutions, especially the institution of the family.

Drunkenness is considered an evil in most of the world's major religious traditions, and Islam has for centuries forbidden even the moderate use of fermented drink. In the West, however, efforts to ban the consumption of alcohol have been a relatively recent phenomenon. Their origin can be traced to the apparently rapid spread of the technology of distillation and of alcohol abuse in 18th-century Europe, which alarmed those concerned with public health and morals.

The Anti-Saloon League

In reaction to this, the extraordinary "Women's War" broke out across the nation in 1873. Thousands of women marched from church meetings to saloons, where with prayer and song they demanded—with transitory results—that saloonkeepers give up their businesses. By 1900, millions of men and women were beginning to share this hostility toward the saloon and to regard it as the most dangerous social institution then threatening the family. The Anti-Saloon League of America (ASL), organized in Ohio, effectively marshaled such people into political action.

R

S

Index